THE GREATER GOOD

THE GREATER GOOD

How Philanthropy Drives the American Economy and Can Save Capitalism

CLAIRE GAUDIANI

Times Books
Henry Holt and Company • New York

Times Books
Henry Holt and Company, LLC
Publishers since 1866
115 West 18th Street
New York, New York 10011

Henry Holt® is a registered trademark of
Henry Holt and Company, LLC.

Distributed in Canada by H. B. Fenn and Company Ltd.

Library of Congress Cataloging-in-Publication Data

Gaudiani, Claire.
The greater good : how philanthropy drives the American economy and can save capitalism / Claire Gaudiani.
p. cm.
Includes bibliographical references and index.
ISBN: 0-8050-7196-2
1. Charities—Economic aspects—United States. 2. Endowments—Economic aspects—United States. 3. Generosity—Economic aspects. 4. Capitalism—United States. I. Title.
HV91.G37 2003
330.973—dc21 2003050702

Henry Holt books are available for special promotions and premiums. For details contact: Director, Special Markets.

First Edition 2003

Designed by Kelly S. Too

Printed in the United States of America

3 5 7 9 10 8 6 4 2

CONTENTS

THE GREATER GOOD

INTRODUCTION

HOW PHILANTHROPY SAVES AMERICAN CAPITALISM

> *The raising of extraordinarily large sums of money, given voluntarily and freely by millions of our fellow Americans, is a unique American tradition. . . . Philanthropy . . . charity . . . giving voluntarily and freely . . . call it what you like, but it is truly a jewel of American tradition.*
>
> —PRESIDENT JOHN F. KENNEDY

It's a pretty strong statement, isn't it, to say that philanthropy saves American capitalism? On the other hand, *something* certainly saved capitalism in the United States. It works here in a way it doesn't work anywhere else. In fact, both capitalism and democracy work here better than they have any right to. There must be a reason. I will argue that it's philanthropy, or, more generally, generosity. I will argue that citizen generosity has, for almost two hundred years, created a social environment where capitalism could flourish without destroying democracy. Generosity has also served as an economic engine to complement capitalism.

Citizen philanthropy did not save capitalism at some particular historical moment when it needed rescue. Generosity has saved capitalism over many, many decades, like a smart, kind friend watches out for a somewhat intemperate but gifted colleague, advising him throughout his life on the need for self-restraint and better judgment.

Why has this happened in America? Principally because generosity is one of the most widely shared values in the United States. It reflects our compassion and our entrepreneurial spirit, as well as our democratic values. It is the work of everyone, not just the extremely wealthy or the religiously oriented. Large numbers of Americans tend to feel personally responsible to address individual and collective challenges by making contributions designed to improve things, to correct injustices, to make our society more democratic. So, not only did 89 percent of Americans make a voluntary contribution in 2001, but the gifts addressed a wide array of needs. Thirty-eight percent went to support peoples' religions. The rest went to education, health, human services, and areas such as arts, culture, humanities, the environment, international affairs, and general public benefit funds like United Way. Individuals gave $177.05 billion in gifts and bequests, and that is 75.8 percent of the more than $212 billion given to philanthropic causes in 2001. People from all races, economic levels, and ethnicities and both genders are givers at significant levels. This breadth of commitment to citizen generosity in America stimulates a spirit of mutuality and shared values that is profoundly important, especially to control cynicism among the people in a democracy.

I am focusing exclusively on the generosity of individual Americans when I use the term philanthropy. Philanthropy has grown beyond the generosity of individual citizens to include public and private foundations and donations from corporations, and sometimes these donations are included here, but usually when the wealth creator was still alive and participating in the foundation's giving. It is, after all, the individual donors who give over 75 percent of all the donations in the country. That is 75 percent of $212 billion! Some of the people we meet in the coming chapters are (or were) as rich as Rockefeller. Others were never able to donate more than a dime at a time. There's no other way to say this: No people on earth are as generous with their money as Americans are. More Americans give than vote.

My argument does not focus on philanthropy as charity. It focuses on philanthropy as investment. Charity is important, of course. Much individual giving goes to help people obtain the basic necessities of life. Millions of private dollars and countless hours go to support soup kitchens for the hungry and shelters for the homeless in America. Our collective response to the tragedy of September 11, 2001, included literally billions of dollars of support to help victims and their families to meet immediate needs for clothing, shelter, and food. And most of us associate generosity with charity because of the Judeo-Christian background that influences U.S. culture. The religious heritage of the United States has shaped our values around generosity. Judeo-Christian beliefs offer the great commandment: Love thy neighbor as thyself. The Good Samaritan defined Jesus' idea of neighbor. He helped the injured man even though he had nothing in common with him—not race, ethnicity, nor religion. The Samaritan treated this mugged neighbor as he would want to be treated himself. He offered him charity.

Charity is the simplest, first step of generosity. The ultimate form of generosity is the investment in people, property, and ideas. Maimonides wrote of the eight stages of Tsedakah (generosity that acknowledges the dignity of the receiver) that the lowest stage is to give as little, as infrequently, as publicly, and with as little regard for the recipient's feelings as the donor chooses. At least you are giving! Surprisingly enough, the highest stage is not to give as much as one can, as often, as modestly, and as respectfully as possible. Such great goodness is only the seventh of the eight stages. The highest level of Tsedakah is to enter into a partnership with the person in need so that he will become productive and eventually independent.

Some 370 years ago, John Winthrop, governor of the Massachusetts colony, called for generosity as a way to build the future of the new land. In his sermon "A Modell of Christian Charity," delivered in Salem harbor on the good ship *Arabella,* which had brought him to the New World in 1630, he claimed that the virtue of charity would need to take a new place. Winthrop writes: ". . . wee must be knitt together in this worke as one man, we must entertaine each other in brotherly Affeccion, we must be willing to abridge our selves of our superfluities, for the supply of other's necessities. . . . We must delight in each other, make other's conditions our own, rejoice together, mourn together, labor and suffer together, always having before our eyes our community as members of the same body."[1]

Winthrop was calling for sharing as a part of the life people would lead. He was asking that all who had any "superfluities," as he called them, should share until all others had met their necessities. He focused on the importance of really implementing the commandment to love your neighbor as yourself and to found a social structure where citizens expected both to give and to get this kind of support.

These teachings underscore the compassion that is part of the Western tradition of generosity. They may seem to place less stress on the investment facet of generosity, but, when the prophet in Deuteronomy says, "Justice, only justice shall you pursue, that you may thrive," he announces prosperity (thriving) for those who nurture justice. Loving your neighbor will mean fairness and honesty, the very elements that capitalism needs to sustain investor confidence. While the Samaritan offered the immediate care to the wounded man that most people would define as charity, further consideration reveals that the Samaritan's generosity was restoring a member of the community to his active and productive life with his family. These elements are part of investment.

Cotton Mather, who was Ben Franklin's mentor, but much more deeply religious than Franklin, published in 1710 his *Essays to Do Good*. In these essays, he called for the practice of "silent generosity" and "pious contempt" against the obviously uncharitable.[2] Franklin's more secular orientation to why and how to be generous had a practicality about it that was eventually connected to "utilitarian individualism," one of the great elements of American tradition since colonial time. Franklin envisioned upward mobility in a way that still rings true for many today: "If they are poor they begin first as Servants or Journeymen; establish themselves in Business, marry, raise Families, and become responsible Citizens."[3]

I believe strongly that a wider knowledge of American history and traditions of generosity will help guarantee that new philanthropic endeavors will actually work here in the United States. The current generation is living better than at any time in U.S. history. Our forebears laid the groundwork for our well-being. The only way to express our gratitude is to follow their example and structure a way for advances to continue that will benefit future Americans and those beyond this country who will share future times with them. Each year we continue without the express effort to build a new model, we are wasting time we may not be able to recover if cynicism and economic class isolationism grow stronger.

Chapter 1 of this book will define citizen generosity in America and how it has worked, what roles it has played, and its origins in the religions and philosophies of the Western tradition. A crucial distinction will be made between generosity as charity and generosity as investment. The investment approach distinguishes the most significant kind of American generosity from the "poorhouse and soup line" method and expresses our values of freedom, the individual, and entrepreneurialism.

The second and third chapters present the case for how gifts to education, and to programs beyond education, built human capital. They trace the influence such generosity has had on the U.S. economy in the past. They show how generosity has enabled capitalism and democracy to work together, each strengthening the other, in spite of apparent contradictions between the two. The fourth and fifth chapters recount the effects of generosity on the development of the country's physical capital and its intellectual capital. Of particular importance in these chapters is the exploration of how the impulse toward democracy has inspired philanthropy that has, in turn, served as an economic engine. We have progressed economically as a result of efforts to affirm the unique value of each person and diverse peoples.

Chapter 6 is, in a sense, the heart of the book. After documenting our history of generosity, I will show why that generosity is a direct result of the philosophies and beliefs of the founders of our country. I will focus on their declaration of the unalienable right to "the pursuit of happiness" and what that means in terms of both the individual and the society as a whole. The right to pursue happiness may not link citizens directly to wealth, but it does instill a spirit of hope that is often supported through the philanthropic investments of fellow Americans. That hope manifests itself as a belief in the possibility of upward mobility. In countries where education is generally restricted to the children of the first and second wealthiest quintiles, the children of those in the fourth and fifth quintiles have a difficult time moving up from their parents' level and into one of the first three quintiles. Likewise, when the decision about who gets jobs is based on who has special connections rather than on individuals' merit and readiness to do the work, the upward mobility of those in the bottom two quintiles stagnates. This, so far, is not the situation in the United States.

In this country, each person's insight, ambition, and way of seeing the world is meant to create new possibilities. To the extent that my talents can work with my motivation and self-discipline to make something happen in society, progress occurs. The entrepreneurial spirit of Americans is, I think, a direct result of our right to pursue our own happiness. Each age, and, in fact, each person, defines this pursuit a bit differently, but the result over hundreds of years is a flexibility and responsiveness to the future and change. The status quo, the way things have always been, has less status in the United States. The pursuit of happiness is at the core of change, which is, of course, imbedded in the power of the individual to see the world in a particular way.

Chapters 7 and 8 lay out the challenges and resources that may be involved in improving the levels of generosity. The next fifty years will see the largest private intergenerational wealth transfer in human history. Experts Paul Schervish and John Havens at the Boston College Social Welfare Research Institute have projected that between 1998 and 2052, between $31 trillion and $41 trillion of wealth (in 1998 dollars) will move from one generation to another. They estimate that during this fifty-four-year period, our economy will produce 10.1 *million* new millionaires. Our economy currently enables Americans to accumulate and hand down more wealth, with little of it siphoned off by taxes. In the future, what principles, what values will shape how we share these funds and preserve the character of the American spirit? How will the growing wealth change us as individual citizens and as a whole society? Both the coming wealth transfer and the omnipresent diversity in the U.S. population, the subject of chapter 8, need to be nudged into the resources column and not be permitted to drift into the problem category. The money potentially available in the wealth transfer, as well as the rich ideas available from recent immigrants from other cultures, can help our deliberations.

Chapter 9 opens with an examination of the dangerous donations that can occur and, as a result, can have the potential to undermine the positive power of investment giving in our society. It lays out some pragmatic examples of generosity that do more harm than good. This investigation of the negative effects of philanthropy is crucial in trying to shape a new vision of the role of generosity in the United States.

Chapter 10 describes some of the successful generosity ventures that are currently working. We need to acknowledge them before we consider what can be done in the future. We need to have in mind how contemporary Americans are improving the way our democracy and economy actually work. Then we can consider who might ultimately be able to do what to achieve new goals through generosity and cooperation.

The book closes with an outline for a new American Revolution in generosity. We need to develop ways to give much more money to investments in our society and then make goals and make the gifts. Within a specific time frame, we need to achieve specific goals *with, not for* people who need to live better and contribute more of their gifts to our society. We can do much better to really honor our forebears and preserve their endowment. Generosity has served us too powerfully to let it slip away while we adjust to self-centeredness that will make neither us nor our children happier, will not stabilize the relations between income groups, and will not serve the tenets in our founding documents about freedom and equality. We have work to do. We have built a strong economy, and we can now use its strengths to assure that the middle 60 percent as well as the bottom 20 percent make progress with the top 20 percent. Justice and fairness have marked the best moments in our history. We can have them again, but we need to act powerfully. The fragile balance we maintain between capitalism and democracy is always in the hands of the current generation.

1

DEMOCRACY, CAPITALISM, AND GENEROSITY: THE FRAGILE BALANCE

Most people think that Americans are generous because we are rich. The truth is that we are rich, in significant part, because we are generous. It is not surprising that Americans know so little about the economic impact of citizen generosity on the country's growth. We tend to see giving as something that is just *good* and *nice* to do, which it is. We do not, unfortunately, recognize it as a major contributing factor in our economic, social, and political achievements as a nation.

Just imagine, for instance, how your city or New York City or San Francisco would look if every building funded by individual donors were suddenly to disappear. The hospitals, museums, universities, theaters—gone. Imagine the workday the rest of us would experience if all the people educated thanks to privately donated, need-based scholarships were suddenly to stay home for a week—their offices, labs, operating rooms, studios, classrooms, courtrooms, empty. What if all the inventions, all the research funded by private gifts likewise suddenly disappeared, sucked out of the system and no longer available for our society's benefit? Just imagine if the medicines, penicillin among others, initially developed with funding from donations, were no longer available in your local pharmacy. What if the thousands of organizations funded by citizens' contributions vanished? No United Way or American Cancer Society, no Alcoholics Anonymous, no Mothers Against Drunk Driving.

Fifty-one percent of all hospital beds are funded by citizen generosity. Forty-nine percent of all two- and four-year institutions of higher learning are not-for-profit. Citizen generosity funds a little more than 20 percent of all students in institutions of higher learning, 95 percent of all orchestras, and 60 percent of social service organizations.[1] In 1997, not-for-profit organizations spent $700 billion in cash. That's cash. It does not include volunteered time. And it's about 8 percent of the economy. Generosity is not a luxury in this country. It is a cultural norm, a defining characteristic of our successful economy and our reasonably successful society.

The use we make of generosity, or philanthropy, has historically been very different from that of other countries. We use it to address societal problems. When something is wrong, we don't wait for the government to fix it. Once we've donated money and time to the problem, we may then ask government to take it from there, but we are philanthropically entrepreneurial. Because philanthropy is an investment in our democracy and our economy, we give considerably larger amounts than the citizens of other countries do. While many countries have significantly higher tax rates, we give about 2 percent of our Gross Domestic Product annually. The next highest figure in the world is 0.7 percent in the United Kingdom. This is a very large difference, but it was once much larger. In the past ten to fifteen years, other countries have begun to copy our use of nonprofit organizations to help government and industry solve problems. It's a method that works.

This is more than a story worth telling; it's a case worth making, since today we sit at a critical economic and critical juncture in our country's history. But let me start with a favorite story of my own.

In 1894, Dr. Daniel Hale Williams performed the first successful open-heart surgery in the world at Provident Hospital in Chicago. In 1890, just four years earlier, Provident Hospital did not even exist. The personal generosity of Americans, wealthy and poor, black and white, male and female, brought the hospital into existence and then to prominence—in four years.

In 1889, a young woman named Emma Reynolds wanted to be a nurse. She sought admission at each of Chicago's various nursing schools and was turned down because she was African American. Her brother, who was minister of St. Stephen's African Methodist Episcopal Church, turned to another prominent member of the black community for help. He asked Dr. Williams, a respected surgeon, to intercede for Emma Reynolds at the white nursing schools. Williams tried but was unsuccessful.

Williams and the Reverend Mr. Reynolds were angry and frustrated by this situation, and in the great American tradition of entrepreneurialism, they decided to remedy it. In 1890, Williams gathered a group of black ministers, physicians, and businessmen to talk about founding an interracial hospital and nurse-training school in Chicago. With their pledge of support, he and Reynolds began their task. Soon they had the enthusiastic support not only of the black community but of several prominent white Chicagoans as well. At the time, it was shamefully difficult for a black physician to hospitalize a patient, and these supporters recognized the desperate need. They held rallies and fund-raising events all over Chicago's south and west sides. And the people gave.

The group knew they were going to make it when the Reverend Mr. Jenkins Jones and black nurse Nahyoke Sockum Curtis persuaded the Armour Meat Packing Company to donate the down payment for a three-story brick house. It became Provident Hospital, with a total of twelve beds. Equipment and supplies for the hospital were donated or paid for by financial contributions from the community. Volunteers provided a large part of the staff. Black women who cleaned the homes of white families during the day then donated their "spare" time to scrub the hospital's floors. Male volunteers whose color made them ineligible to join the local carpenter's union nonetheless built the hospital's interior walls. Donations came in from such prominent, wealthy white businessmen as George M. Pullman, department store owner Marshall Field, Cyrus

McCormick of McCormick reaper fame, and hotelier Potter Palmer. Many of these contributors acknowledged the benefit of making sure that medical treatment would be available to their black employees.

The story of Provident did not end when the last walls were up and the beds in place. The hospital grew in size to sixty-five beds. Emma Reynolds became a nurse, and so did hundreds of other young women. There were seven young women in the first class with Emma Reynolds, but as the hospital grew, so did the nursing class. During the tenure of George Cleveland Hall as chief of staff, from 1894 to 1928, more than two hundred black nurses were trained at Provident.

After Williams performed the first successful open-heart surgery, Provident trained doctors such as William Warrick Cardozo, who served a residency at Provident and went on to do groundbreaking research into sickle-cell anemia. Other benefits followed. Curtis organized a contingent of black nurses, many from Provident, to serve during the Spanish-American War. One of the women who helped found the hospital was Fannie Barrier Williams, wife of a prominent black attorney. Her work with the hospital not only served the community but also paved her own way to become the first black member of the prestigious Chicago Women's Club in 1895, sponsored by a white woman doctor from the Provident staff. Eventually Fannie Williams became the first woman of any race or ethnicity to serve on the Chicago Library Board.

The hospital's growth also created jobs. Businesses developed to address the needs of the hospital. The hospital also helped to transform the neighborhood in which it was located. It is a given that the proximity of a hospital is a major factor in the desirability of a community to prospective home owners. Consider, then, how important a hospital would be to middle-class and upper-class African Americans in the first decades of the twentieth century. At that time, most white hospitals did not accept black patients. When they did, the patients were lodged in poorly maintained, separate wards, often in the basement. It didn't matter whether you could afford the best or not; you couldn't get it. Most black doctors were not allowed to perform surgery in white operating rooms. You could have a brilliant doctor of your own race, but he or she would be unable to take out your appendix. In 1919, there were roughly thirty black hospitals in the North. Most of them were small, did not provide full service to their patients, and were sorely deficient in the basics of science and technology. There were five that managed to provide anything like sufficient medical care. Two were in Philadelphia, two were in New York, and then there was Provident.

Obviously, Provident was a great attraction to African American professionals, and not only doctors. It moved to a new location in 1896, now a sixty-five-bed hospital, and became the hub of a community called Bronzeville. Within a few blocks of the hospital, and within a few decades of its founding, there grew up a thriving business district. Two newspapers, the *Chicago Bee* and the *Chicago Defender,* established their headquarters there. The Overton Hygienic Building—a four-story, block-long construction—went up directly across the street, to house the banking and other enterprises of black entrepreneur Anthony Overton and to provide rental space for other black professionals. The Wabash YWCA went up in 1911. Prominent black citizens, such as Ida B. Wells and her husband, Frederick Barnett, moved into the neighborhood in the teens and twenties. During the 1920s, in fact, Bronzeville shared in the cultural blossoming that was called the Harlem Renaissance. It is difficult to imagine that this remarkable community could have grown up without a source of medical care for its affluent, as well as its not-so-affluent, citizens.

The Provident Hospital is today part of the Cook County Bureau of Health. Provident has developed programs with the Chicago Board of Education to reduce out-of-wedlock pregnancy and to teach pregnant teens good prenatal habits while completing high school. Other Provident programs offer ambulatory care and home visits to permit the elderly, diabetics, and cancer patients as well as expectant mothers to get regular medical services close to home, while assuring that patients with high risks or specialized needs get their help directly from Cook County Hospital.

• • •

Perhaps you can see why I like this story so much. The story of Provident Hospital dramatizes the way in which philanthropy—that is, citizen generosity—creates remarkable social *and* economic value. Like the proverbial pebble dropped in still waters, generosity generates ever-expanding rings of benefit that wash over many layers of society. It produces a virtuous cycle of self-reinforcing benefits.

The outstanding characteristic of American generosity is its entrepreneurial character. By this I mean a drive to build something of value through hard work and risk taking. Identifying a problem or an opportunity is the critical starting point. But the entrepreneurial spirit drives the individual or group to take action and to do so with a sense of urgency. Over the decades, and in fact centuries, private donors in America have typically made their gifts far earlier and far more quickly than other funders and investors, such as business or government, usually even before the market or our legislators have realized that there is a critical need. This is generally true because generous citizens are individually prepared to take higher risks and invest in more experimental efforts than businesses or government. Markets and shareholders make high and hard demands on the rate of return on invested funds in the business world. And government funding typically requires extensive time to achieve broad political consensus.

Thus philanthropy has provided a dynamic and dependable third option, beyond markets and government, for capital infusion into areas that go on to build the American economy. These voluntary gifts have initiated the first stages of tremendous change and development. And, over the years, since they were not tied to a financial return, donors used a moral or social calculus to measure the value of their gifts.

The Provident story also illustrates another dimension of American philanthropy, its boundary-crossing character. The Chicagoans who decided that the city needed an interracial hospital and training school so that blacks could become nurses were not all part of the same group. They shared neither class, nor race, nor religion, nor gender. What they did share was a common goal, an aspiration, and an idea to which they were willing to contribute. They ended up integrating social space as a product of their collaboration.

And as Johns Hopkins political economist Francis Fukuyama confirms, such bonds of trust and mutuality also create the best chances for a productive economy.[2] The broader the range of capital sources for the entrepreneur, the faster the needed assets are accumulated. One's own family or ethnic community is entirely too narrow a source of resources to produce flourishing economic growth. So the entrepreneurial spirit of American generosity also encompasses a readiness to invest across boundaries, leading to rich economic and social growth and a confluence between democracy and capitalism. For highly individualistic systems to coexist and to prosper, bonds of trust must be built. David Hume, the eighteenth-century Scottish philosopher/statesman, tells a memorable parable:

> Your corn is ripe today; mine will be so tomorrow. Tis profitable for us both, that I should labour with you today, and that you should aid me tomorrow. I have no kindness for you, and know you have as little for me. I will not, therefore, take any pains upon your account. And should I labour with you upon my own account, in expectation of a return, I know I should be disappointed, and that I should in vain depend upon your gratitude. Here then I leave you to labour alone; You treat me in the same manner, The seasons change; and both of us lose our harvests for want of mutual confidence and security.[3]

We really have no way of knowing all of the motivations of people, like Marshall Field, who gave to Provident. Was he thinking of the economic benefit that he might obtain in the form of more dependable labor if his black employees had better health care? Was it pure generosity driven by the thought of the future well-being of an unknown group of children who might someday become nurses? And what about the motivation of the African American organizers? Were they seeking a future economic benefit for themselves as well? Cheaper labor to assist the black physicians perhaps? Or more social status? Or simply a better chance for their own daughters to get an education? Indeed, the parties to the project at the time, black and white, could not have known for certain the motivations of their counterparts in the venture. They were taking a measure of risk, reaching across boundaries real or imagined, with the sense that the promised benefits justified the risk taking.

Trust builds on itself, meaning that, assuming success, each subsequent venture is less risky and easier to complete. The product of mutuality is "social" capital, nicely defined by Robert Putnam as "the features of social organization, such as networks, norms, and trust, that facilitate coordination and cooperation for mutual benefit. Social capital enhances the benefits of investment in physical and human capital."[4]

Such networks were built and enhanced by the Provident Hospital development effort, and we can see that generosity created rich social capital, so essential to the functioning of a democratic society. All contributors, whether volunteer laborers or wealthy patrons, acted to produce something of common value, a greater good for a larger group than themselves as individuals. In recognizing that the best way to enjoy the personal benefits of democratic capitalism was to help others achieve these goals, they were following a civic tradition that has carried us to the position we occupy in the world today.

But the argument of this book isn't simply that philanthropy creates a strong social environment for democracy (which it does). It's that investment-oriented citizen generosity has built real assets in the very areas of our society that economists associate with accelerating economic growth, as witness the assets created by Provident in its own community and the medical community.

As the first step, the dynamic marketplace of ideas essential to successful capitalism is significantly enhanced by new ideas, many of which are initially tested and implemented because of philanthropy. This third way of funding—beyond the government and private, return-expecting investors—opens the door to ideas that are still too young to have gained the backing of a majority of voters or shareholders, and brings dynamism and prosperity to our economy. Such new ideas are essential.

Paul Romer, an economist at Stanford University, has turned the world of economic theory on its head by proposing that an economy is based on ideas rather than on material things. Rather than accepting the classic view that economic growth is defined by the availability of material resources and their allocation among alternative uses, Romer focuses economic progress on ideas, putting scarcity and even price systems in a secondary position. Wealth creation, according to Romer, is pegged to the capacity of the country to hatch new ideas that regroup and reuse material resources in new ways.

Philanthropy, at its essence, creates additional avenues to launch ideas in our society. Those with wealth can push money out to support their ideas or other people's ideas. Those with ideas and few assets can pull money from the wealthy or from foundations to a special sector of tax-exempt organizations set up for funding and piloting projects without a profit-making aim.

These ideas are the fuel for three major areas of democratic capital investment. The first is donations to develop people, or human capital. The second is donations to property, or physical capital. The third is donations to support ideas, or intellectual capital.

First, Americans have developed people—that is, the human potential—more extensively and more deeply into the lower income levels of our population than any other country with our levels of diversity. The knowledge, skills, and diversity of our people make a substantial impact on our economic growth. Donations by citizens have increased the quality, quantity, and variety of the labor pool available to our country.

Provident Hospital provides an example of this. The project furthered the development of nursing as a career option for black women. Because the hospital was one of the few in the nation where a black physician could serve an internship or residency, it furthered the development of black physicians. The children of these doctors and nurses at Provident almost certainly advanced further in the use of their talents than if their parents had done domestic work or manual labor all their lives. Human capital grows generation by generation from the initial investment. Society is rewarded with more highly contributing citizens.

For hundreds of years, need-based scholarships, internships, training programs, and many other kinds of educational-advancement programs have made individual progress a real possibility for every citizen, at any income level, a greater good for the person and a greater good for society. American generosity sent millions of students to college, including Ralph Waldo Emerson, Milton Friedman, Alice Walker, Oprah Winfrey, Bella Abzug, Ruth Bader Ginsburg, Itzhak Perlman, Mark Rothko, John Updike, W. E. B. Du Bois, Gregory Peck, Bill Clinton, Saul Bellow, Mae Jemison, and Leontyne Price. The list could go on and on. No field would be where it is today without this most basic, and earliest, area of private philanthropy, the scholarship. But we need to continue to use philanthropy to find innovative ways to expand the exercise of human potential as the challenges that face our society change.

Second, individual acts of generosity have gone to build up home ownership and community assets. Donations have also targeted physical facilities, increasing the value of our property and tangible assets. Donations, both large and small, built most of the nation's best museums, hospitals, theaters, community centers, and private colleges and universities. These investments in physical capital create economic engines for their sites. More jobs become available. Businesses grow around these spaces to meet the demands of the new enterprise and its employees.

Again, Provident provides an example of this. When the hospital moved from the 1891 twelve-bed frame building, a new hospital was built. Again, white contributors joined with black professionals and community members to raise $100,000 for the facility. This was not only, in itself, a significant asset for the community, but it also inspired the building or conversion of dozens of other buildings in the area, including, as I mentioned above, the Overton Hygienic Building and the Wabash YMCA. For well over one hundred years, that hospital secured the neighborhood it was a part of, providing work for smaller businesses and people who were additions to the community. A gift brought that economic activity. And on the Chicago note, that city's nine philanthropically supported museums bring more revenue to the city than all of its major sports franchises (all businesses) together! And the generosity that funds these facilities raises the value of property in the surrounding communities.

In the past century, philanthropy began to invest in physical capital to develop low-income communities. Think of Habitat for Humanity's building and selling sixty thousand homes to low-income people at prices they could afford and maintain, or St. Paul's Community Baptist Church in East Brooklyn, which built twenty-five hundred homes for low-income citizens in a specific neighborhood. These buildings affect not only the lives of the individuals who occupy them but also the growth of capital, in the form of property values, in the communities in which they are built.

Third, by supporting new ideas, including inventions, innovations, and new institutions, generosity has created dramatic advances at a fast rate in U.S. society. This voluntary support for change has enhanced the opportunities for rapid progress, particularly in science, technology, and social change. Successful inventions themselves advance economic growth by improving the quality, quantity, and diversity of goods and services available and by improving the means of production. Again, let us turn to Provident. Even in this small hospital in Chicago's Bronzeville, major medical innovations were made. Daniel Hale Williams's groundbreaking open-heart surgery and William Warrick Cardozo's sickle-cell discoveries furthered medical science.

Major donors such as the Guggenheims, John D. Rockefeller III, and Andrew Carnegie funded new ideas and inventions ranging from aviation, space rocketry, and radar, to the electron microscope and penicillin, to guaranteed pensions for teachers. In direct contrast, the drive against polio was funded in bulk by 4 billion *dimes* contributed to the March of Dimes by our parents, grandparents, and greatgrandparents, until the vaccine was discovered. Scientific, technological, and cultural knowledge has sprouted in the wake of the discoveries and initiatives funded by these donations. They have also frequently given Americans a sense of their collective power to solve new problems and newly critical problems, all kinds of problems.

I would like to return one last time to the Provident story. We've already seen that it illustrates a solid investment strategy to ensure the accumulation of human capital, physical capital, and, last but not least, intellectual capital. But the Provident story also shows how citizen generosity has contributed to the progress we continue to make toward achieving the ideals our founding fathers laid out. As Americans, one of our important democratic values says we believe that all men are created equal. Thirty years after the Civil War, the moral entrepreneurs involved in the Provident project were pushing reality closer to that ideal by giving black women the opportunity to become nurses long before a majority of Americans were prepared to give them this opportunity. This diverse group, acting in the entrepreneurial spirit, pressed and achieved a measure of practical progress toward the awesome goal of equality in our democracy, while pressing toward the better utilization of talent in our capitalist economy.

More than a century after the founding of Provident, the United States has emerged from the cold war with extraordinary economic and social strengths. A greater percentage of our population has achieved a higher standard of living than any other country with our levels of diversity. The greatest share of the credit for this success often goes to the abundance of our natural resources, the large size of our markets, and our increasing success with technologies, and well it should. But we ignore at our peril the economic growth that has come from the way Americans practice generosity. This unique national trait has complemented the strong features and tempered the negative features of capitalism.

It is the balance struck between capitalism and democracy that matters. Generosity toward our fellow citizens feeds innovative risk taking and economic growth from which we all profit. By releasing new potential in human capital, physical capital, and intellectual capital, individuals who have reaped the rewards of capitalism are reinvesting in economic growth, democratically. Why is the interplay between democracy and capitalism so delicate and so vital? In the United States, our form of democracy protects the individual from the power of the state, insisting that the state exists to assure the greatest amount of happiness to the largest number of people. "We hold these truths to be self-evident, that all men are created equal, that they are endowed by their Creator with certain unalienable Rights, that among these are Life, Liberty and the pursuit of Happiness." That maxim, held as basic teaching in our country, implies that each of us as citizens will act with respect toward our fellows as we move through one another's lives. Politically, democracy has always struggled with the strain between individual freedoms granted and individual freedoms protected. How can these rights be assured for everyone?

The solution is, indeed, delicate. Democracy inspires optimism, fairness, and, dare I say it, even altruism. Because individual freedom does not come easily or remain in place without effort, guaranteeing it in our democracy puts an enormous burden on each of us to live with our interdependence in mind. Democratic life includes vigilant commitment to voluntary civic engagement and respect for the laws of the land while they advance our collective independence and personal pursuit of happiness. Early in our days as a country, Alexis de Tocqueville saw these traits as stabilizing practices that rightly understood the boundaries of self-interest.[5]

In the United States, business operates under the expectations of this political system. Democracy, which admittedly makes the world safer for capitalism because of the freedom it assures, is routinely tackled and thrown down by the lack of self-restraint, by the greed and materialism of capitalism. In general, neither democracy nor capitalism enshrines authority with the power it has in monarchic systems, so the exercise of good judgment, personal ethics, and mindfulness of the common, not just the individual, good constitute the authority people need to operate within democracy.

Capitalism needs democracy's values to remain defensible in society. Conversely, democracy needs capitalism's wealth creation for pursuing justice and opportunity for all. Capitalism offers the broadest set of options for expanding wealth. It invests assets along a spectrum, from the low risk and low return of bonds to the high risk and high return of venture capital. It tolerates high risk and creative thrust into new opportunities in the quest for calculated material gain. Along the way, however, democracy can be taken advantage of, and capitalism knows how to do it.

Capitalism stimulates competition, winner-take-all approaches, and optimization of the individual's assets. It is vigorous and thrives on freedom and light bureaucracy. It is robustly risk tolerant and self-confident. It also can be pessimistic. "Things may get worse, so I had better take mine now." Capitalism tends toward accepting the starker Hobbesian view of a world where "the notions of right and wrong, justice and injustice . . . have no place," a state "called war; and such a war as is of every man against every man."[6] One of the awesome personal challenges is to be a great humanist and a great capitalist.

Unless capitalism has a governor on its motor it can easily race out of control and do real harm to others and eventually to itself. Look at the market chaos and lost investor confidence that resulted from the apparent self-dealing greed of Enron, Anderson, Tyco, Adelphi, and other recent examples of corporate destruction. They illustrate what happens when some people think they are smarter than the majority of the people and can exempt themselves from the rules of ethics. Capitalism itself does not make out well under these circumstances. This, as most Wall Street people said at the time, is *not* "just the way business works." No enterprise can work that way for long. Cynicism is the enemy of trust. Thus, capitalism and democracy both depend on trust and transparency. In fact, the great self-correcting mechanism that is the market punishes those who self-deal or forget the importance of transparency.

As many economists and historians have argued effectively, capitalism works best in democracies in part because of the ways in which those democracies promote honesty and fairness in exchanges between citizens. More laws and rules to codify the values of democracy may not be the answer, but they tend to look appealing when employees, retirees, and stockholders are being hurt by the "I will take mine first" attitude of some corporate officers. On the other hand, pure capitalism does not care about race, gender, religion, or ethnicity, just performance. It is a great leveler, thriving more on good ideas than on the social status of the thinkers. As political scientist John Mueller puts it, "We're very fortunate that democracy doesn't require people to be good or noble, but merely to calculate what is best for them or their society, and then to act only if they happen to be so inclined. We are very fortunate that capitalism raises and transforms selfishness and acquisitiveness into higher purposes. Democracy and capitalism are about as romantic as, in Charlotte Brontë's phrase, Monday morning. But that is a good thing."[7]

Capitalism and democracy need each other as they have evolved in the United States, and their broker is generosity. Yes, taxes are the prescriptions we vote on ourselves—and more or less carry out—but just as the guarantee of individual rights balances a democracy's political majority, philanthropy provides individual financial investments to balance the legislative direction of our taxes. And while companies infuse our economy with money to serve their bottom-line interests, often with anticipated or unanticipated social profits, generosity offers a channel for taking high risks without strings attached, except for those that tie us to the people with whom we share this country.

Philanthropy makes a real witness to our social contract and a real investment in our economy's future. Generosity is capitalism's open and pragmatic acknowledgment that, since democracy's freedoms enhance capitalism's economic powers, then democracy deserves assets from capitalism that contribute to its strength. By sharing assets beyond those prescribed by taxes or the cost of doing business, capitalism can improve social cohesion as well as justice and opportunity for all citizens. Citizen generosity works as a mitigator to soften capitalism's more destructive features: cut-throat competition and wealth concentration. Generosity blunts some of the destructive facets of competitiveness, "the survival of the fittest" elements of unfettered capitalism. Generosity expands toward those who have not been favored in the game of life, and, seeing their potential as an asset to them and to the rest of us, it offers them a chance to play and win.

Generosity helps to distribute rather than concentrate wealth and opportunities in society. The broad implications of this feature of citizen generosity are upward mobility for an astonishing percentage of America's underclass population, good for democracy and good for the economy. Generosity is the moral juice that has kept us heading toward the founders' ideals, despite many mistakes along the way. Finally, in practice, American philanthropy uses the best features of capitalism to do its work. Generosity is entrepreneurial, individualistic, creative, visionary, and idea generating.

In the coming chapters I will demonstrate the real economic impact philanthropy has had in these areas, contributing to making us grow during the past 150 years into the dominant economic and political power in the world. However, before we get much further in this adventure, I want to acknowledge that, in the course of the interviews I have done for this book, I have spoken to many brilliant people who do not agree with me on this. Some of their objections are very much worth mentioning.[8]

Let's look at what these critics claim:

Philanthropy is a self-serving way that elites and wanna-be elites provide social standing for themselves with modest benefit to the causes they espouse.

That's true in some instances. There are charity balls that raise less for their charities than they spend on the champagne they serve. And there are "vanity foundations" that spend more on publicizing their good works than on the works themselves. But as a blanket indictment of philanthropy in this country, the accusation doesn't hold up. That's something I hope to prove conclusively in the next four chapters.

People who give are mostly inspired by the tax write-offs and not by high-minded goals.

That may be true. And I really couldn't care less. Whether I have given a scholarship to get a tax deduction or to give your daughter a high-quality education on me, her education will not be changed. Capitalism and our economy are bound up in self-interest, and self-interest rightly understood should weigh just as much on the individual and social benefits of democracy as it does on dollars and cents. It is acceptable to watch out for yourself as long as you are also watching out for your fellow citizens. I am resistant to letting perfect motives drive out good motives. In our current environment, it will be hard enough to keep generosity increasing among all citizens without insisting on perfect idealistic motives.

Wealth is becoming more concentrated, in the aftermath of the economic boom of the 1990s, in the hands of a small percentage of the population who do not use it to serve the interests of democracy.

I'm tempted to say, "Exactly! That's my point!" It is the very fact that wealth is becoming more concentrated that makes my call for increased philanthropy necessary. The urgency of this book resides first in the fact that we have stopped nurturing and building our giving habits at just the wrong time. Even with the downturn of the market in 2001–2002, a massive wealth transfer will move an estimated $31 trillion from one generation to another through bequests over the next fifty years, according to Paul Schervish and John Havens of Boston College.[9] This wealth transfer poses one big problem and one great opportunity.

For the first time in U.S. history, we are looking at mass affluence. In 2001, there were 5 million millionaire-plus families in America. The children and grandchildren in these families will not have to work if they do not choose to. They can, if they like, decide not to struggle with education and career preparation, and they may not feel much connection with those who do. They may feel little or no responsibility for or link to the quality of social and economic life of their fellow citizens. Conspicuous consumption and unchecked materialism among a few could increasingly dominate the culture. If philanthropy atrophies, the results could be dire. The people in the middle 60 percent as well as the bottom 20 percent of the income distribution in the United States will start to feel definitively left behind, alienated from a fair chance to do better. The bonds between democracy and capitalism will begin to loosen, as those who feel they have no economic opportunities will, rightly, consider themselves as less equal citizens.

But think of the good fortune this wealth transfer offers. The funds in private hands available for this "third" way of funding could, for the first time, stand powerfully ready to improve areas that still need attention in our society. We can get serious as a nation about fixing what is still broken in our democracy by fostering more generosity that will sustain our way of life, economically as well as politically.

Philanthropy enables the power that wealth accumulates to persist through generations and create the American equivalent of a ruling class. The views of this small elite have an inappropriately large impact on any issue they choose to deploy their money to shape.

If I were advocating philanthropy *instead of* government activity, this would be a knockout blow. But I'm not. I'm saying that philanthropy is the third factor in our economic and social well-being, not the first or second. *Of course,* government has to continue to work to preserve a functioning democracy in this country. But government should not be relied on to make all the decisions and the initiatives with regard to important institutions. Where public goods such as museums and hospitals are the result only of government spending, not of philanthropic investments by fellow citizens, people learn to wait for something good to happen rather than helping to make it happen, as is our culture. If ideas are doomed to falter unless they can attract government funding or create a profit, many people will stop trying to innovate. Rather than a foolish either/or trade-off, we should be able develop a better blend of both/and. A great civic loss would result if we discouraged individual citizens from providing beyond the required tax payments for the well-being and sustainable growth of the country in whatever way most motivates them. This kind of freedom is also radical and has contributed to the radically imaginative opportunities that characterize our country. The challenge over the next twenty years is to sustain and increase giving by people in all categories.

Generosity is no substitute for more significantly redistributive tax structures and government-supported health care, early childhood care, and eldercare, as well as more government support for the arts. We should come closer to the social welfare system operating in Sweden and other northern European countries.

I believe that Americans have a primary and critical responsibility to maintain a strong redistributive tax structure. On the other hand, while European countries, especially the Scandinavian countries, have significantly higher tax rates and less domestic philanthropy, nothing in our own national temperament suggests that the United States will move dramatically in this direction. But let me be clear, *absolutely nothing* in this book should be construed to suggest that generosity should actually be counted on to replace taxes as the appropriate way to achieve desired outcomes in American society.

However, private generosity has made a defining difference in our country. More citizen generosity could help to energize our economy now when this is exactly what is needed. More government funding for inert or ineffectual bureaucracies could actually be worse instead of better, speeding the death of civic engagement that was born before the abolitionist days. The government, by its nature, moves slowly, and what we need is to foster more efficient change. As problems appear to become intractable, notions of welfare and mutual help become increasingly difficult to defend, and it will become harder and harder to find a political consensus for higher government funding to support people while they try to make economic progress in our country.

In fact, American society and economy are not *highly successful and do* not *provide a higher quality of life to a larger percentage of a highly diverse population than any other country in the world. You have far too rosy a view of life in this country.*

Life is certainly not ideal in the United States, not for those living below the poverty line, not for many people of color, nor for some immigrants. Yet the poor in America, particularly the elderly poor, live better—according to the social health indices—than those in many European countries where taxes and their benefits are higher.[10] Upward mobility for the poor is higher in the United States.[11] People from poor countries choose to immigrate here for just this reason. Within the first generation, immigrants' children go to college in significant numbers in America.

It's somewhat difficult to argue that life in the United States is really good at the same time that I'm arguing for improving it, but that's exactly the position in which I find myself. I want to say that the U.S. system works pretty well, but that the system includes a very important mechanism—philanthropy—that we must acknowledge as crucial and that we must continue to encourage. And we must do it right away. The earliest signs of significant increases in the size of the gap between have's and have not's appear in the 2000 census data. The new data is alarming. The United States may be on the verge of losing the fragile balance that citizen generosity has maintained with the forces of capitalism. This balance has enabled America to make dramatic economic progress in an atmosphere of relative social order and little class conflict. Taking the past for granted may spell real doom for our future. Citizen generosity matters. Without it, cynicism and class conflict could pervade and change the very parts of America's spirit that make us successful. Social trends are shifting the ground from under us in ways that could be devastating. The handwriting is already on the wall. Without determination we could find that the spirit of generosity that has made us so great has been forgotten.

This is especially true since, over the last three decades, the United States has undergone a massive cultural diversification, as new immigration laws have beckoned an infusion of new citizens from around the globe. While many of them will share in the wealth, a major proportion of these newer Americans do not share ethnicity, race, or religion with Americans of European descent. The cultural traditions of Islam, Hinduism, Buddhism, and Confucianism each have a unique way of inspiring care and compassion for others, which could provide for an even richer, more diverse economy of ideas and assets. Their points of view are even embodied in economic structures, such as the *kye, hui,* and *niangis,* as well as in spiritual traditions. But to enfold those traditions and structures into our social capital, we must take steps now to ensure that the philanthropic tradition is not quelled or narrowed.

From my own work in economic development in New London, Connecticut, and from my assessment of the social health indices and the most recent census, I believe the United States clearly needs to improve our social progress. The old codes of conservative and liberal, of Democrat and Republican, of right wing and left wing, seem very tired. In corporate board meetings I was assumed to be "the liberal academic"; in faculty meetings, I was assumed to be "the conservative management." To businesspeople and to the poor in New London these labels were worthless and the debate tired; what they needed was creative problem solving. In New London, we needed new businesses to bring jobs and strengthen the tax base. We needed new productive, not competitive or exploitative, alliances among ethnic and racial groups. Moreover, citizens needed to bring these changes about.

In the country today, we need something new that respects our American, independent, entrepreneurial spirit and resists the pessimism of statist, confiscatory policies and demeaning pass-throughs. Something that insists on the partnership of citizen generosity with the corporate and government sectors to reduce poverty and increase investments in human capital, facilities and communities, and new ideas. We could trigger and develop innovative national goals for personal well-being, including such hot-button issues as suitable education, home ownership, urban economic development, and intellectual capital. It's time to realize that we get only so far relying on government as our surrogate and that we, as private citizens, must all be invested. Douglass North, one of only two economic historians to win the Nobel Prize, has focused much of his work on economic growth on the institutional aspects of the economic past. His conclusion is that institutions that protected property rights and lowered transaction costs created the decisive contributions to economic growth. More recently the work of Hernando De Soto focuses on the value of deeds and documentation of ownership (financial instruments and institutions) to the growth of capitalism and reduction of poverty. He makes a brilliant case for how in developing countries the evolution of these institutions could transform the condition of the poor.

We cannot afford to defer our attention longer. By inspiring Americans at all income levels to use a portion of their income to exercise some choice about where in society their money goes, we can drive economic growth and civic engagement hand in hand. Will Americans of the future be able to make even more progress toward the aspirations of the founding fathers? I believe we will be, and, with some good leadership and sound information, I believe that American citizens will commit to the work ahead, just as we did during the Progressive Era in the first decades of the twentieth century. Those who disagree with these premises or find these views too idealistic will not like much in this book.

2

MAKING THE MOST OF PEOPLE THROUGH EDUCATION: HUMAN CAPITAL, PART ONE

I still believe the American Revolution to be big with important consequences to the world and that the labor of no individual, however feeble his contributions were, could have been spared.

—BENJAMIN RUSH, 1788

The founding fathers had certainly never heard of the concept of human capital, but Benjamin Rush seems to have had an intuitive understanding of this twentieth-century term. It was recently defined in "The Well-being of Nations," a special report prepared by the Organization for Economic Cooperation and Development, as "the knowledge, skills, competencies and attributes embodied in individuals that facilitate the creation of personal social and economic well-being. . . ."[1] Many of the founders understood that the new nation would profit from investments made in developing the knowledge and skills of all citizens and that in many cases this would require personal generosity toward those fellow citizens. All of us may have been created equal, but life hardly offers a level playing field. For democracy to work, these practical men understood that people would have to help one another across a variety of natural divisions in order to make the rights to life, liberty, and the pursuit of happiness a reality for all. The fierce arguments about slavery that figured in the writing of the Constitution testify that this issue of equal opportunity was before them. While some were slave owners, others had already begun an Abolitionist Society in 1774. They were on the threshold of revolutionary thinking about slavery and women's rights. And they knew it. They eventually compromised in a way that, while it might have made union possible, has also haunted the nation to this day. But they knew what the issues were.

Paul Schervish noted recently that in our knowledge society, each person can and does own the means of production: the human brain. Human intelligence is the fundamental means of production for our common future. This insight changes everything. Education, in particular, must be looked at even more seriously. Early health care and education are also more critical than ever. It doesn't make sense, whether to a nonsentimental capitalist or a deeply committed liberal, to allow human capital to be wasted. No one is expendable.

Human capital—along with its sister term, social capital—has become a fundamental concept of modern economic theory. Human capital resides within human beings, as the sum of an individual's attributes, skills, and knowledge. It goes beyond what someone knows and what someone knows how to do. It extends to knowing "why"—a conceptual understanding of "systems" such as family life or scientific reasoning—and knowing "who"—the ability to understand how to deploy a variety of people and groups effectively and work with them toward common goals. Human capital should not be confused with social capital. Social capital is the asset developed in society as a result of the many relationships people form while engaging in civic activities. It is productive networks that support progress and make up for losses. Social capital is an important source of mutual trust that connects people in bonds as strong as family ties, but does not involve blood relations. Human capital can be isolated and deprived of social capital, yet still be highly developed and have significant impact.

Collectively, the enormous pool of human potential is a nation's greatest economic asset. In fact, Nobel Prize–winning economist Gary Becker estimates that it accounts for 75 percent of national wealth.[2] If Becker is correct, then combining the remaining assets, which includes corporate capital, capital in unincorporated businesses, all housing and facilities, consumer durables, government capital, and cash,[3] accounts for only 25 percent of the nation's wealth. Among others, economists Lester Thurow and Robert Barro and management consultant Peter Drucker concur that investments in human capital make the greatest impact on long-term productivity of the society. This became all the more evident in the twentieth century as growth was fueled less by physical labor and more by ideas and services. It is now a cliché to say that employees are a company's most valuable assets, but historically employees were viewed as an expense, the "cost of labor."

For human capital to work and grow, though, it must be mobilized. Just as with the physical assets and resources so dear to economists at earlier points in time, it does little good if human capital is dormant, unshared, and perhaps even unrecognized by its possessor. Like hidden ore and coal deposits of the nineteenth century, the benefits of human capital can be realized only when it is developed. In both cases, this requires investment. There is an important up-front, or sunk, cost associated with the initial development, and it must be borne by someone or some part of the "system." As with most economic development, there are important considerations about the size of the investment required and who should bear the cost.

Developing human capital involves three kinds of investments in people. Investing in a person's physical well-being requires providing better health care, nutrition, housing, and personal security. As is all too clear, especially in the less-developed world, a country cannot move forward economically when disease and poor public health conditions limit the ability of its people to function in society. Investing in people's minds occurs by support for their education, scholarships, training, and mentoring. Investing in justice and individual rights ultimately aims at developing every person's character and capabilities to the fullest. Each area advances the potential of people to work, produce, create, earn, advance, live, and help others. This activity expands the economy.

After basic needs are provided for, education is the most powerful way to invest in people. The benefits of this investment come to individuals, and to their families and heirs, in higher earnings during a lifetime of work. For instance, research shows that, on average, college graduates earn 80 percent more over the course of their careers than those whose education ended with high school. In 1989, earnings for those who had not completed high school averaged $20,504. For those who had received graduate or professional degrees, average earnings in 1989 were $58,837.[4] The additional investment in education develops skills in the individual beyond any specific knowledge of the law, or medicine, or architecture; it also develops writing and analytical skills, problem-solving and interpersonal skills. Job readiness makes people with advanced degrees worth more to their employers and their society, to themselves and their families over their lifetimes. People with higher salaries also tend to have better health and longer life spans than those who face low incomes or chronic dependency.

The benefits of education also accrue to society. A better-educated population increases the social stock of knowledge, promotes a general receptivity to new technologies and change, and, Becker shows, strengthens both democratic values and economic growth. In 1999, 84 percent of the adult U.S. population over twenty-five had received a high school diploma, and 26 percent of adults age twenty-five and over had at least a bachelor's degree. Both of these are record highs for the United States. Blacks are now graduating from high school at the same rate as whites. In 1999, 54 percent of college students were women. This continued their majority status, which began in 1979.

Recent studies by Barro and Becker confirm that the higher the rate of secondary and higher education, the higher the rates of economic growth and investment. Furthermore, democracy correlates with gross domestic product (GDP). This means the higher the GDP, the more likely democracy is to flourish. Remember Aristotle's claim about the relationship between wealth, democracy, and poverty:

> Yet the true friend of the people should see that they be not too poor, for extreme poverty lowers the character of the democracy;

> measures therefore should be taken which will give them lasting prosperity; and as this is equally the interest of all classes, the proceeds of the public revenues should be accumulated and distributed among its poor, if possible, in such quantities as may enable them to purchase a little farm, or, at any rate, make a beginning in trade or husbandry.[5]

It is secondary and higher education, not elementary, that builds GDP. Secondary and higher education among men is associated with increased economic growth and investment. In addition, education of women is correlated with reduced birth rates per female, which in turn correlates with improving the growth of the economy.

So, the formula for developing human capital is to provide for the physical well-being of the people, to educate the people, and to treat the people with justice so that human potential is not wasted. Our history suggests that the United States has tried to follow this formula, which involves taking the best characteristics of capitalism (wealth creation) and the best aspects of democracy (equality and human dignity) and making them work together. Not everything works fairly for everyone all the time, and things do not work as well as they should, but the strong drive to share assets so that others can advance has consistently been understood as a way to advance both the economy and democratic society.

Citizen generosity has again and again been the leader in all three of these areas. Generosity of spirit combines with financial generosity to initiate social movement. Slowly, this approach makes the environment of our society change. Then, opinions and laws change. The democracy and the economy grow stronger. Generosity in America has saved what might be called the normal course of things from, well, taking its normal course. So extraordinary things happen and set new standards of what can be achieved.

INVESTING IN HUMAN CAPITAL THROUGH EDUCATION

In 1643, Harvard's president Thomas Weld secured a significant gift from the elderly, childless daughter of Anthony Radcliffe, Lady

Anne Mowlson, to support "some poore scholler through the completion of his Master of Arts degree."[6] This gift became one of the earliest scholarships in the New World. What was the motivation?

President Weld and Lady Mowlson did not want financial constraints to stop a student from finishing his education. They saw the degree as an asset to the student. But in 1663, shortly after this gift, a pamphlet seeking funds from colonists added another reason why generosity to higher education deserved such importance. It encouraged: "let us creep as we can" to donate funds for higher education "lest degeneracy, Barbarism, Ignorance, and irreligion doe by degrees breake in upon us."[7] These donations began to make social change. In today's language, we might even say that these gifts encouraged upward mobility and changed the mix of students in higher education. We learn that:

> By the 1670s, around one-fifth of the fathers of Harvard students were artisans—millers, bakers, butchers and the like—and a few more were small farmers and manual workers. The growth of endowed scholarships, in addition to some paid college jobs, played a part here—almost all required neediness.
>
> From the university's earliest years, supporting needy students had been part of popular pride in Harvard and respect for learning, hence the "corn scholarships" (1645–55) funded from the sale of corn contributed by townships in Massachusetts and Connecticut.[8]

A bit more than a hundred years later, this enlightened thinking was well articulated at Yale. The University's Treasurer's Papers, December 1, 1831, make a clear case:

> The College is also in want of funds for the relief of necessitous students. Individuals of this class have not unfrequently risen to the highest stations of influence and authority in the nation. The welfare of our republic requires that such men be educated. Other colleges very generally offer education to them at reduced price. Yale must therefore do the same, both to promote the interest of the community and to secure her own prosperity.[9]

The Yale Treasurer's report starts out with the idea that the needy student is important as an individual, but then it moves on. Talent is clearly to be found among "necessitous students" and deserves to be developed through education. "The welfare of our republic requires" it and for two good reasons: "to promote the interest of the community and to secure" Yale's "own prosperity." What an idea! "The welfare of our republic requires that such men be educated."

Indeed it did. Benjamin Rush, one of the less famous signers of the Declaration of Independence, exemplifies the benefit the republic received in its earliest days from support for a needy scholar's education. Rush was himself the beneficiary of an early "investor" in human capital, Benjamin Franklin. It was Franklin who personally paid for Rush's medical education in Europe, making Rush an early "scholarship boy made good."

He really did make good, too. Later on in his life, he became committed to the establishment of public schools to assure the education of all citizens. And he took the idea of *all* citizens literally, reflecting a moderately modern understanding of investment in human capital. He wanted African Americans freed and also educated. In addition to serving as president of the Abolitionist Society started by Benjamin Franklin in 1774, Rush vigorously supported the education of women and girls. He advocated the importance of removing "the present disparity which subsists between the sexes in the degrees of their education and knowledge."[10] He supported the Young Ladies Academy in Philadelphia in 1787 and became an incorporator. He believed in the republican ideal that women should be educated in order to instill the values and virtues of citizenship in their sons. Rush was convinced that women "must concur in all our plans of education for young men, or no laws will ever render them effectual."[11] He worked, without success, to have his views on the importance of universal public education incorporated into the constitution of the state of Pennsylvania. Interestingly, Rush also advocated the humane treatment of the mentally ill and of prisoners. He supported the first studies of mental illness with his own money, although he was not a wealthy man, just an American philanthropist.

It would be generations before a political consensus would emerge that favored a government investment in ending slavery, or the education of blacks and women, or support for the mentally ill. But as we shall see, personal generosity and moral entrepreneurship have always led the way in courageous investments like these.

At the founding of Cornell University, Ezra Cornell gave three or four times more funding to the university than it got from the state of New York through the state land-grant funds obtained from the federal Morrill Act of 1862. Cornell University announced at its founding that it intended to enable a large number of citizens, including those who emerged from the state's poorest families, to attend. Specifically, that "poor, young men and . . . young women . . . without distinction as to class, previous occupation or locality" would be welcomed to the education they deserved.[12] In 1896, in a special report on financial aid, the trustees affirmed their commitment to the policy of giving two-thirds of the tuition to over a third of the nonscience students as need-based financial aid.

Princeton's administrators saw this "two-thirds policy," which had been viewed by many people as too generous, and decided, on the contrary, to adopt it, making it one important way Princeton would continue to assure that students from ministers' families could go on being educated at the university. Princeton saw this policy as a way to be certain that the most able students would have a Princeton education regardless of the financial circumstances of their parents.[13]

These institutions and hundreds of other private colleges and universities set out to raise the money from individual donors who could enable qualified students to attend despite a lack of financial resources. Some givers focused on the education of women or the education of African Americans as Benjamin Rush had. Others focused on special subject matter such as scholarships for science education or medical education. Some were wealthy enough to endow or launch entire institutions.

Philanthropist Mary Garrett, for example, made a remarkable investment in human capital. It was her idea and funded by her money. Perhaps the first philanthropist to practice what has been called "coercive philanthropy," she used her philanthropic contributions as leverage to assure improvements in medical education and to force the provision of opportunities to women within the male-dominated worlds of medicine and higher education. A century later, her work still shapes our economy.

In 1892, Garrett decided to give $354,000 to Johns Hopkins University to found a medical school. She knew her funds were critical to the growth of the university. She also knew that improved medical education for both men and women was equally critical to the greater good of society. At the time, medical education in America was poorly organized, and many essential courses were optional—and that was for the men. Women who studied medicine in the United States were limited to female medical colleges. Garrett's radical answer was twofold: She demanded that Johns Hopkins make its new medical school a graduate-level institution and that 5 percent of the entrants be women.

Her biographer Kathleen Waters Sander summarizes the effect of these demands in her article "Sharing a Love of History":

> Because of Garrett's largesse and insistence on higher standards, the new Hopkins medical school became the national model of academic medicine by the end of the 19th century, as gender barriers in medicine began to fall and the quality of medical education and practice rose. . . .
>
> One historian at the time referred to Garrett's gift to start the country's first coeducational, graduate-level medical school as the "crowning achievement of American feminism" in the 19th century.[14]

As a result of Garrett's gift, changes in social and professional life that might have been delayed for decades occurred along with the opening of the medical school. Those changes are still felt today. By 1998, women were 49 percent of the applicant pool and graduation class at Hopkins in medicine and 36 percent of the house staff and faculty in medicine. Garrett's gift helped change the face of medical education. As a moral entrepreneur, she advanced both the Johns Hopkins's medical school and broader social changes. In fact, when Garrett became a contributor to Columbia University, she sought and received the same conditions for women as she had at Hopkins.

It was not only people with hereditary wealth, like Garrett, who invested in human capital by developing institutions that changed opportunities for people. People from poor backgrounds took up the same challenge. Take Charles Pratt. As a young man, he struggled and worked long hours in farming and trade. Eventually he got a job in business where he achieved considerable success. That enabled him to start his own company, which he sold to Standard Oil in 1874, where he continued as an executive. Turning his wealth to philanthropy, he endowed the Pratt Institute, which focused on what was considered at the time a utilitarian (as contrasted with a classical) education. Pratt intended to help students help themselves through practical, skill-based courses of study such as architecture and bookkeeping. He once noted that his "interest in the young led me to feel that, as soon as my business promised a competency, I would try and do something for young people situated as I had been."[15] I am noting here that few of us remember what Pratt did in business. His name lives on because of his philanthropy. It was his generosity that secured his immortality.

Caroline Phelps-Stokes, the daughter and granddaughter of highly successful businessmen-entrepreneurs, spent her own life in philanthropic activities that, paralleling Garrett's contribution to women in medicine, made a dramatic change in the education of African Americans and Native Americans in the United States. She left a substantial estate that, in 1911, founded the Phelps-Stokes Fund.[16] She directed that the fund be focused on "the creation and improvement of dwellings in the City of New York for the poor families of the city, and for the education of Africans, African-Americans, and American Indians, and needy white students."[17]

The Phelps-Stokes Fund contributed to basic change in American society. It commissioned studies and reports that presented the statistics needed to develop new policies. Its mission statement says: "The Fund's charter interests include the education of African Americans, Native Americans, Africans, and needy white youth. Its logo, four open books, symbolizes the importance of education in promoting the fullest development and use of human talent. Over its ninety-year history, the Fund has sponsored educational surveys and research studies, administered scholarship and fellowship programs, organized training and professional development programs, and advocated on behalf of its constituents through public education programs."

One of the fund's first studies, "Negro Education in the United States," completed in 1912, detailed the differences between white and black schools and presented the inadequacies of the segregated system. It demonstrated the flaws in the effort to sustain "separate but equal" schools, almost fifty years before *Brown v. the Board of Education*. The work of the fund and of Caroline Phelps-Stokes developed human capital among African Americans and Indians and poor Americans generally. Through the dissemination of its studies, it also raised the social conscience of other Americans who became convinced that the nation could improve its treatment of these peoples and experience a greater good in society.

The fund went beyond commissioning reports; it acted on their findings and implemented changes, most often by supporting new or grassroots organizations that carried out the work. Among many others, the Phelps-Stokes Fund nurtured the Citizens Housing Council of New York, the Boys Choir of Harlem, the Harlem Youth Development Foundation, and the Jackie Robinson Foundation. Each of these organizations is now independent and embarked on significant projects that create opportunities for minorities both in the United States and in Africa.

However impressive this list of organizations, the Phelps-Stokes Fund may have made its most lasting impression with one single effort. Endeavoring to build strength in schools and colleges focused on minority students, it began supporting the best of the historically black colleges and funding scholarships for black students to attend these schools. The nation's 105 historically black colleges and universities (HBCUs) consist of private liberal arts colleges such as Spelman, land-grant institutions such as Tennessee State University, graduate and professional schools such as Howard Medical School, as well as two-year community colleges.

Ultimately, Phelps-Stokes Fund president Dr. Frederick Douglass Patterson conceived and developed the United Negro College Fund, which became an independent entity in 1944. UNCF now collects and distributes hundreds of millions of dollars of scholarship funds to a select forty-one of the country's historically black colleges. The funds raised are remarkable. In 1945, the first year of UNCF fund-raising, the fund raised less than $25 million. When their last campaign ended in 1996, UNCF had raised $280 million, seven times more than in 1945, and 12 percent more than their stated goal for that year. The fund received $15 million from individuals, $125 million from corporations, and $102 million from foundations. (This breakdown illustrates how an initial commitment from generous citizens induces dramatic contributions from other sectors, like private industry.) The remaining moneys came from organizations and public development funds.[18] By 2000, UNCF had amassed contributions totaling $1.6 billion for its fifty-five year history.

African Americans make up 94 percent of the students enrolled in UNCF colleges. Sixty percent of those students are female. Ninety-two percent of the students enrolled receive scholarship aid. The results are astonishing. HBCUs enroll only 18 percent of all black college students, yet they graduate 40 percent of all African Americans with B.A. degrees. Seventy-five percent of blacks with Ph.D.s graduate from an HBCU, as do 75 percent of military officers and 50 percent of black elected officials and business executives.[19]

African Americans, the city of New York, and the country as a whole derived benefits from the philanthropic investments of the Phelps-Stokes Fund. The opportunities held out to the thousands of young people affected by the fund have contributed to the growth of black middle- and upper-middle-income families in the country. Phelps-Stokes' work and the investments made by UNCF, like the work of most investors in human capital, leveraged or built capacity. This term, *capacity building,* can be best defined as developing core skills and capabilities so as to assure productivity and sustainability in others who are advancing the development of human capital.

Beyond these incredible achievements, the Phelps-Stokes Fund provides us with another story of how human-capital development works through education, this time from one of its employees.

Franklin Williams, an African American, became president of the Phelps-Stokes Fund in 1970. When he was growing up, his mother had been a maid for a wealthy family. A neighbor, May Edward Chinn, was the first African American woman to graduate from Bellevue Hospital Medical School (1926). Dr. Chinn was also the first black woman to intern at Harlem Hospital, and for many years she served as the only black female physician in Harlem. Her father had been a slave who escaped from the Chinn plantation in Virginia in 1864, and her mother was born on a Chickahominy Indian reservation near Norfolk, Virginia. Dr. Chinn funded Franklin Williams's college education at Lincoln University and Fordham Law School. Williams himself was very generous throughout his life, often beginning sentences by remembering his own benefactor saying, "But for Dr. Chinn, I would be . . ."

Williams served in a segregated unit in the U.S. Army, where he learned lessons about the role of race in America that inspired him to focus on civil rights cases when he later set up his law practice. Eventually, he was tapped to run the Africa division of the Peace Corps, served on the Board of Chemical Bank, and subsequently became U.S. ambassador to Ghana. Returning from this assignment, he launched the Urban Institute. Chinn's generosity in the case of Franklin Williams led to a significant set of initiatives to expand justice, equality, and opportunity in the United States.

So how has all this giving to education worked out to benefit the nation? Simply in terms of scholarships, it doesn't take much effort to find an impressive list of leaders in our country who benefited from a private scholarship of some kind. In every field of endeavor, of every race and ethnic origin, there are hundreds of recognizable names, people who developed their skills and attributes because they received this kind of scholarship to college, whether they attended public or private higher education. Examples of the benefits to society are not difficult to find. In addition to Dr. Daniel Hale Williams and Dr. William Warrick Cardozo, whom we met at Provident Hospital, Dr. Benjamin Carson was the first surgeon to separate twins who were conjoined at the head, and he regularly performed brain surgery on epileptic children to give them normal lives. They are joined by University of Chicago economist Milton

Friedman; Dr. Jane Cooke Wright, cancer research pioneer; Henry Bacon, designer of the Lincoln Memorial; Itzhak Perlman; Leo Hendrik Baekeland, inventor of Bakelite; Arthur Mitchell, who founded the Dance Theater of Harlem; former surgeon general Joycelyn Elders; and Selma Burke, Meta Vaux Warrick Fuller, Lois Mailou Jones, Augusta Savage, and Lee Krasner, five of the most significant women in American art history; as well as all of the people listed in the end note and literally millions of others.[20]

Private philanthropy often leads the way long before government policy and funding or for-profit ventures, and this is exactly what happened in the area of need-based support for students attending postsecondary education. Today, the federal government is deeply involved in student financial aid. In fact, together, the states and federal government account for 80 percent of all financial aid dollars. But when do you think the government (state or federal) got *seriously* committed to funding higher education? Not in the eighteenth or nineteenth centuries. Very few states provided any financial aid before the 1930s, and the federal government did not become engaged until Congress passed the GI Bill in 1944.

THE GI BILL AND BEYOND

The GI Bill authorized the first significant dollars from the federal budget for tuition, and it was private-citizen generosity that spurred the government's decision to fund the bill at all. Probably no story better illustrates the impact of personal generosity on government's attitude toward education than the American Legion's struggle to get the GI Bill passed.

With 15 million veterans returning to the United States after World War II, the economy was threatened with a huge influx of people into the workforce. The country could have struggled through high unemployment, anger, and cynicism among servicemen and their families, or it could invest in any veteran who wanted to attend college to expand his or her capacity, choosing a life that person might not have envisioned before going off to war.

The American Legion, founded in 1919, had nearly 3 million members in fifteen thousand American Legion posts worldwide, almost all volunteers. Prior to World War II, the members of the organization had a strong interest in their shared experience as veterans, but many of their most active efforts tended to focus on the needs of other segments of society, and with great success.[21] But in 1944, the American Legion vigorously and innovatively supported the GI Bill. At the time, Congress was dragging its feet. The bill was considered too expensive, a pipe dream that would bankrupt our budget. Higher education leaders rejected the bill because they foresaw a negative impact if millions of older and mostly male students arrived on campuses, lowering university standards and upsetting collegiate social norms and interactions. It was the vision and generosity of thousands of American Legion members in chapters big and small all across the country that helped to get the GI Bill passed. The Legionnaires' donations and their fund-raising efforts created the funds needed to support visits, telegrams, letters, and telephone calls to congressmen and newspaper contacts across the country. This commitment of citizen generosity to the passage of the GI Bill mobilized local fellow citizens to support it. Ultimately, this work changed the course of American history. Left alone, without the funds collected and spent to change things, Congress and higher education leaders would probably have buried the GI Bill and the untold assets it released into our postwar economy. Prior to this period, Congress had already failed to act on no fewer than 640 bills concerning veterans.

By 1947, 49 percent of all college students were returning GIs receiving full tuition coverage as well as support for other needs through the GI Bill.[22] The colleges were crowded, but the returning GIs were highly motivated and successful students. Colleges "made money" and launched millions of men from low- and moderate-income families toward moderate- and high-income careers. In many cases these GI Bill graduates were entering new fields, born during wartime: high technology, manufacturing, and engineering-based industries.

The bill changed the lives of more than 8 million servicemen and women returning after World War II. It also propelled the postwar economy forward. Not only paying for college education, the GI Bill also allowed veterans to finance home ownership with government-supported loans and without a down payment. This one provision of the bill enabled the first major increase in wealth among substantial numbers of Americans. This wealth was, of course, imbedded in home equity. It helped these first-time, young veteran home owners to upgrade their housing several times throughout their lives and to continue growing their wealth as their incomes increased through the 1950s. This wealth was handed down to the next generation, enabling them to buy homes earlier in their lives and grow their wealth as their parents did on the back of the GI Bill funds. The cascading effect of that citizen-inspired investment in human capital provided a vital underpinning for the success of the United States in the 1950s and 1960s. Interestingly enough, the more recently updated provisions of the GI Bill are currently some of the best recruiting and retaining devices of the all-volunteer armed services of today.

It must be remembered that the GI Bill was, and is, not for needy students. The only criterion for government aid was veteran status. But the passage of the bill drew the federal government into the funding of needs-based scholarships as well, by graphically showing the impact on the nation of investing in human capital through the financial support of advanced education for our people. At the level of the GI Bill, this became a new endeavor for the federal government and one in which it is still a major player, to the advantage of individuals and for the greater good of the nation. But there is more to be done.

In 2000, one in every eight undergraduate students came from a family whose income is less than $20,000, and 55 percent of all undergraduates received financial aid. Thirty-nine percent of this aid was from the federal government.[23] The federal government provides Pell Grants, Student Equal Opportunity Grants (SEOG), and Stafford and Perkins Loans, as well as veterans' benefits, PLUS loans, or ROTC scholarships. While this is an enormous amount of money, much of it is in loans, not in grants. By 2000, loans accounted for 54 percent of federal financial aid.[24] In addition, the grants do not go as far as they used to. In 1986, typical Pell Grants—the largest needs-based financial aid program—covered 98 percent of a student's tuition. By 1999, it only covered 57 percent.[25]

State governments provide scholarships and loans as well. Colleges, both public and private, also offer aid. Yet, unbeknownst to most citizens, many public institutions like the University of Virginia and the University of Michigan, among others, receive a very small percentage of their funding from their state, often less than 20 percent of the institution's budget. Consequently, their presidents are raising funds with the same intensity as the presidents of private institutions. Most important, financial reasons still prevent some very gifted students from going to college. This is a continuing challenge, one that deserves attention as we deliberate innovations in human-capital investment.

Even given the remarkable increase in federal funding for need-based scholarships, private funds are desperately needed to reduce student debt. Only the best endowed universities and colleges are able to give financial aid that does not include a significant loan to the student recipient. Beginning life with heavy indebtedness alters the kinds of jobs students can afford to take after graduation. In addition to simply continuing to give scholarships for needy students, generous citizens in the twenty-first century should consider offering debt-forgiveness funds to colleges so that under specific conditions, students with loans could have those repaid by the donor's fund.

Precollege education offers another area for private generosity for supporting America's tradition of investment in human capital. For many students, the low quality of primary and secondary education all but assures that students will not achieve preparedness for quality higher education. Scholarship support for needy students at the elementary and secondary levels can enable those with the most potential to get the early education that will prepare them for admission to the very colleges and universities that have scholarships for their postsecondary education. As is our tradition, new efforts at generosity should reach out beyond areas of current success and address new challenges. The American dream doesn't change very much. The pathways to get to it do.

At the moment, even though federal and state governments are now heavily involved in student financial aid, philanthropy still provides a great deal of scholarship support. The largest single private sector organization offering scholarships is Scholarship America, which is an example of grassroots philanthropy by large numbers of ordinary American citizens, joined by wealthy donors and corporations. Like the donors to UNCF and the members of the American Legion, the power comes from the sheer numbers of ordinary people who step forward to give.

Initiated in 1958 by a Massachusetts optometrist worried about the number of young people in his community who needed financial aid to attend college, Scholarship America was created with a simple idea, asking everyone in town to offer $1 to build scholarship aid for the town's youth. The fund's founder, Dr. Irving Fradkin, reflected on the fact that when he was a young man, people in his community had assisted him. The first effort Fradkin organized raised $6,000, and nearly 20 students from Fall River went to college, students who without Scholarship America's help could not have attended school that fall. This idea spread quickly to other cities and towns.

In 2000, Scholarship America raised more than $100 million, which went to more than 90,000 students across the country. Growing from one chapter in 1958, by 2000 Dollars for Scholars, the name given to the local chapters of Scholarship America, had grown to almost one thousand chapters nationwide, spending all year putting fund-raising events together. Over a hundred chapters are established in inner-city communities alone. Young people receiving these funds know how involved other members of their neighborhoods are in investing in their success. This connectedness is part of the advantage they get from the Dollars for Scholars grants. The 90,000 recipients are likely to be interested in helping other students just as they were helped as youth. The 2000 Annual Report of Scholarship America reports that in 1990 the organization was serving the scholarship needs of 24,000 students across the United States. Through the year 2000, Scholarship America has distributed $911.5 million to 850,000 students since 1958.

In addition to the fund-raising done in the local Dollars for Scholars chapters, Scholarship America has developed the Scholarship Management Service, designed to offer corporations and corporate foundations support in managing the collection and distribution of scholarship funds made available to the children of employees. Scholarship America has contracts with nine hundred companies to provide this service and help the companies support the students who need aid to pay for college. It has also developed another way to invest in human capital, ScholarShop, which counsels younger students, some still in junior high school, on what they will need in order to be academically and financially ready for college entrance.

The impulse to "give back" when one is successful is also still strong, despite government involvement in scholarship funding. Although data have never been collected, most colleges can attest to the fact that successful scholarship students often prove to be dependable benefactors for the next generation.

A Connecticut College trustee who had been a scholarship student in the early 1960s went into finance and then into the investment field specializing in start-up high-tech companies. She had told me that if she "ever made it big" on an investment, she wanted to give the college a gift of 10 percent. One fine day a few years ago, I got a call in the president's office. This woman said that she would be sending a check for $10 million in the coming weeks. She said she could never have had the life she had enjoyed all these years if the college had not invested in her before her potential looked so certain. Now she could give something back. And so she did. A smaller donor had another way of putting it. "Someone sent the elevator down to pick me up when I could not have gotten to the right floor in life without that help. Now I want my gift to send the elevator down for someone else."

A civil rights lawyer in Los Angeles named Crispus Attucks Wright (after the African American who was the first to die in the Boston Massacre) left his law school an endowment of $2 million for scholarships. They are for academically qualified and financially deserving law students of any minority ethnicity who are willing to practice law in an underserved community. "I feel a deep obligation to the USC Law School," he said. "The professors—as well as many of my classmates—brought out the best in me and made me work at my optimum level. I am both proud and glad that my contribution will help make the law school more accessible to talented students." Wright was the grandson of a slave, and a scholarship took him to law school and a career that stretched from 1940 to 1987. "We don't climb the ladder to success alone. We stand on the shoulders of hundreds who have sacrificed and paved the way for us and what better way to repay those brave and wonderful souls than to give something back."[26]

My favorite story of scholarship support, however, is the story of Oseola McCarty. It is a favorite because McCarty was so practical. She herself had never received a scholarship and yet she still gave them. McCarty grew up in Hattiesburg, Mississippi. From an early age, she worked with her grandmother and aunt, washing and ironing bundles of clothes for white families in town. She quit school in the sixth grade to take care of her aunt, who had fallen ill. Although her aunt recovered, McCarty did not want to return to school. She spent a lonely life washing, ironing, taking care of elderly relatives, and living frugally. She read the Bible daily and opened a bank account as a teenager. She put money into her account each week, but never withdrew any. Early on she learned the secret of compounding interest. In her book, *Simple Wisdom for Rich Living,* she says, "The secret to building a fortune is compounding interest. It's not the ones that make the big money, but the ones who know how to save who get ahead."[27]

In 1995, at the age of eighty-seven, she decided she did not want what she had earned and carefully saved to go to waste. "I had been thinking for a long time. . . . I wanted to give it to the college. They used to not let colored people go out there, but now they do, and I think they should have it. . . . I just want the scholarship to go to some child who needs it. I'm too old to get an education, but they can."[28] McCarty's life savings, $150,000, went to endow scholarships at the University of Southern Mississippi. Her example inspired many others. Her gift was augmented by money from over six hundred other donors who wanted to honor her. The scholarship endowment eventually grew to over $480,000.

The Oseola McCarty story reminds me as well of a different story of personal generosity by a very different person. In looking at these stories side by side, we see the remarkable diversity of philanthropists and their powerful imaginations. The innovative philanthropy of Eugene Lang, and other donors, has reached out to young people long before they enter the doors of a university.

PREPARING FOR COLLEGE

Eugene Lang, a scholarship student, successful businessman, and chair of the Board of Trustees at Swarthmore College, grew up poor and worked hard. Lang was born and raised in New York City. He washed dishes after school as a teenager during the Depression. When he was fourteen, a trustee of Swarthmore College happened to be a guest at the restaurant where he worked. The trustee arranged for Lang to be interviewed for admission. Lang received a scholarship to Swarthmore and then went on to the Columbia University School of Business. He eventually started his own high-tech company and became successful, wealthy, and generous.

His old school, P.S. 121 in East Harlem, was still serving low-income children as it had in his day. When he returned to give a commencement speech in 1981, he got an idea as he spoke with the students. He made an impromptu offer to the sixth graders: he would give financial aid to every student who was admitted to a four-year college program. He went on to take the entire class under his wing through high school, providing his own time—he was available to them on Saturdays—as well as money. He also arranged workshops, trips to colleges, and visits by social workers, because he saw that financial need was not the only problem that needed to be addressed in these children's lives. "This program has given me a tremendous sense of purpose and a feeling that I've done something with my life," Lang said.[29]

Lang's early funding for college dreams for inner-city children has proven to be both innovative and essential. His example inspired others—individuals, community groups, and corporations—and the "I Have a Dream" Program spread throughout the country. As of 2002, 13,000 Dreamers worked toward college in twenty-seven states and 180 cities. The "I Have a Dream" model shows a significant positive impact on life outcomes for its students. Studies done by outside evaluators show results. For instance, in

New York in 1992, a study of eight "I Have a Dream" projects found that the on-time graduation rate was 63 percent higher among Dreamers than their peers and that 73 percent of the graduating Dreamers were enrolled in college the following year.

In 2000–2001, East Palo Alto, California, Dreamers showed an 89 percent graduation/GED-completion rate with 85 percent of the graduates pursuing a college education. Studies in Chicago conducted in 1996 showed that Dreamers attended college at three times the rate of peers not in the program. Sixty-nine percent of these Chicago Dreamers in the classes of 1993 and 1994 graduated from high school in districts where the high school dropout rate was 60 percent. By 1996, the graduating class achieved a 75 percent completion rate, more than double the rate of control groups. In Portland, Oregon, Dreamers did not, unfortunately, show a drop in teen pregnancies, but 73 percent of the girls who got pregnant were expected to graduate from high school. Nationally, by comparison, 30 percent of girls involved in teen pregnancies graduated from high school.

Moreover, the increase in combined incomes of just the young mothers enrolled in the program (over their lifetimes) was estimated to amount to $943,000, very close to the entire cost of the "I Have a Dream" project for all the boys and girls enrolled. Just as impressive are the statistics on delinquency among Dreamer males. Referrals to the criminal justice system were only 57 to 58 percent as high as males in the control group. Given that the total cost of processing a juvenile for one overnight stay in the criminal justice system is about $3,000, these statistics speak eloquently. Evaluators estimate that Portland saved about $374,000 over six years just from Dreamers' lower juvenile delinquency rates.

Not every project has the same statistics, but taken as a whole, the successes have made "I Have a Dream" the model for hundreds of educational support initiatives, both public and private. The message is that investments in children pay off. But most Americans know this. The rest of us should be asking ourselves why we are not involved in making "I Have a Dream" projects work in our towns. Any prescription drug that created the desired health improvement at these rates would be approved by the FDA, prescribed by doctors, and described as a miracle cure. Successful social change is adopted more slowly. Other data are even more convincing. We just do not succeed in applying this knowledge to our personal philanthropy often enough, and we don't insist that it shape public-policy decisions on the uses of tax funds. Furthermore, "I Have a Dream" illustrates again how the initiative and generosity of individual citizens leads state and federal funding efforts. New York's Liberty Partnership Program is a state-funded program based on "I Have a Dream," as is a new federal program, called GEAR UP (Gaining Early Awareness and Readiness for Undergraduate Programs).[30]

Lang inspired donors to locate school systems, individual schools—indeed, classrooms—where an insufficient number of children graduated and went on to higher education. Generous donor investment was applied directly to the problem. Like Lang, Mississippi native Jim Barksdale, the former CEO of Netscape, took on systematic change, too. In 2000, Barksdale and his wife, Sally, gave $100 million to the state of Mississippi. The money was given to fund reading education programs at elementary schools throughout the state and to buy books and materials for ongoing literacy programs, as well as, through the University of Mississippi, to support teachers. Said University of Mississippi chancellor Robert C. Khayat: "What makes me tear up is that this really does address one of the major challenges we face as a society, and that's what higher education should be doing and what private wealth should be doing. My sense is that the measure of wealth is moving from how much is a person worth to how much does a person give."[31]

To set the stage for the Barksdales' gift: Mississippi's academic outcomes are, and have been, very poor. In many southern states students take the ACT test instead of the SAT. In 2000, Mississippi's ACT scores ranked twenty-sixth out of twenty-six states. Also in 2000, only 32 percent of fourth graders scored at the proficient or advanced level on national reading tests. This was an improvement from 1998 when only 29 percent read at those levels. Worse results showed up in national math tests, where 80 percent of the fourth graders rated at basic or below basic levels. Sadly, eighth graders did not show an increase in test scores. Scores were worse on eighth-grade science tests, where 89 percent scored basic or below.[32] Industry does not typically invest where educational outcomes are so weak for such a significant majority of the population.

The Barkesdales' investment has the potential to advance the human capital in individual students but also in the state as a whole. As in the case of Lang's gift, the Barkesdales' shows that individual benefit can also create greater good. The Barksdales announced further that they intend to give *all* their money to philanthropic projects. Jim Barksdale had faced a literacy crisis in his own youth. He could not read in the third grade. He eventually worked with a tutor and later went on to become CEO for companies such as AT&T Wireless Services and Netscape Communications Corporation. "It [reading] is a skill that must be acquired if a child is going to grow up and become a functioning, contributing adult. . . . I invest in starting businesses, so to me this is not a gift. Gifts get squandered. This is an investment and this program will and must work. . . . I know it works if it is one on one, it's time on task, it's attitude, it's love, it's whatever it takes."[33]

The Barksdales, Lang, and McCarty have something vital in common as donors, even though they have much less in common in the rest of their lives. They do not share the same race, religion, ethnicity, region of the country, educational background or level, or work. They do share a great American tradition in their patterns of generosity. All three give abundantly. They remember where they came from and their own struggles when they were young. They are all entrepreneurial and independent and believe they can substantially change life, making it better with a combination of their funds, their dedication, and their imagination. They are, of course, right.

There are a number of other programs, funded by both grassroots philanthropy and major donors, which support precollegiate students. Among these, I want briefly to explore Prep for Prep and A Better Chance (ABC), which inspired the government-funded program called Upward Bound. These successes have engendered countless summer prep programs on college campuses that serve students from low-income families from all kinds of backgrounds and that are funded by citizens. These organizations are locating and preparing children to enter America's most selective institutions, public and private. This investment in human capital is making a difference in who goes to what colleges in the United States.

A Better Chance began in 1963 with the mission to identify, recruit, and develop leadership among young people of color throughout the United States. "If there is to be an 'elite' system of education in the United States then children of color must be a part of it," wrote ABC director Judith Berry Griffin.[34] Individual generosity provided the majority of the $14.5 million raised in 2000. Corporate support also came from the Goldman Sachs Foundation. Thousands of students have been prepared for the nation's most elite schools through ABC. More than one-third of the ABC scholars come from families on welfare, and 65 percent come from single parent families. More than eleven thousand middle school children have been placed in elite prep schools and 99 percent of them enroll immediately in college upon graduation. An estimated $20 million is leveraged at the high school level to support these young people's advancing education.

Like ABC, Prep for Prep, founded in 1978, searches for leaders among low-income, minority children and gives them a chance to attend elite secondary schools. Upward Bound, on the other hand, was started with a slightly different mission: "To help economically disadvantaged students complete high school and to enter and succeed in postsecondary education." A federal program started by the Department of Education, it is the oldest and largest of the TRIO programs (Talent Search and Student Support Services are the other two), all of which share the objective of helping disadvantaged students achieve success at the postsecondary level. Currently 566 Upward Bound projects serve about forty-two thousand students. At least two-thirds of each project's participants must be from households that have low income (which is defined as earning less than one and a half times the designated official poverty level for a family of four) and in which neither parent has graduated from college. Even though Upward Bound is an example of the government's involvement in helping disadvantaged children finish high school, it must be remembered that it was initiated two years *after* A Better Chance, giving us yet another example of the private sector teaching the public sector about good ideas.

So why should we care? Well, apart from the moral imperative, it is important to remember that, statistically, all the children helped by these programs were at high risk to fail in school and end up in poverty, in need of prolonged social service support, or in the criminal justice system. Many would have become unmarried early parents. Instead, they now make contributions to society and improve their own and their families' chances to benefit from our society and economy. Investments in them make sense.

These three organizations and many hundreds of others all across the country have added thousands of students to the ranks of those who could be admitted to competitive institutions, get college scholarships, and proceed to appropriate positions in the work world and sustaining communities. This is the result of dedication from the students themselves, their families, and the staff and supporters of the programs.

You might ask if I am content with this record. I am not. We are missing those countless millions, some of whom have ended up in prison costing taxpayers $25,000 to $30,000 per year for the duration of their sentences. Conservative estimates by specialists in the field estimate that there are more than 2 million gifted children of color in the nation who would benefit greatly by expanded learning opportunities. Think of the statistics associated with the students involved in the "I Have a Dream" programs. If Portland can save $374,000 over six years through one private program, how much could the nation save if the Dream programs spread to all communities? Even though crime rates are going down, incarceration rates are increasing. In 1999, over 108,000 juveniles were held in residential placement.[35] Do the math. If we project as a national average the amount that Michigan paid per day in 2000 ($200),[36] then the country as a whole is paying $21.6 million *per day* for juvenile prisoners' care. That makes $7.884 billion annually! Even if only one-tenth of them could have been kept out of the justice system, this country would have saved the taxpayers $2.16 million per day and $788.4 million per year.

The programs discussed above have been proven successful. If they were scaled up and scaled out to address this much larger number of prospective highly successful youngsters, would our nation be stronger or weaker? It seems self-evident that, as the Yale Treasurer's Papers said in 1830, "the welfare of the republic requires" that our philanthropy stretch to address these opportunities. We must do as our ancestors did: cease seeing needs and start seeing opportunities.

Our American traditions head us in the right direction, making a difference especially in the lives of children of the lowest quintile of the income distribution. Generous citizens have developed a significant set of good ideas that advance human capital ever more effectively for the current challenges. However, the country is not scaling up these good ideas as fast as we should to make the progress our ancestors and our future deserve. Our giving needs to increase dramatically, and citizens need to invest and to put their new gifts into expanding the models of human development that have already proven successful.

America's tradition of investing in people sustains an environment where people of diverse income, education, and class, as well as of different races and ethnicities, have a chance to succeed. Our history shows that a growing number of our own diverse citizens actually do achieve and contribute. Moreover, people from all over the world are attracted to come, work, stay, and raise families in the United States because it is no secret that American generosity creates real opportunities for the children of hardworking people, even if they do not have the financial assets to advance their own or their children's education. This area of effort has been so successful that citizens could it take to a whole new level over the next three decades.

For the past fifty years, the Council for Financial Aid to Education has measured the investments made in human capital through education. During the last half of the twentieth century, as the data shows, America's most elite institutions built a dramatic increase in the percentage of students admitted on need-based scholarship. Currently, most offer financial support to 35 to 55 percent of their students. Many of these students from the lowest-income homes are not burdened with loans, and some even receive travel and clothing allowances, depending on their need. I have watched the pride of families, wealthy for generations, as they meet the current recipients of their scholarship endowments: young people from core inner cities, from Appalachia, or from other countries who have come to the United States as refugees. Some of these young people have become, through philanthropy, warmly accepted members of the wealthy endowing families. The scholarships and the connections the young people make at these selective institutions enable them, through their intelligence and personal discipline, to compete for the positions they deserve rather than the ones their families could afford. Many succeed in a range of fields. Our society is the richer for their achievement.

Their stories, and those of millions of other Americans from different backgrounds, show how powerfully we believe in investing our own money in other people, people we are not even related to, people with potential that deserves to be developed for their sake and for the sake of the country. You can call what they did the optimization of human capital, or, more specifically, funding financial aid, but the other way to see these citizen gifts is as investments in the most important asset of any society—its people.

3

MAKING THE MOST OF PEOPLE BEYOND EDUCATION: HUMAN CAPITAL, PART TWO

Human-capital development does not happen only through education. Some investments link physical well-being (the founding fathers' idea of "life") with the development of the individual as an adult and a contributor to the economy. Individuals' needs can be met and their capacities developed at many stages in life. Ideally, these efforts connect across boundaries of religion, ethnicity, and race in an effort to cultivate common bonds. Philanthropists who choose this approach often take an interest in one important system that dooms or develops human capital.

Social transitions can, and usually do, make waves in a nation's economy. In the nineteenth century, one such transition threw a significant percentage of the female population into an economic no-man's-land. In the first centuries of this country's history, the primary economic unit was the family farm. At its center were a husband and a wife, but the unit included, as both workers and dependents, their children, their servants or slaves, and any other relations who needed to be absorbed. Everyone was valuable as a worker, either in the fields or in the kitchen and garden, or both. In the nineteenth century, however, the financial face of the country began its change from agrarian to industrial and mercantile.

Increasingly, families moved into towns and cities. Often, entire families went to work in factories and mills. When necessary, infants and small children were cared for by an older sibling or a neighbor, but it was considered best when the mother was able to care for them herself.

In time, a family ideal began to emerge for the middle and upper classes. The father worked. The mother stayed at home to care for children and household. There was no longer any room in this model for "extra hands." Unmarried men did not now need families in order to form a viable economic unit, as they had when farming was dominant. Unmarried women were more problematic. The family ideal, which had emerged from an economic change, grew more and more powerful as a social construct. Strongly influenced by England's strait-laced Queen Victoria, this ideal began to have a tyrannical effect on the lives of American women, particularly white, middle-class women.

Of course, many women continued to work, as they always had, on farms or as domestic workers and cottage labor. Among African Americans, even middle-class women worked. That is to say, black women who worked could be part of the middle class, so long as they were respectable and, usually, educated. But for white, middle-class women, options shrank desperately. Working outside the home meant an immediate and devastating loss of class. Any job, other than teacher or perhaps domestic companion, carried with it a stigma that was almost equivalent to that of prostitution. No woman who worked in a factory or shop could expect that she would ever be asked to marry by a respectable man. And if she were married, the disgrace to her husband would almost certainly cause him to lose his own position. She would be ostracized by family and friends and lose whatever support she might have hoped from them.

And yet, there were many white, middle-class women who were unmarried or widowed. After the Civil War, the situation became even worse, as tens of thousands of women lost their husbands and were left destitute, often with children to care for. Here was a large pool of workers whose labor could not be utilized for the good of the economy. Worse, they and their children could only be a burden on what limited social services nineteenth-century government attempted to provide. They were a serious economic liability. What's more, the power of the Victorian social construct made it almost impossible to help them, without finding them all husbands.

This is the kind of situation for which private generosity is best suited because it needed new thinking and new applications of solutions to complex concerns. Only other women who had a clear understanding of the problem and the discretion to deal with the social constraints could address it. Fortunately, they did. Beginning in the first half of the nineteenth century, affluent, philanthropic women who were concerned about the condition of women in society in general developed women's exchanges. It was an idea the average male reformer would not have taken seriously for an instant, but it was highly effective.

Very simply, a group of wealthy women in Philadelphia opened a shop in 1832, at which goods were sold on consignment. The organizers provided all or part of the materials used to produce these handmade goods, and the proceeds went to those who made them, middle-class women without husbands. The crucial part of the operation is that the makers of the goods remained anonymous. They could work at home to support themselves and their children, and no one would know it. After the 1876 Centennial Exhibition, exchanges opened in cities and towns around the country, eventually forming into the National Federation of Women's Exchanges, an organization that still exists today.

The women who ran the exchanges used the structures of capital markets to develop the human capital they were concerned about. The founders of the Richmond Exchange, for example, set it up as a joint stock company. They amassed the initial capital by selling shares at $25 per share. One annual report of the Exchange for Women's Work in Richmond, Virginia, notes, "Surely such a charity will bear scrutiny and criticism even at this day, when people have learned to distinguish so accurately between the benevolence that helps and that which only harms the recipient."[1]

Now, as we look back from a society that is more open about both class and gender, the women's exchanges may seem merely quaint. The "decayed gentlewomen" who were forced to feed their children and themselves by crocheting doilies and making jars of relish are as likely to inspire our condescension as our compassion. But their plight was very real, and the solution was both generous and ingenious.

The women's exchanges also addressed, both directly and indirectly, the problem of the social transition itself. No nation can tolerate for long a large group of unemployable people who nonetheless drain the country's resources, which is what the concept of Victorian womanhood had created. That pool of labor had to be tapped if the U.S. economy was to thrive and it was. From 1870 to 1920 the female workforce grew from less than two million to almost nine million. And women made up a growing proportion of the workforce, going from 13 to 21 percent.[2] But the transition was incredibly rocky.

First, working-class and poor women were increasingly forced to go away from their families and into factories and mills. Because they worked, they did not qualify for the protections extended to the "pure woman" who was the Victorian ideal. There was no precedent set for their treatment, and so they were often exploited, sexually and otherwise. Second, middle-class women and upper-class women were becoming more and more educated—and therefore more potentially valuable to the economy—and they were barred from working. Clearly, social forces were seriously interfering with the ability of the market economy to function smoothly.

The women's exchanges became part of the solution to both of these problems. Because the exchanges put women of different economic levels in close working contact, they eventually went beyond their original agenda to become champions of the rights of workingwomen. They also became training grounds for the educated woman's entry into the vocations that would support them, helping them to hone skills in organization and finance. (More about that later.)

These affluent women did not operate from a base of social and economic naïveté. They were purposeful in their attempts to mitigate the effects of capitalism as a way of preserving the essential system. The leaders of the St. Louis Exchange explicitly expressed their intention that it would become "a bridge between capital and labor, this at a time when labor unrest was a source of much concern to society."[3] They represented a force that would become far more important in the early decades of the twentieth century. Through their access to capital, in the form of the wealth of their husbands and fathers, and through their own need to engage productively and pragmatically in the nation's business, they had a tremendous impact on what has come to be called the Progressive Era.

Take Mrs. Russell Sage, for example. The United States had just celebrated fifty years of nationhood when she was born. She was three when the Yale Treasurer's Papers noted the importance of investing in people who would, with their talents and a scholarship, "rise to the highest stations of influence and authority in the nation." Her life's work might have made someone think that Benjamin Rush was her role model. She connected the wealthy like herself to middle-class reformers. Like many wealthy women before and after her, and many, many today, she got personally involved, took risks, and taught the wealthy and the poor new ways to look at the world of which they were a part.

For our purposes, though, what is most important is that she used the huge fortune left in her hands by her husband, Russell Sage, in ways that greatly improved the quality of the labor force in this country. And she did this at a time of crisis for American business.

Between 1870 and 1920, about 27 million immigrants came to the United States from Europe. Almost 9 million of those arrived between 1900 and 1910. At about the same time, about 8 percent of the black population of the South fled the oppression of Jim Crow and arrived in the urban North. At first glance, this was good news for American industry. More workers meant higher production and lower wages—and thus more economic success. But there was a problem. The quality of the labor force was just not good enough. In fact, it was terrible. And economic growth depends upon the quality as well as on the quantity of workers.

The factors involved in the quality of the labor force are simple. Indeed, they are so simple and so widely accepted that you can look them up in the encyclopedia, the *Britannica*, at any rate. "The quality of the labour force depends on education and training, physique and health."[4] In other words, a strong, healthy worker who can speak English and read a training manual is more valuable than a sick, undernourished worker who has difficulty following the simplest verbal instructions in an unknown language. The latter description fit most of the tens of millions of new workers in the cities around the turn of the twentieth century.

These millions poured into northern and some western U.S. cities without resources to help them stay afloat, isolated from the support of the families and villages they had left behind in Europe and the South, and not yet connected to any such support systems in their new locations. Most did not speak English. They were crowded into cities that were not ready to deal with them. Soon, their numbers were depleted by sickness and starvation. Daphne Spain gives this description of the situation in *How Women Saved the Cities:*

> Late nineteenth-century American cities were nasty places. People threw swill out their windows onto muddy, unpaved streets where pigs scavenged for garbage. Open cesspools fouled the air. Public transit, consisting of horse-drawn trolleys, relied on thousands of draft animals that produced tons of manure every day. Horses dropped dead on the streets. Children played in those same streets unless they were in school or working in factories. Tenement residents had to carry water from the street up to their rooms if they wanted to wash, so it was impossible to keep families or homes clean for long. Inadequate municipal water supplies and delivery systems meant that fires regularly killed vast numbers of people and destroyed acres of property. Contaminated drinking water was almost as dangerous as fire, contributing to lethal epidemics and high infant mortality.[5]

People who lived in these conditions were not prepared for work. Not to put too fine a point on it, they did not offer an ideal labor supply. Moreover, there were no government social services to help them. Government, from the local to the federal level, had not yet taken on the provision of social services. The stage was set for a serious threat to the capitalist system on a variety of economic, social, and political fronts.

Into this crisis stepped a group of unlikely saviors, willing to invest in other people with no models to show how to do the job they had in mind. Educated middle-class women, both white and black, who were not accepted into American businesses and professions—other than teaching—took it upon themselves to do what the institutions would not or could not do. Jane Addams, Mary Church Terrell, Florence Kelley, Nannie Helen Burroughs, Charlotte Perkins Gilman, Rose Schneiderman, and their financial supporters, such as Grace Dodge and Mrs. Russell Sage, redefined citizenship. "As men earned their citizenship through their readiness and ability to defend their city, so perhaps woman, if she takes a citizen's place in the modern industrial city, will have to earn it by devotion and self-abnegation in the service of its complex needs."[6]

Margaret Olivia Slocum Sage was typical of these women. She was born in Syracuse, New York, the daughter of a successful promoter of American agricultural tools and equipment. She attended Emma Willard's Troy Female Seminary and then became a teacher for a time. She became friends with Russell Sage and his first wife, Maria Winne Sage. She taught in settlement houses and, like Benjamin Rush, wrote essays and took up unfashionable causes. Two years after Maria's death, she married Russell Sage. Here, she becomes less typical. When Sage died in 1906, he left her more than $60 million, his entire fortune, saying that she was better suited "temperamentally" to dispose of it than he was. ("Uncle" Russell Sage would squeeze a quarter 'til the eagle screamed.) Fortunately for the American economy, he was right. She could, and would, do a lot to change the labor force with that $60 million.

A polymorph investor in human potential, she supported education directly through funding to women's colleges and major universities. She also became a great proponent of women's suffrage and, as we will see later, their productive engagement in society. She was also one of the primary funders of social services to that vast pool of potential workers that flooded into the cities at the turn of the century. So similar in background, education, and sentiments to others in the small army of women who took it upon themselves to clean up the cities, she had, in addition, the force of her vast financial resources.

Sage's foundation was a primary source of funding for these efforts, with a particular focus on health. The foundation funded work to control tuberculosis and upgrade sanitary conditions in poor neighborhoods, as well as hospitals and emergency relief efforts. Sage also supported people's spiritual needs with contributions to her own Dutch Reformed Church, as well as to Presbyterians and Methodists, black and also Catholic church communities, but let's continue to focus on the issue of improving the quality of the labor force.

The College Settlements Association, the National Association of Colored Women, the Young Men's and Young Women's Christian Association, the Salvation Army, and others provided housing for workingwomen and for transients. They cleaned up the streets in urban slum areas and built bathhouses for the millions who had no indoor plumbing and no way to keep themselves and their families clean. They built hospitals. In their settlement houses and community centers, they provided libraries, vocational training, child care and kindergartens, employment bureaus, and English classes. They organized penny-savings clubs and gave scholarships.

Between 1890 and 1910, these women and the men who worked with them established four hundred settlement houses.[7] The bathhouses were the sole source of hygiene for more than 10 million people in Chicago, New York, Boston, and Baltimore. The YWCA alone provided residences for more than 150,000 single women who were called "women adrift" in a federal report if they were not living with their families or the families of their employers.[8]

Without funding from Sage, Grace Dodge, Nettie Fowler McCormick, Bertha Honore Palmer, and a handful of other major donors, would the best efforts of such social reformers as Jane Addams, Florence Kelley, and Mary McLeod Bethune have made a difference? Yes, of course. Would that difference have been enough? Would the American economy have been able to swallow and digest that huge lump of desperate humanity, much less transform it into a pool of healthy, trained, English-speaking workers? It seems unlikely. The situation required a productive cooperation between people who controlled large sums of money and people who were willing to commit their lives to hands-on work. The result certainly saved America's cities, as Daphne Spain points out, and filled America's factories with healthy, trainable labor. It may also have saved us from the kind of uprising of the proletariat predicted by the Marxist theorists, but I'll just let you think about that one. I'm certainly not going to try to prove it.

A great many of the social services provided by all these philanthropic organizations were eventually taken over by local, state, or federal government agencies as American society changed the way it looked at its responsibilities. Ultimately, Sage's greatest impact may have been on the way policy makers would understand the poor and their conditions in America's cities. She realized that in an American society increasingly driven by success in science and technology, she needed to create a way for policy leaders and regular citizens to understand in quantitative terms the challenges human beings faced with poverty and how they could be addressed. She began a foundation with $10 million and began to fund surveys. The first, the "Pittsburgh Survey," done in 1914, attempted to examine the social problems of the whole city. This approach changed the way the country learned about public health and other issues that bore directly on how improvements in the lives of working people and the poor could occur. The rest of the century is the story of how this work progressed.

As I mentioned earlier, there was one last economic equation at work: the women who organized the women's exchanges and settlement houses were themselves "surplus" human capital. Between 1870 and 1880, the number of women enrolled in institutions of higher education nearly quadrupled. Educated for work but unemployed because of employers' and society's prejudices, these women were looking for a toehold in the labor market. In 1911, for example, the alumnae associations of the Seven Sisters colleges, as well as those of Wells College and Cornell University, formed an organization in New York City called the Intercollegiate Bureau of Occupations. Its purpose was to seek out and to develop vocational opportunities for educated women. The functions of the organization were taken over in 1919 by the Bureau of Vocational

Information (BVI), which continued the task. In 1926, the BVI closed for lack of funding. And yet, the philanthropic organizations that college-educated women set up for the well-being of others ended up creating, as a by-product, an entirely new vocation for educated women: social work.

The leaders in this new profession included Sophonisba Breckinridge and Edith Abbott; Florence Kelley, the director of the National Consumers League; Julia Lathrop, the first head of the Children's Bureau, and her successor, Grace Abbott; and Alice Hamilton, a Hull House veteran who became the first woman professor at Harvard Medical School and an innovator in industrial medicine. By 1921, there was a professional organization, the American Association of Social Workers. In 1952, it merged with several other professional groups to become the National Association of Social Workers. By 1999, there were 377 schools of social work in colleges and universities in this country. According to the Bureau of Labor Statistics, there were 813,000 people holding jobs in social work in this country in 1999. More than 71 percent of them were women. In funding new and innovative ways to develop human capital, this movement created an entire industry employing and developing hundreds of thousands of people.

Many of the women—and men—who came out of this movement also played important roles in the New Deal, from Frances Perkins and Harry Hopkins to Eleanor Roosevelt herself, who was a settlement house volunteer in her early days. When the Great Depression struck in 1929, more Americans became more needy, and, in 1935, Congress approved the Works Progress Administration (WPA) at the request of President Franklin Roosevelt. The WPA greatly expanded on the work of the settlement houses and exchanges and related donor-supported programs, all of which, like the WPA, were aimed at relieving the economic hardship of America's depression. The WPA employed more than 8.5 million people on 1.4 million public projects from 1935 to 1943, when it was disbanded. New Deal programs, whether you believe they saved the American economy or not, certainly had an enormous impact on it and were directly influenced by the philanthropically inspired activities of the Progressive movement.

So far in this chapter, we have shared a wide range of programs supported by philanthropy that developed human capital both within and beyond educational institutions. These few stories have only begun to demonstrate all that has gone on in the United States during our century of economic boom. Junior Achievement—the business clubs for youth—and 4H—the farm clubs for young people—show other ideas that have helped us develop a more efficient and skilled workforce at various times in our economic growth.

If we are to emulate our ancestors and protect our future, we must keep investing in human capital. To do this we need to support existing programs that work, such as "I Have a Dream" and 4H. We need to emulate Oseola McCarty and continue to support and create scholarship programs. Why would people pay for the education of other people's children? Some might want to give others what someone gave to them. Others might want to be sure other children get the very thing they missed out on in life. Still others without children might want to share parenthood by providing higher education for a child who will live differently because of the opportunity the benefactor provided. For the individual and for the country the outcome is the same: the dreams of both come closer to coming true. An education takes the students closer to where they are needed in society and closer to where their gifts call them to be.

We also need to identify the current unmet challenges and develop a stronger workforce. Look at literacy nationally, as the Barksdales did in Mississippi. According to the 1993 National Literacy Survey, 21 to 23 percent of American adults (representing 41 to 44 million people) scored at the lowest level of proficiency. Twenty-five percent were new immigrants just learning English, and 62 percent had never completed high school. The report goes further and states that 20 percent of the people in this lowest level were receiving food stamps, half were living in poverty, and less than half voted in a state or national election. They worked less, and they earned less. Even if the low-proficiency elderly in the study (33 percent) are discounted, that leaves over 27 million people in America who might benefit from English-as-a-second-language classes and from basic literacy training.[9]

The Return to College programs at the University of Pennsylvania and at Smith College (Comstock Scholars), among others, help at a higher level. They offer adults the opportunity to get advanced degrees at elite institutions on scholarships, even if they did not attend college as young people and even if, as adults, they still need financial support. Why is this important? Because, as we saw in the beginning of the chapter, more education means a higher income, and a higher income means less dependency in the future.

Prisons are another system where new philanthropy invests in human capital now. Many are comforted by the fact that the crime rate is down and the arrest rate is leveling off, which is good news. Tough-on-crime policies have worked. America is safer. Prisoners seem to no longer be an important issue. But consider the explosion in America's prison population to an incredible 2 million. In the next ten to twenty years, many of these people will be released, unprepared and more violent than when they entered the system. Without intervention, by some estimates, nearly 70 percent of these released prisoners will be rearrested within three years. They will cost society with the crimes they commit when they get out and then they will cost society when they return to prison.

Compiling high-quality data on the annual cost to taxpayers of incarceration offers many problems. The numbers are so impressive, however, that it is worth risking a margin of error to estimate these costs. States' costs of incarceration are very different from each other. They are very different from costs in the federal prison system and from local jails; incarcerated juveniles have different costs from adult prisoners and the costs of the different levels of security also vary. Some sources include the costs of building and maintaining prison facilities in their annual estimate of each prisoner's cost of maintenance. Others do not. The cost per inmate in the federal prison system alone was $24,000 annually in 2002.[10] In Massachusetts, prisoners cost over $32,000 annually.[11] Maryland pays about $23,000 annually to incarcerate an inmate.[12] The cost of building the prison must be added into the equation: by a 1997 estimate between $45,000 and $125,000 per cell.[13]

So for our estimation purposes, let's take an average roughly between Maryland's estimated cost per year of $23,000 and that of Massachusetts, $32,000. We could decide to estimate that the average annual cost of maintaining one prisoner for one year including all expenses is about $28,000. Remember that we have 2 million adults incarcerated in the United States, so we are spending roughly $56 billion annually to imprison them.

Add in the economic loss of each crime itself. Ed Zedlewski, an economist with the National Institute of Justice, calculated that in 1995, on average, each crime cost $2,300.[14] Even if the recidivism rates are wrong and only half of all prisoners return to prison, then based on Zedlewski's numbers, they will cost society $2.3 billion in terms of their crimes alone. The cost to reincarcerate the recidivists will be at least $25 billion annually, money taxpayers could save or spend in other ways if more of these people experienced a basic change while in prison. Not all can, but recidivism is too high and not a small price to pay, in any terms, human or economic.

That estimate of $56 billion annually represents more than one-fourth of all the money Americans gave to philanthropic causes last year ($212 billion)! Even modest changes in our expenditures for incarceration could free these funds for other critical needs in our society. We should operate prisons differently, following some of the successful pilot projects that have been funded, developed, and tested with philanthropic dollars. Such decisions need not make us soft on crime—but they can allow us to be smart about society and the power of philanthropy in American capitalism.

The answer is to ensure that the prisoners do not return to a life of crime. Prisoners, it turns out, are human capital with an interesting and challenging set of needs that must be addressed before they can bring their assets back to society. According to a Community Resources for Justice policy brief written in 2001, "National statistics indicate that seven in 10 prison inmates function at the two lowest levels of both prose and numeric literacy, meaning that they are unable to fill out a Social Security or job application, write a business letter, calculate a price discount, read a bus schedule, or perform many other text- and number-based tasks of daily life." The report goes on to say that, nationally, 80 percent of prisoners report drug use and that voluntary drug-treatment programs are not enough: "Inmates who receive in-prison treatment followed by a six-month aftercare program did significantly better than their counterparts. These inmates were two to three times more likely to be drug free 18 months post release than offenders who received no treatment, or only in-prison treatment for substance abuse."[15]

However, because of tougher attitudes toward prisoners, state and federal government programs within prisons have largely disappeared. Today's released prisoners are less likely to have been educated in prison. They are less likely to have gone through a drug-treatment program. They are less likely to be on parole when they go back to their families and neighborhoods. They have served their full sentences and return home after their term in prison with no supervision and no aftercare.

One innovator in this area is Chuck Colson, who, in 1976, after leaving prison in the days post-Watergate, founded Prison Fellowship Ministries, a privately funded program that currently operates in fifty states and ninety-three countries worldwide. Prison Fellowship is based on the idea that recidivism occurs only when the prisoner has not experienced a change of heart for the better while in prison. A faith-based organization, the program acknowledges that the people in America's prisons need help to develop positive relationships with people outside of prison and need to receive encouragement, acceptance, and accountability from those on the outside. The prisoners need educational and spiritual training to build and practice the life skills likely to aid their transitions to successful postprison life in society. Does the program work? The answer is simple. Only 6 percent of those who have experienced Colson's InnerChange Freedom Initiative return to prison within three years. The citizens who succeed return to their families, work, pay taxes, and perhaps even volunteer in programs to improve their communities.

Another program created to address this problem is a joint effort between the Maryland Department of Correction and the Enterprise Foundation (an organization that will be discussed at length in the next chapter). Together they created the Maryland Reentry Partnership, which began in 2001. As the foundation's *Annual Report 2001* points out, the cost of giving 250 men (in the pilot program) a chance to change their lives is a great deal cheaper than to ignore them. "Annually, it costs about $23,000 to house an inmate versus $2,500 to provide the services and resources that help people become productive citizens through the Maryland Reentry Partnership."[16]

In economic terms, prisoners who do not return to prison become assets to society instead of cost centers—costs in the prison system and in the expenses that crimes and violence impose on tax-paying citizens. The person and his or her family clearly get great advantages, too, from this generosity. Prison programs such as Pioneer and the Maryland Reentry Partnership greatly reduce recidivism and advance the human capital that has fallen out of society's reach, behind bars. The moral of this story is that personal generosity by citizens who feel personally responsible for the quality of society and the economy makes a difference no other factor can make.

Finally, one of the most important areas in need of similar imaginative work by generous citizens is home ownership for low-income families, which will be discussed in more detail in the next chapter. Citizens who wish to reproduce a version of the human-capital development done by settlement houses and women's exchanges over one hundred years ago should work with banks to develop access to credit, down payments, and mortgages for families at the low and low-moderate income level. Citizens can help reduce the down payments and support portions of monthly payments so people can get into homes they own and begin to develop equity. Home ownership is a critical factor in improving school performance of children from low-income families.

America's tradition of investing in people sustains an environment where people of very diverse income, educational and social levels, different races and ethnicities, all have a chance to succeed. This effort advances as well with the education that people can get in the community college system at very low cost. These institutions have grown significantly in the last thirty years. They are an important reason for upward mobility. As these stories show, recipients of generosity help perpetuate the tradition, and scholarship recipients rate among the more generous contributors. Those who succeed are inspired to fund opportunities for education, home ownership, improved access to health care, and jobs for those who have not yet succeeded. Consequently, U.S. history shows that a growing percentage of our highly diverse citizens actually do achieve and contribute. Moreover, people from all over the world are attracted to come, work, stay, and raise families in the United States. It is no secret that American generosity creates real opportunities for talented, hardworking people. It really is the gift that keeps on giving.

4

EXPANDING THE BUILT ENVIRONMENT: PHYSICAL CAPITAL

We are, after all, only trustees of the wealth we possess. . . . Without the community and its resources . . . there would be little wealth for anyone. The community where a man has lived and worked has a real claim to a portion of the results of a successful life. . . . If it be known that a generous measure of the wealth one accumulates is ultimately to be devoted to community use, it may be deemed honorable . . . for men who prefer struggle and achievement to idleness and leisure to continue the pursuit of wealth.

—JOHN RUSKIN, *Of Seven Lamps of Architecture*

"If you build it, they will come." They did, and they have. It is easy for Americans to take our communities for granted. Citizen donations have constructed billions of dollars worth of buildings and parks all over the country. Some of these amenities—the museums, libraries, hospitals, universities, observatories, and theaters—provide assets to serve the citizens of an entire community; others fulfill the American dream of home ownership, one family at a time. Generous donors have given private capital to build our physical capital. In addition to raising the American quality of life, these facilities became economic engines in their communities. Economic impact studies now prove, quantitatively, how critical these facilities have been. Where studies have not been done, qualitative data augment the statistics.

Of course, donated buildings do not supplant the construction of factories and offices where business investors set up industry; instead, they support existing industry. On a basic level, these facilities contribute to higher property values in the communities surrounding them. They also do much more. Donated buildings create jobs. They attract visitors. The visitors need new businesses to serve them. Homes must be built for the new employees of the donated building and the new businesses it required. In fact, decisions about which towns would be chosen for philanthropic investment, like where colleges would be placed, have often determined which towns grew to be important commercial centers for American industry.

Philanthropist Robert Wood Johnson understood the relationship between buildings and a stronger economy and a healthier society. He said: "We build not only structures in which men and women of the future will work, but also the patterns of society in which they will work. We are building not only frameworks of stone and steel but frameworks of ideas and ideals."[1] Donations to physical capital reinforce confidence in the long-term strength of the economy and often inspire significant partnerships with local governments to advance the goals of improving a city or community. All over the country, institutions exist that were built by far-sighted philanthropists. These institutions have stunning effects on the economy.

ECONOMIC GROWTH AND DONATED FACILITIES

Think of your hometown, the town where you live, or any great American city. Now as your mind's eye surveys the main streets, identify all the buildings constructed by donors' funds. Now remove them and see how the quality of life would be affected. Where would the community meet to share the *Nutcracker Suite* if the donated theater were gone? And the library? What would the town do without it? By the way, the hospital was probably a gift, too. If tax dollars had had to pay for these amenities instead, what would be missing from the town? How much direct federal and state government support would have been necessary to make up for the loss?

City building has been at the core of good deeds back to the days of the prophet Jeremiah: "Build houses, and dwell in them; and plant gardens, and eat the fruit of them; take wives, and beget sons and daughters; . . . that you may be increased there, and not diminished. And seek the peace of the city where I have caused you to be carried away captives, and pray to the Lord for it: for in the peace of the city you shall have peace."[2] Anyone who has worked to build a city knows that residential *living* is critical to the success of urban restoration just as the prophet suggests. Politics, personalities, and luck touch almost all city-planning decisions and certainly touch the decisions to rebuild a community or building, whether the source of funds is tax dollars or private donations.

When it comes to our cities, the United States is particularly fortunate to have three robust systems that can provide funding for ventures. Most countries have a for-profit or corporate sector that makes investments, they also have government funding that can be accessed in various ways. In the United States we enjoy a very large and responsive third sector—donated or philanthropic funds that stand as a source of support necessary to launch efforts. Each one of the three works independently and with different rules and expectations, but our history is full of examples where all three have worked together to expand the possibilities for growth and to meet pressing needs.

Baltimore is the first stop in our tour of cities affected by philanthropic investment in physical capital. It is the site of an institution we have already visited and will visit again: Johns Hopkins University. But first, we must look to the man who inspired Johns Hopkins and gave Baltimore a major donation of physical capital: George Peabody.

In 1857, George Peabody spent $1.5 million to construct the nation's first major urban cultural center, which included an art gallery, a library, and a school of music. His gift stimulated the cultural life of Baltimore and anticipated the "American Renaissance" that occurred between Reconstruction and World War I. The diverse facilities attracted new visitors to the city, enabling the Peabody Institute to play a major role in its development. Perhaps even more important, Peabody's early generosity paved the way for later donors and set the standard for improving the cultural life of the nation through facilities. Not only did the Peabody Institute serve as a model for subsequent donors such as the Fricks, Morgans, and Carnegies; in Baltimore, it directly inspired the development of the Enoch Pratt Free Library, the Baltimore Museum of Art, the Walters Art Gallery, and Johns Hopkins University.

Johns Hopkins University was founded in 1876. Johns Hopkins himself was the grandson of Margaret Johns and Gerard Hopkins, both devout Quakers who, in 1807, freed their slaves and put the young Hopkins's father and uncle to work in the fields. After working as an accountant in his uncle's grocery store, Hopkins built his own grocery business, accepting whiskey as payment for goods, which his uncle would not. His company was a huge success, enabling Hopkins to become an investor and board member in the Baltimore and Ohio Railroad, where he made his millions. Like many other wealthy people, Johns Hopkins then concentrated on philanthropy. He prepared his estate plans under the influence of George Peabody (who funded the Peabody Museums at Yale and Harvard, as well as Baltimore's Peabody Institute). Also advising him was John W. Garrett, father of Mary Garrett (who later founded the Johns Hopkins Medical School).

In 1867, Hopkins incorporated the Johns Hopkins University and the Johns Hopkins Hospital and established a twelve-member board of trustees for each. When he died in 1873, he left $7 million to be divided equally between the two institutions. It was, at the time, the largest philanthropic bequest in U.S. history. Its size made Johns Hopkins University's endowment larger than either Harvard's or Princeton's.

Johns Hopkins's first president, Daniel Coit Gilman, described the aims of the university as "the encouragement of research . . . and the advancement of individual scholars, who by their excellence will advance the sciences they pursue, and the society where they dwell."[3] Modeled after the great German research universities, Johns Hopkins was the first of its kind in the United States. As we have seen, its medical school redefined teaching in the field and is still one of the foremost schools in the country; its school of public health and its applied physics laboratory rank first among schools for the amount of research support they are awarded each year. Philanthropists have revitalized the institution throughout the university's history, from Mary Garrett's gift to build that coeducational medical school to recent gifts from the likes of Michael Bloomberg, who endowed the school of public health.

The "Bay Area Economic Study," an economic impact report conducted in 2000, offers detailed information about the force that the university and the hospital exert on the city of Baltimore, and it shows a direct impact on jobs and income. Measures similar to those in the "Bay Area Economic Study" could be done in any city and have been done in many, expressly to record the financial assets that come with donations from generous citizens making investments in public buildings. Impact studies typically describe three economic multipliers of facilities like museums, theaters, hospitals, and libraries: total output, which, as we have seen, estimates the aggregate total spending that takes place; earnings, which describes the successive rounds of respending that occurs as wage earners trade dollars for goods and services; and jobs, which estimates the aggregate force created by employment spending.

The "Bay Area Economic Study" applies all of these measures to Johns Hopkins. In 1999, the year the study examines, Johns Hopkins University and Health System was the largest private employer in the state, with 37,900 employees. Forty-three percent of them lived in the city of Baltimore. They were (and are) a major sustaining force in the city. Hopkins also hosts six independent research centers, including the Space Telescope Science Institute, the Kennedy Krieger Institute, and the Gerontology Research Center of the National Institute on Aging. These had a combined payroll of 2,940 men and women. In 1999, *direct* expenditure by Hopkins and its affiliates into the local economy totaled $2.41 billion.

Of course, economic impact is not limited to who gets paid

directly by the institution. It spirals out, affecting everyone in the community. For example, in 1999, Hopkins provided $63 million in health care to those too poor to pay for it themselves. More than two thousand construction workers owed their jobs that year to Hopkins building projects. Fourteen start-up companies were founded in Maryland to capitalize on the inventions created at Hopkins. When Johns Hopkins received the $108 million contract from NASA for the FUSE telescope mission, it subcontracted to local firms such as Orbital Sciences Corporation, Swales Aerospace, Interface Control Systems, and AlliedSignal Technical Services Corporation, bringing the money to Maryland and spreading it into the local economy.

Further, to get a true picture of the economic impact of Johns Hopkins, we should include the dollars spent by consultants, researchers, and applicants coming to Baltimore to visit the university. The "Bay Area Economics Study" did just that, and the results are astonishing. Taking into account the jobs that would have existed anyway, Hopkins can, directly and indirectly, be credited with generating close to eighty thousand net *new* jobs in the state of Maryland. As the study says: "For every direct Johns Hopkins employee, in fact, there's at least one other Marylander putting dinner on the table with salary dollars that started at Hopkins." The "spinoff spending" alone adds up to an additional $2.74 billion, making Johns Hopkins's net contribution to the state of Maryland a whopping $5.15 billion, or one out of every $33 spent in the state.[4]

Of course, not all of this money qualifies as philanthropic dollars. The point is that philanthropic dollars built, and continue to expand, the institution that generates so much. Whether we count jobs, income, or assets to the quality of life, Hopkins has made a dramatic and positive impact on the city of Baltimore. Largely because of its existence, Baltimore and, in fact, the state of Maryland appeal to leaders of companies in a wide range of fields including biotechnology. The biotechnology cluster in the Baltimore-Washington area has sprouted nineteen companies with nearly $800 million in revenue, many of which trace their founding and staffing to a Hopkins lab. Carnegie Mellon University professor Richard Florida notes in his recent book *The Rise of the Creative Class* that the

Baltimore-Washington area is number eight among the fifty American cities where the most creative people live.[5]

Harvard University offers another example of the impact of gift buildings on the local economy. Harvard is a major employer in its host city of Cambridge and in Boston. More than fifteen thousand people work at the university and over half of its $1.8 billion budget goes immediately into the local economy: equipment purchases, student financial aid, building and maintenance and support services; largely local companies and individuals. Moreover, just payment of taxes, payments in lieu of taxes, municipal fees, and purchases of goods and services along with payroll for employees who are Cambridge and Boston residents come to more than half a billion dollars.[6]

Harvard and the other major research universities in the Boston area catalyzed the economic development of Route 128 in Massachusetts. This development, which focused on high-tech companies, changed the economic base of the area as well as most of the state. In addition to Harvard, they include the Massachusetts Institute of Technology, Boston College, Tufts University, and Boston University, as well as the nearly one hundred other academic institutions around Boston.

Other towns, indeed whole regions, have experienced this same growth because of an initial philanthropic investment in physical capital. Stanford's facilities and graduates helped develop high-tech industries in the region around Palo Alto. North Carolina's Research Triangle, with cutting-edge infrastructure in the labs at Duke University, the University of North Carolina, and North Carolina State University, created a robust environment for high tech. Many other sites, such as Seattle and Austin, offer related examples. More recently, efforts of Yale in New Haven and the University of Pennsylvania in West Philadelphia have extended this same kind of force, with the participation of their states and cities, as well as non-profits and private industries.

Obviously, proximity to any major research university offers major assets for building creativity, and therefore universities offer significant advantages to businesses: a well-educated potential workforce, cultural and educational opportunities for employees and their families, and access to first-rate health care, among many others. As more businesses and new industries surround the university, real estate values rise. Some businesses count on the university as a customer; others draw on the university as a supplier, a mutual gain for the business environment in the city. Besides retail and high-technology companies, other industries flock to these sites. Biotechnology, financial services, banking, insurance companies, and knowledge industries tend to be attracted to the workforce and the cultural environment of the academic settings.

The over nineteen hundred private colleges and universities all over the country can tell similar stories about their impact on the economies of their towns or regions. These stories generally do not involve the same huge sums as the major research universities discussed above, but they are as important. Throughout American history, small towns have sought to sustain community pride and revitalize their prospects by attracting a college. People donated land to start colleges, realizing that any surrounding land would grow significantly in value. Many towns attracted their colleges with financial commitments from local donors who could give only small gifts, but they did just that, and the gifts mounted up. Western Reserve University was attracted to Hudson, Ohio, in 1826, when farmers in the area promised to commit cash, in-kind gifts, or their own labor to secure the university. One farmer's wife supposedly even pledged to contribute $50 a year from her egg and butter money and fulfilled her promise for ten full years.[7]

Of course, major donors were also important, but the term *major* was relative to fortunes of the time, and colleges of all sizes often relied on various size gifts to get under way. Williams College started with an initial collection of gifts amounting to $14,000, and Amherst, $50,000. Princeton, in a major campaign in the 1830s, recorded its largest gift at the level of $5,000.[8] All of them and countless others started or stabilized academic institutions that became economic engines in their communities and in their states.

The contributions by individual donors over hundreds of years to academic institutions are still delivering assets and not just the assets that come from the strong investment returns those schools get. As well, the strong facilities built over the centuries have made the universities' built environment too precious to abandon. Thirty years ago, the University of Pennsylvania did not leave inner-city Philadelphia and go to the end of the main line to King of Prussia to make a new campus in the green suburbs. It remained committed to the city. Its magnificent campus buildings and hospital grounded it in Ben Franklin's city, even with all of the challenges inner cities and old buildings provide.

Across the country from Philadelphia, Baltimore, and Boston, another philanthropist had an enormous effect on her city's built environment. Ellen Browning Scripps was an investor in education and health care. She was born poor (one of eleven children) but ultimately became extremely wealthy by investing in and working for her brothers' various newspapers. Settling in San Diego, she founded the Scripps Institution of Oceanography (from a $600,000 bequest from her brother), Scripps College for Women, and Scripps Memorial Hospital (later the Scripps Clinic and Research Foundation).

As important and impressive as this list is, Scripps gave still more. She was among the founders of the Bishop's School, to which she also provided scholarship funds, and bought land to make public parks. She gave large sums to the San Diego Zoo, the San Diego Museum of Natural History, and the YMCA/YWCA. Her money built the La Jolla Woman's Club, the first La Jolla Library, and the Children's Pool. Scripps built physical capital throughout San Diego. As we will see, this diversity of donated physical capital builds stronger cities, communities, and people.

As Ellen Browning Scripps knew, universities and colleges are not the only areas where philanthropists can build the physical environment and achieve stunning economic and social results. Nor are they the only places where the "educated populace," so essential to our democracy, develops. Many kinds of buildings have changed the character of our cities. For instance, most Americans know that Ben Franklin, who was a printer's apprentice and so had access to many books, advanced the idea that all towns should have free libraries so that the citizenry could have access to learning for self-education—another sign of the entrepreneurial U.S. spirit. Some of us know that Andrew Carnegie, initially a poor Scottish immigrant working as a sweeper in a steel factory, funded no fewer than 2,509 free public libraries in towns and cities all across the country and throughout the English-speaking world. He spent more than $56 million on this effort.[9]

Very few of us know that Julius Rosenwald, like Peabody before him and Carnegie after him, was a builder of economic assets by funding and building several kinds of new construction. He built hundreds of public schools and community centers. Like Peabody and Carnegie and hundreds of similarly inspired individual donors of both large and small gifts to build property, he saw the connection between creating facilities, building human capital, and improving the quality of daily life while building the local economy. He made his commitment by connecting his confidence in buildings as engines of change to his commitment to social justice and self-help as it was taught by Rabbi Emil Hirsch in the Chicago Sinai Congregation. Julius Rosenwald is a stellar example of American philanthropy. His story is important to the story of American generosity because, like Rush, Rosenwald gave both to people like himself and to those very different from him. He provided support to the range of needs his fellow citizens were confronting. He saw the connection between his generosity and economic advancement for people and the nation. He also saw the importance of linking his commitment to change with the commitment of the local community. He often asked that individual local donors show their enthusiasm for his investment by raising a pool of matching donations.

Rosenwald came from a poor immigrant family of German Jews. He developed Sears, Roebuck, Inc. into a mighty corporation and became a wealthy man. A major supporter of Jewish causes, especially assistance for some one hundred thousand recently arrived Jews at the beginning of the twentieth century, he also invested in the human capital of his own employees. His enlightened social conscience made him offer health and dental coverage and profit sharing to them and their families. But Rosenwald's most significant contribution came in his support of the founding of YMCA-YWCAs for African Americans in twenty-five communities throughout the country and his commitment of funds to construct hundreds of "Rosenwald" schools: new, modern buildings for the education of African Americans. None of this made him a paragon of virtue. His own family members say he was not an easy man to deal with. Opinionated and sometimes harsh, he was also a risk taker and a shrewd businessman. In so being, he saw the benefits of improving America's human capital through physical capital, and he set about making those improvements.

Rosenwald knew that black communities would benefit from YMCAs as much as white communities, but African Americans were consistently denied membership in the early decades of the twentieth century. He pledged $25,000 to any city able to raise $75,000 to build a Y in its black neighborhood. He ended up contributing almost $4 million to help build twenty-five YMCA-YWCA facilities in black neighborhoods all over the country. Rosenwald's gift, and the challenge format that structured it, created new buildings, new donors, and new levels of social cohesion, as Martin Morse Wooster explains:

> Rosenwald's plan stimulated major philanthropic effort. In Washington, D.C., 4,500 African Americans—five percent of the black population—contributed $27,000 to the YMCA construction fund. In Chicago, 10,000 donors—a fourth of the black population—gave $67,000. Several of the donors were former slaves who parted with their life savings. [Booker T.] Washington remarked that "the organizing of the colored people for the gathering and collection of subscriptions, the inspiration that comes from labor in common for the common good—all this is in itself a character-building process, and has had a far-reaching influence upon the churches and other religious organizations throughout the country."[10]

Then Rosenwald began building schools. Convinced that education offered the most productive approach to strengthening the economic future of African Americans, he became committed to the issue even when other philanthropists—worried about upsetting southern white supremacists—moved more slowly on it.

Rosenwald recognized a problem when he saw one. At the time, in Alabama for example, only 20 percent of black children were enrolled in the public schools, while 60 percent of white children were. With the building of the schools, Julius Rosenwald helped over six hundred thousand black children attend school. Again, Wooster details the story:

> In May 1911, Rosenwald and [Booker T.] Washington met at Chicago's Blackstone Hotel to discuss projects. Rosenwald's first act was to agree to lead an effort to raise $50,000 for Tuskegee, allowing Washington to spend more time at the school and less time fundraising. A year later, Washington and Rosenwald began plans to build schools for blacks. Rosenwald agreed to let Washington select the schools that would participate in the program. If the schools raised enough money, Rosenwald said, "I will agree to pay a total of twenty-five thousand dollars (25,000) to such schools as soon as they furnish a list of bonafide subscriptions equal to the amount you have designated."[11]

Wooster also recounts a powerful story of African American participation in the school fund drives:

> . . . in Boligee, Alabama, in 1916 . . . an anonymous observer wrote a firsthand account. Local cotton farmers had just been ravaged by the boll weevil, and most contributors walked four miles through the mud to get to the meeting site. "You would have been overawed with emotion if you could have seen these poor people walking up to the table, emptying their pockets for a school," the observer wrote. "One old man, who had seen slavery days, with all of his life's earnings in an old greasy sack, slowly drew it from his pocket, and emptied it on the table. I have never seen such a pile of nickels, pennies, dimes, and dollars, etc. in my life. He put thirty-eight dollars on the table, which was his entire savings."[12]

In total, Rosenwald gave $4.4 million to build 5,357 schools in the South. His donations were augmented by $18.1 million from the government, $1.2 million from foundations, and $4.7 million from individual African Americans. The latter is perhaps the most important. No Rosenwald school was built without the local black community's helping and feeling a sense of its own power to affect change for the better.[13] From Maryland to Texas, the Rosenwald schools are still legend. Charlotte, North Carolina, has just included its Rosenwald school in a documentary on the city.

Estimates are that Rosenwald gave away $63 million, which would be worth at least ten times that amount today. His generosity had an impact on various elements of corporate human resource policy, on Chicago's Jews, and, most profoundly, on African Americans throughout the South. He literally built the capacity for thousands of students to contribute more both to America's democracy and to its economy.

Let's stay with Julius Rosenwald for the moment because he will lead us to another kind of donated building, the museum. In building the Museum of Science and Industry in Chicago, he brought a major asset to the city. Impressed by the science museum he had seen in Munich, he saw the asset it would be to Americans. The concept he brought home involved making the country's first center for "industrial enlightenment," a center for the advancement of education for the public in science and technology. He built the museum in 1929, spending between $6.6 and $7 million, and gave it as a gift to the city. He developed the idea of an interactive museum where visitors could manipulate the displays, not simply view them. He wanted to increase the learning and the excitement around learning. He believed people, but particularly children, needed the stimulation of the museum to connect to the future as the new century progressed. He wanted to have an impact on everybody's children.

Today, the Museum of Science and Industry is the oldest science museum in the Western Hemisphere and has had 160 million visitors since it opened in 1933. Among the top seven most popular museums in the United States, it is also one of the best loved and most frequently visited in the world. As Rosenwald had hoped, it has inspired thousands of young people to become scientists and has set a standard of excellence and innovation for other science museums across the country and throughout the world.[14] And the Museum of Science and Industry is only one of the nine museums that are housed on Chicago Park Service land, making up the Museums in the Park. The others are the Adler Planetarium, the Shedd Aquarium, the Art Institute of Chicago, the Notebaert Nature Museum, the Chicago Historical Society, the DuSable Museum of African American History, the Field Museum, and the Mexican Fine Arts Center. All of these institutions, built with donated funds, are key to the cultural life of the city. They contain world-class collections of historical artifacts, art, exotic creatures, and astronomical treasures, and they create opportunities for cultural richness and space for community engagement. They also bring a powerful economic payoff, even though they are tax exempt.

Question: Which makes a greater impact through visitors and revenue on the economy of Chicago, its five major-league sports franchises or its nine major museums? Answer: The museums.

Between 1996 and 1999, a million more tourists visited these museums than attended all of Chicago's sports events combined. In fact, in 1999, the number of visitors to the Museums in the Park surpassed the attendance at all major sports teams' events combined by 19 percent. In 2000, 8.7 million guests visited the museums while 6.8 million attended games of the Cubs, White Sox, Bulls, Blackhawks, and Bears.[15] These figures are from an economic impact study released by the Metro Chicago Information Center summarizing the contributions of the museums to the city's economy.

And there are more. In 1999, the Museums in the Park required $206.3 million in direct funding. This $206 million in direct spending generated approximately $456 million in total output (which estimates the aggregate total spending that takes place) and $180.25 million in personal earnings. The museums created 10,900 jobs in indirect or support industries such as wholesale supply, manufacturing, transportation, communications, insurance, finance, utilities, and tourism. The museum consortium is also a major Chicago employer in its own right. In 1999, the nine museums directly employed more than sixty-eight hundred people.

Of the 7.9 million tourists who visited Chicago for day trips in

1999, 43 percent mentioned museums as a major reason for their visit, more than three times the number who mentioned sports. Day-trippers spent on average $114 each, so $387.6 million in the city's GDP can be traced to the museums. Of the 15 million overnight visitors who came to Chicago in the same year, 23 percent of them cited museums as the reason for their visit, three times the number who mentioned sports (7 percent). These travelers spent an average of $150 per person per day and stayed an average of 3.9 days, so an additional $2 billion in GDP gets tallied under philanthropy. In addition, 1.3 million overseas travelers visited Chicago in 1999. Thirty percent cited museums and art galleries as a primary activity during their stay, almost four times the number who mentioned sports (8 percent). These travelers spent an average of $258 per person per day and stayed an average of 6.7 days. Ring up another $674 million. Added together, the tourist revenue brought in by the museums came to over $3 billion in 1999.[16]

The Museums in the Park have positioned Chicago as a world-class center of arts and culture, attracting ever more tourists to Illinois and the city. The report concludes: "Support . . . of the Chicago cultural community as a whole is not only an investment in the cultural well-being of those who live and work in the City and the surrounding metropolitan area. It is a sound investment in the economic well-being of the City of Chicago and the State of Illinois."[17] The donated built environment makes a bottom line difference to Chicago's economy. What is significant for our purposes here is that in America the impetus for these structures comes from private citizens and only later on in the process attracts partnerships with government or develops for-profit interests.

The desire to build cultural facilities for the economic, social, and cultural good of cities and towns across America still exists today. The *New York Times* covered this phenomenon in the South, focusing just on the dozen cities where individual donors are funding museums to create local economic assets. Well, yes, of course, they want to increase the presence of the arts in their towns, but they know exactly what the collateral advantages are of investing in buildings. A total of four projects, two each in North Carolina and Georgia, involve projected costs of over $150 million. Others are well under way in Virginia, Louisiana, Tennessee, Alabama, and Mississippi. Many involve name-brand architects like Frank Gehry. All this is part of the dual aim to create an economic asset with dollars from individual generosity and to make a significant space to advance culture and the quality of community life.

> In many cities business leaders are supporting these projects in the hope that they will draw tourists and attract more talented work forces. The economic prosperity of the 1980's and 1990's made many of these business figures rich, and they have contributed millions of dollars to museum fundraising campaigns. Museum directors are acutely aware that donors want to use museums as tools for economic development, are competing with one another to produce the most striking buildings.[18]

Hence the world-class architects. Like their predecessors, the new donors are also giving very generously and getting others to do likewise, spreading the practice of the American gospel of giving. The Gehry museum going up in Biloxi, Mississippi, received a gift of $1 million from Jerry O'Keefe and his family, but the O'Keefes also have raised an additional $7 million toward the projected final cost of $16 million.

Among the newest projects planned to build physical capital is the new Guggenheim Museum project redevelopment of Piers 9, 11, 13, and 14 in New York City. This will benefit the economic interests of lower Manhattan beyond the scope of the city's or the state's budget. This huge effort, on hold in the aftermath of the economic downturn of 2001, will, if it gets restarted, provide 2,550 new jobs for the people of New York. The new museum is ultimately expected to bring in 2 to 3 million visitors per year and generate $280 million in annual economic activity, which will bring New York City $14 million in new tax revenues. In a government-philanthropy partnership, the city will make a contribution of approximately 10 percent toward the new museum's anticipated cost of $678 million.[19] Foundation director Thomas Krens remarked: "The new Guggenheim on the New York City waterfront, I believe, will have a profound impact on the economic and cultural life of New York City. Given the architectural presence of the building design, the scope and quality of the program, it will add tremendously to the quality of life of local residents in Lower Manhattan."[20] This effort and others like it are, of course, linked to the economic health of the time and place where they launch. Philanthropy does not occur in a vacuum. It depends on economic growth and contributes to it.

In addition to the economic assets they bring, almost all of the cultural facilities built with donors' funds have contributed to the democratizing forces in our society. They provide opportunities for all citizens, including those from widely diverse economic levels, races, and ethnicities. In fact, more recently, most have programs designed to draw members of the communities who have traditionally not used them. Museums, theaters, concert halls, and facilities like Provident Hospital have traditionally welcomed a broad range of citizens. As more for-profit hospitals replace the non-profits, we may see a change. Of course, the equivalent cultural facilities on campuses often provide the best access to arts and culture in their communities even though they are also used for events restricted to the campus members and not all citizens. The funders of the Guggenheim, the O'Keefes, and many others are following in the great tradition of Peabody and Rosenwald and, in fact, Benjamin Franklin. The American tradition of generosity has brought the benefits of the gifts of major donors to all citizens as human capital–building assets shared over the decades and even centuries. This tradition may have contributed to the sense of social solidarity many Americans share, though they come from different groups.

Cleveland, like all of the cities we have visited, has relied on a diverse group of philanthropists to build the major facilities that became fundamental assets to the economic and cultural growth of the city and all its diverse inhabitants. Indeed, Cleveland has an even more deeply seated culture of philanthropy than many of these cities. This is because Cleveland's industrial leaders became, as did a similar group in Minneapolis and Hartford, committed to a culture of giving. Major business leaders passed this culture of giving carefully from one generation to another. The well-being of the local community was of paramount concern to them. This proud tradition created an expectation that citizens would make financial and volunteer contributions at a variety of levels to assure that all the features of a strong community would thrive. As a result, it was less possible for a business to succeed in Cleveland unless its executives participated in philanthropy.

One of the major innovations that built this tradition was the development of the nation's first community foundation in 1914. Frederick Goff, president of Cleveland Trust Company, created the Cleveland Community Foundation to assure that clients leaving money would do so in a way that would meet the continually changing needs of the city and the area. Avoiding the snarl created when the intent of a donor is no longer practical or necessary, Goff's idea enables donors to set up named funds designated for specific purposes. The disbursement of funds is then accomplished through a distribution committee of five members elected from among local leaders. The committee assures that all available funds are used to address the needs of the community in a way that most closely matches the intentions of the donor. Pooling these individual donor funds under the management of one organization gives community foundations the advantage of significant giving power. At the same time, the foundations give donors considerable confidence in the "perpetual" usefulness of their bequests, yet frees them from wealth-management concerns and cost. Many communities have seen the wisdom of Goff's idea. In the years since 1914, hundreds of community foundations have developed all over the country.

The Cleveland Community Foundation's influence can be seen throughout the city. The Cleveland Recreation Survey in 1919 resulted in funding for a citywide series of parks called the Emerald Necklace. Much later, in 1977, the Cleveland Lakefront State Park study showed new uses for the waterfront, which the community foundation realized. The foundation also started a multimillion-dollar initiative in the neighborhoods surrounding Cleveland in

1987. The funding for the restoration of Cleveland's theaters and its theater district (sustained for fifteen years) included $2.2 million in grants and an unprecedented $3.8 million of the foundation's capital. These generous investments in physical capital revived the economy all over the city.

Largely because of the foundation's cultural power, Cleveland's philanthropic community has directed the city's future and addressed its problems. It has assembled a diverse coalition of people from business, finance, law, medicine, the ministry, the nonprofit sector, and labor who have all been called upon for a wide range of projects. While banks and most other companies changed hands, arrived in, and then left the city, the Cleveland Community Foundation maintained its focus. This issue is now more important than ever when many corporations move their headquarters and their original cities suffer the loss of corporate commitment to local funding. The foundation's $2 billion endowment, some of it contributed many decades ago, inspires confidence; grantees feel less subject to the vagaries of changes in government or corporate leadership and more confident in their long-range planning and survival. For example, physical facilities need to be sustained and maintained by funders, and the operating budgets for them are often harder to meet without significant philanthropic dedication. In Cleveland, through the foundation, philanthropists have often left funds endowed for the upkeep of buildings they or others initially funded.

It is important to note that when philanthropic groups maintain a long-term commitment to their communities, they can also give those communities the experience and leverage to push through other initiatives. It is interesting, for example, that the school voucher program, which developed in Cleveland as a desperate and determined attempt to assure quality K–12 education, passed the judgment of the Supreme Court. Cleveland's leaders built a knowledgeable and broad-based plan. The Cleveland Community Foundation announced its first study, the comprehensive "Cleveland School Survey" (the education survey) in 1915, and the foundation's leaders' dedication to Cleveland's schools has shown up through the decades since. Consequently, it is impossible to quantify the effect of their collective intelligence and understanding in making the recent voucher program a reality.

All the different types of physical capital discussed above—hospitals, universities and colleges, K–12 schools, libraries and community centers and museums—affect the economies of the cities and towns where they have been built. Thousands of towns and cities across the country could point to this variety of donated facilities and relate the economic benefits they have brought.

New London, Connecticut, for example, my hometown for thirteen years, tells the story of philanthropic investment in physical capital in vivid detail. A typical colonial New England port city, it was founded in 1646 by Governor John Winthrop Jr., son of the man who wrote the sermon on the *Arabella*. Its population has hovered between fifteen thousand and thirty thousand since. It has had 350 years of economic ups and downs and has had citizens of significant wealth and severe poverty. Most would agree that it has had its share of good and bad local leadership along the way. Its citizens had an early and long-standing connection to the Congregational Church, in time adding the Episcopal and eventually the Catholic Church. Waves of immigrants arrived in New London and settled down to fill jobs in retail and merchant work, on the wharves in various maritime-related industries, and in the professions. Because the town was blessed with a wonderful natural harbor, trading and the whaling industry employed many of its residents, at all economic levels. Since New London had access to plenty of timber, shipbuilding became an important industry as well. New London's oldest homes, the Hempstead Houses, were part of the Underground Railroad. With a strong history connected to the military, to sea captains and merchants in international trade, and to free blacks and abolitionists, New London is American history in six square miles. So how has this diverse history been affected by donated physical capital?

As we have seen from Provident and Johns Hopkins, the donation of funds to create hospitals provides huge benefits to the towns and communities in which they are located. New London's hospital was the gift of the children of an immigrant who arrived in 1804 from Venice, Italy. Giuseppe Lorenzo changed his name to Joseph Lawrence, joined the Episcopal Church, and in 1833 entered the whaling industry, where he made his fortune. His son, Sebastian Lawrence, provided the land, Lawrence Hall, and a $400,000 endowment to found the Joseph Lawrence Free Public Hospital, which opened in 1912 with forty beds. Later, Memorial Hospital, established in 1892 by a gift of $10,000 by J. N. Harris, merged with Lawrence, as did the medical facilities funded by the members of the Palmer family. By 1930, New London had established its centrality in the economy of the region as the medical center and home base for the medical families who came to work in the hospital. Doctors' offices opened nearby, as did pharmacies and medical-supply houses. The hospital has continued to expand in the passing years by raising funds from local citizens, thus continuing the generosity of the original donors.

Today, Lawrence & Memorial Hospital is the major health-care provider in southeastern Connecticut. It has a staff of two thousand and serves a population of 180,000 (which expands to 250,000 in the summer months). It is a not-for-profit private hospital and provides the region's only cardiac catheterization lab, inpatient rehabilitation unit, comprehensive community cancer center, and neonatal intensive care unit. A donation at the beginning of the twentieth century has lasted and contributed to New London's economic growth at the beginning of the twenty-first.

Perhaps the greatest accumulation of gifts that came into New London arrived to attract and then construct and sustain the second example of physical-capital donation, Connecticut College. When Wesleyan announced it would no longer accept women students, a group met in Hartford to find a place to launch an excellent private liberal arts college for women. A number of cities competed to attract the new college. A variety of sources worked to place the college in New London. The town of New London gave $50,000, and Harriet Allyn offered fifty acres of beautiful land on a hilltop. But it was the individual citizens, running fund-raisers and going door to door to collect pennies, who finally secured the college for

New London. By raising $135,000, they ensured the main gift, $1 million from industrialist Morton Plant. Plant was determined to see matching funds from the citizens of the town where he would agree to place his gift and therefore where the new college would settle. Again, as with Rosenwald and others, the small gifts from individual citizens attracted and captured the larger generosity.

The college was chartered in 1911, and the first students came in September 1915. In the years following its founding, the college expanded. The Bolles family, among others, made gifts that increased the size of the college's arboretum, and the Palmer family made a set of important gifts to the Palmer Library and the Palmer Auditorium. Mary Harkness gave a dormitory and the Harkness Chapel. In just nine years, the college had extended to 341 acres, and another $850,000 had been given for new buildings and other needs.

Since then, the college has joined the ranks of the nation's most selective liberal arts colleges and has raised several hundred million dollars, much of it in endowments. Some has been spent for buildings, programs, salaries, and scholarships. Generous givers have donated all but a very small percentage of these millions. The college has attracted many thousands of visitors to New London each year, including those from surrounding towns who want to hear lectures, use the library, or hear music. The gifts that people gave almost one hundred years ago are being repaid now, in particular, as the college spearheads the economic development of the city and opens it to an industry—pharmaceuticals—that is likely to have an economic impact in the twenty-first century.

Connecticut College is not the only educational institution in New London built with donated funds. Unbeknownst to many of us today, many "public" schools in New England towns in the eighteenth and nineteenth centuries were not tax-supported but were gifts of donors. The boost to education in New London came early when Robert Bartlett willed his property to the town to provide a free school for poor children. He died in 1673, leaving more than 250 acres for education. With various missteps and failures, including a 1682 fine for not maintaining a grammar school despite

Bartlett's gift, a school was eventually established in 1701. Girls were taught before and after normal school hours. In 1873, a private school for boys opened. It was named the Bulkeley School after Leonard H. Bulkeley, who had given $25,000 to trustees to invest for a local secondary school. When this initial investment had grown to $70,000, the new school was built and endowed. Major donors increased this endowment over the next fifty years. Another benefactor decided to establish a school just for girls in memory of her son, Thomas W. Williams II. The Williams Memorial Institute opened in 1891. The city of New London paid for the tuition of local girls. In 1896, the Henry Chapman family made a set of gifts to establish a technical-vocational school for both boys and girls. In 1952, the Bulkeley and Chapman Schools merged and became totally coeducational. It was New London's first lasting public high school.

From the seventeenth through the mid-twentieth centuries, there was no public high school in New London. Yet, education during that period, as it does today, meant a leap for poor children from the low-paid work of an unskilled laborer to the possibility of better-paid employment as a skilled laborer or for a job in trade. Even more to the point, the better educated the populace of the town, the more it could attract and sustain advancing industries. When the whaling industry declined, the industry that advanced in its place was shipbuilding. Where would New London have been if it hadn't been able to offer workers with the math and reading skills necessary for the industry?

Libraries, like private schools, improved the quality of life in New London, educated its populace, and helped it to grow faster than neighboring towns. Downtown, at the top of the hill overlooking the city, the New London Library commands the view. The library opened in 1891 but not without great effort to open one earlier. As early as 1784, a New London Library Company met, and, in 1838, a New London Young Men's Reading Association met. In 1840, a New London Young Men's Library Association began. It was Henry Haven's will that set the firm future for the New London Public Library. In 1876, Haven left property to be held in trust until

1890, when the principal could be used for charity. The trustees of the will determined that it should go to build the library and endow its future.

Haven made his fortune in the maritime merchant firm that later bore his name. He first spent six years as an indentured servant of the firm's head.[21] He was deeply engaged in civic and church-related duties all through his life and served a term as mayor. He died leaving his ample estate evenly divided among his two surviving children and charity, one third for each. The final third turned out to be the long-awaited library. An architect from the Richardson school was selected. The endowment left to tend to the library's needs meant that it was funded by its own resources until the 1970s, when the trustees decided to use the remaining funds to expand the library. The city then accepted the financial responsibility for the annual budget costs. The building still stands today. It is a functioning library that is still educating the populace as well as serving as an economic engine because of its strong tourist attraction as a "Richardson library."

New London's major museum is also a gift of a generous citizen whose riches came from the whaling industry that supported New London for many decades. One of the most famous whaling captains is memorialized in the $1 million gift his daughter made to found a museum of art in New London. Harriet Upson Allyn founded the Lyman-Allyn Art Museum for the benefit of the citizens of New London and hired Charles Platt, like Richardson a well-regarded contemporary architect, to design the building. It is a classic Greek Revival mansion–style structure in marble and continues to draw thousands of visitors each year. It also runs many programs to enrich the arts education for New London schoolchildren.

All of these donated buildings helped support the economic and social development of New London. Yet, New London still fell on hard times. During the late twentieth century, after the cold war ended, a good deal of the defense industry was dismantled. The so-called peace dividend that might have been good for the nation was bad for New London, as the submarine base and submarine building and related industries downsized. By the 1990s, New London had the fourth-weakest economy among the 169 towns in the state of Connecticut. Its population was dropping, as was its tax base. Much of its residential real estate was selling for less than the current owners' purchase prices. About 70 percent of the children in the New London school system were receiving government assistance in 2000. The scores of New London's children on the State Mastery Tests ranked in the lowest, or seventh out of seven, groups in the state. The dropout rate in New London High School was between 50 and 70 percent, depending on who offers the statistics and how they are counted.

Four years ago, as president of the college, I gathered a group of citizens who formed a not-for-profit corporation named the New London Development Corporation (NLDC). The city needed an economic shot in the arm, and its political structure and current top staff kept failing to mobilize the city's assets on behalf of its own future. The NLDC tried to remedy some of these problems. The highly diverse board of NLDC had three goals: increase the tax base, increase jobs at all levels, and improve the quality of life for all citizens. This meant improve the K–12 schools in New London to improve property values, improve home ownership among low- and moderate-income people, and improve access to health care. Citizens gave over $1 million to support the NLDC.

The board focused on the city's assets. Among these was a large tract of land on the water downtown. It had monumental drawbacks. It was a highly contaminated brownfield with a scrap-metal company nearby that had leaked environmental hazards onto the land and into the nearby creek and Thames River for many decades. A significantly deteriorated wastewater treatment plant loomed adjacent to the brownfield. We set about to purvey the acreage on the water to a Fortune 500 company that could create a local industry, jobs, and an asset to the tax base. With the cooperation of the state of Connecticut, the biggest goal was met: the NLDC was able to bring the Pfizer Global Research Center to the brownfield in the center of the city shoreline. It built a $300 million facility with twenty-one hundred employees. This one addition to the city has brought an increase of 25 percent in the tax base. The rest of the building projects approved for the remaining land will bring a $30 million Coast Guard museum, a four-star hotel and conference center, more science park building space, and a park and apartments on the waterfront. A lot of work remains ahead for the citizen leaders, but a new era has begun, spearheaded by private-citizen generosity and partnerships with government and the very important private industry sector, Pfizer, Inc.

In addition to NLDC, many other non-profits are working to develop and rejuvenate New London. The NLDC forged a partnership with the United Way and the Southeastern Connecticut Community Foundation to work with the New London schools to improve early childhood, K–12, and after-school education as well as job training. A housing initiative is renovating old houses and returning them to livability. Renovations of large abandoned buildings are under way to permit more citizens to live downtown and rebuild a core American city—not by federal, state, or private handouts, but by productive partnerships with a top Fortune 500 company, state government, and non-profits.

As our last stop on the national tour, let's return to Baltimore. Like New London, it is a major port, but its economy is particularly diversified and balanced so that no single industry has made its destiny critical to the city. In addition, the large number of facilities built by philanthropists has helped strengthen Baltimore, giving it an infrastructure that survived the city's darker economic periods. This infrastructure attracted some of the twentieth century's most notable commercial developers. Their work—in productive partnerships with philanthropists, government, and citizens who voted bond issues—has stimulated recent improvements in the city. As we have seen, it is these types of partnerships that have the best chance to continue repairing America's cities. Individual citizens with big dreams and the willingness to invest in the greater good energize these partnerships.

One such generous citizen was developer James Rouse, who brought his social conscience and his professional expertise to many cities. Through the idea of a festival marketplace, Rouse secured the heart of Baltimore, as well as Boston, New York, Milwaukee, and other cities. In fact, when awarding him the Medal of

Honor shortly before Rouse's death in 1996, President Clinton said that if more developers had followed Rouse's lead, "we would have lower crime rates, fewer gangs, less drugs. Our children would have a better future. Our cities would be delightful places to live. We would not walk in fear. We would walk in pride down the streets of our cities."[22]

In 1955, Rouse organized Baltimore businesspeople to form the Greater Baltimore Committee. Together they developed the massive Charles Center office and apartment complexes that revived downtown. Eventually, they initiated the Inner Harbor project. The federal government was very supportive of these innovative revitalization efforts and provided funding through Community Development Block Grants (CDBG) and Urban Development Action Grants (UDAG). Here is where Rouse's marketplace, Harborplace, opened in 1980. It created an exciting draw for tourists and gave Baltimore's citizens a beautiful and practical access to their water's edge.[23]

The power of private donations to create facilities for education and culture, for economic and social improvement, is no longer a secret shared by a few major donors, if it ever was such a secret. The kind of commitment exhibited by the Cleveland Community Foundation and Jim Rouse are powerful examples. As the twenty-first century courses through its first decade, hundreds of projects of this sort are rising all over the country. The donors often express quite clearly their intention of advancing the arts or the sciences and also attracting further investments to their city, bringing tourists with their money and appreciation to spend time in their town.

ECONOMIC GROWTH AND INCREASING HOME OWNERSHIP

Sharing wealth to increase the economic assets and the cultural and educational richness of communities makes sense, even though the property remains in the nonprofit sector and so remains untaxable. It still contributes indirectly to taxes, as we have seen; the buildings attract other enterprises that are taxpaying and create jobs that bring earners into the community whose needs must be filled by additional jobholders at various levels.

Jim Rouse recognized another way, a very direct way, to build assets from increased values in property: increasing home ownership. Rouse's friend, journalist Neal Peirce, notes that Rouse thought people should be cocreators with God. Peirce quotes Rouse: "The progressive spread of poverty, crime, joblessness, increases every year. The wealthy and powerful fundamentally believe nothing can be done with human conditions of our poor. We must find a way to transform the life of poor people at the bottom of American society. Our country, our cities, are severely threatened. This civilization can fail."[24]

Rouse acted on his beliefs. He launched the Enterprise Foundation in 1982 with a simple, though ambitious, mission in mind: to see that all low-income people in the United States would have the opportunity for fit and affordable housing and respectfully shared support to get up and out of poverty. The foundation has a national network of more than twenty-two hundred organizations in eight hundred locations and, working with partners across the country, has raised and invested $3.9 billion in loans, equity, and grants to create more than 132,000 homes for low-income people. In Baltimore alone, the foundation constructed or rehabilitated nearly three thousand affordable homes for low-income residents.

Why is home ownership so important? Because the single most significant way that Americans develop wealth is through the equity we build up in the homes we own. Besides the stunning impact on wealth generation, home ownership also affects the social well-being of family members. Children of home owners have fewer problems in school, less absenteeism, higher graduation rates. More home-owning families have jobs and are two-parent units. No surprises here. Home owners are less often poor. Tax policy favors home owners. A home owner both builds equity and deducts interest on mortgage payments from taxes. Renters have no such federal deductions, of course.

From the colonial days, Americans have been participating in citizen generosity to develop home owners and home ownership. Barn raisings have always been a part of the U.S. landscape. People donated time and materials and support to erect the buildings a new family needed to become productive members of the community. They were expected to offer their time and materials and support to others in return. On Friday, a plot of land might lie empty; the contributions of other members of the community could make a barn rise by Monday. Some gave wood or nails. Others fed the builders. Everyone worked. The couple who received the barn was very quickly set up to be productive, and the whole community benefited from the asset they had made together and the productivity of the new owners. The whole experience reinforced the civic values and beliefs that have made America strong over centuries.

Increasingly, generous individual Americans see this area of the economy as an opportunity to make a difference in the lives of individuals, families, and communities. Home ownership is a productive way that many communities can leverage the dollars they are already spending on education and social services. They can enter partnerships that support increased home ownership for lower-income families and watch for improvements in school performance; reduction in teen pregnancy, violence, and drug use; and a more stable and efficient economy. For example, the Cleveland Community Foundation, introduced earlier, partnered with and matched funds from the Lutheran Housing Corporation to create the East Cleveland Housing Program. This program focuses on improving housing conditions and increasing home ownership among low- and moderate-income residents. The buildings constructed met precise needs of the poor that the foundation had identified through extensive research.

Another way home ownership is being promoted is through community land trusts (CLTs). These are nonprofit membership organizations created to hold land for the benefit of a community. Currently there are well over one thousand websites that describe their work. Community land trust projects have minimal defaults on loans and maximum efficiency in getting low-income people successfully placed in home ownership.

The Litchfield Housing Trust in Connecticut is an excellent example of a community land trust. Andrew and Jamie Garagrin helped set up the trust in 1989 and then donated thirty-five wooded acres, called Tanner Brook, for affordable housing. Using $1.5 million in grants and loans from the state, the Litchfield Housing Trust built twelve cooperative town houses and one single-story building with four units. Co-op unit owners each contributed three hundred hours of sweat equity as down payment for the units, equivalent to $1,500 in cash equity. Monthly fees are based on the occupants' incomes and range from $350 to $550, including maintenance funds. Residents meet monthly to make decisions together. This effort and many like it are relying on citizen generosity and partnerships with government to make equity building a reality for those who had no chance to achieve it all alone.

Another way to develop housing is through revolving-loan funds. Thousands of contributions of money and time create these funds. For instance, through the Institute for Community Economics, $35 million in revolving funds, representing over four hundred loans to community organizations, have launched more than 3,850 housing units in thirty states. Interestingly, a number of asset-management firms now offer clients the opportunity to invest in these revolving-loan funds, thereby making real investments in social change. The investors can see the results of their investments advancing their own portfolios and strengthening the wider economy.

Family foundations, such as the Melville Trust in Connecticut, have also focused on housing needs. The Melvilles, in cooperation with the Connecticut Housing Finance Authority, recently awarded $250,000 for a Predevelopment Loan Program. They are assuring that ventures unlikely to succeed without the investment of moral entrepreneurs can indeed move forward.

In the same spirit of moral entrepreneurship, Millard and Linda Fuller started Habitat for Humanity with a letter to their colleagues:

> What the poor need is not charity but capital, not caseworkers but coworkers. And what the rich need is a wise, honorable and just way of divesting themselves of their overabundance. The Fund for Humanity will meet both of these needs. Money for the fund will come from shared gifts by those who feel they have more than they need and from non-interest-bearing loans from those who cannot afford to make a gift but who do want to provide working

> capital for the disinherited. The fund will give away no money. It is not a handout.[25]

In 1968, the model for Habitat for Humanity began with the development of forty-two half-acre house sites and a four-acre park and recreational area. Contributions from individuals all over the country permitted the work to go forward. As they were completed, the homes were sold to needy families at cost. Since its official founding in 1976, Habitat has built sixty thousand homes for low- and very low-income families. Almost half of the sixty thousand homes went to families that earned less than half the median income for households in the United States. The zero-interest-rate loans and subsidized purchase prices were critical to the capacity of people to become home owners at all.

All these programs utilize land and buildings to assure that the American dream of home ownership can come true. They build the quality of life for individual citizens and for the community through the wealth-building possibilities of that dream. Like many of today's most successful philanthropic endeavors, they create critical partnerships between government, for-profit and not-for-profit organizations, and individuals. And they build to last. The impact of generous gifts that build property persists through generations.

Businessman James Rouse made his living and his donations in Baltimore to the great advantage of the city and its citizens. He created partnerships where none had existed before. This same story could be told about hundreds of American cities. What all of us can learn from the Baltimore story is just how successful Rouse's Enterprise Foundation has been. Like Lang's "I Have a Dream" Program, Rouse's dream needs to be replicated all over the country until the quality of life of the bottom 20 percent of the income distribution of America's population approaches that of the middle 20 percent. Citizen generosity has led change in local areas all over the nation. It is the only force that can lead them where they have not yet developed.

Not only do philanthropic gifts in facilities, public or private, provide important investments that impact the economy, they also raise the philanthropic investments in human resources to the next power. For instance, children raised in stable housing do better in school. Adults who own homes are more secure than those who do not. Home owners use facilities such as parks, museums, theaters, and colleges, all of which contribute to the quality of life in a community. They see the progress in their health care in the donated hospitals. The environment of the democracy improves as well-being and mutuality grow. Generous donations increase capital by improving property, and they raise the power of other gifts.

5

ADVANCING NEW IDEAS: INTELLECTUAL CAPITAL

It is 1970. Millions of Americans, eyes riveted on the screen, watch without breathing while the *Saturn V* rocket spins a frothy trail into the Florida sky. Dramatically, its spent fuel tanks drop away as Neil Armstrong and the Eagle hurtle toward their rendezvous with the moon. The next day, some number of these same millions are launched into the air themselves, as they board commercial flights for business or pleasure. And many of these individuals will naturally check the stock market listings this week, or perhaps tune into *Wall Street Week* on Friday evening to see how the market has reacted to this American space triumph.

Each of these events, unique and routine, can be directly traced to philanthropy. Rocketry, commercial aviation, stock market portfolio analysis, and radar are just a few of the important ideas that have flourished because innovative donors supported innovative thinkers and built prosperity in America through gifts to grow intellectual capital. This chapter shows how donations have animated new ideas in American society and, as in the case of the development of human and physical capital, how these donations led the government into new, productive funding areas. Stretch your mind and ask where we would be if these breakthroughs had been delayed by decades, waiting for government or some profit-seeking investors to put money down.

This chapter focuses on intellectual capital—knowledge imbedded in people, in organizations and institutions, and in culture and technology. Intellectual capital resides in history and relationships and in values and virtues.[1] In chapter 1 of this book, I shared briefly the economic research of Paul Romer, who theorizes that it is ideas, not things and needs, that are the fuel of an economy. Traditional concepts such as scarcity and diminishing returns do not have a prominent place in Romer's economic model.

John Maynard Keynes, one of the most distinguished economists of the twentieth century, proposed that the finite nature of material assets would limit the rate of growth of economies. Keynes was among those who predicted the limits of growth and the gradual development of a kind of communitarianism. These notions led to a mind-set that growth has limits, which Romer disputes. Romer's thinking was inspired by the fact that economic growth has actually increased during the twentieth century rather than declined.[2] He describes economic development thus:

> A traditional explanation for the persistent poverty of many less developed countries is that they lack objects such as natural resources or capital goods. But Japan had little of either in 1950 and still has few natural resources, so something else must be involved. Increasingly, emphasis is shifting to the notion that it is ideas, not objects, that poor countries lack. The knowledge needed to provide citizens of the poorest countries with a vastly improved standard of living already exists in the advanced countries. If a poor nation invests in education and does not destroy the incentives for its citizens to acquire ideas from the rest of the world, it can rapidly take advantage of the publicly available part of the worldwide stock of knowledge.[3]

If it's that simple for poor countries, it's that simple for any country. In the information age, ideas have become the fourth part of the classic economic triumvirate of land, labor, and capital. Indeed, knowledge might be said to be nudging out land (natural resources). In order to come out on top economically, a country must produce ideas. It must produce scientific ideas that will lead to new products, architectural ideas that will lead to improved housing, wacko ideas that will turn out to be brilliant insights into government and politics. An economically successful country needs incentives for innovation, support for the process of idea producing, and an atmosphere in which ideas can thrive.

We know there have to be inventors. We do not always realize that in most cases it takes two kinds of people, inventors and investors, to get results, and that some of the most significant ideas take years to develop. Government support for speculative research may not be justified, given the demands on the budget. Corporate research and development may not be able to defend funding to their stockholders when success is a long shot. Even risk-oriented individual investors often step away from counterintuitive or seemingly far-fetched ideas. In such situations, philanthropy has made the difference in America. Very often in the United States, individual generous people make it possible to develop and test new ideas, then to scale up and scale out, as we saw so often with human and physical capital projects. American scientific and economic progress has accelerated as a result of direct connections between the person with the new idea and the person with the money to support its development and testing.

America's brand of "generosity as investment" not only has enabled more (and a greater diversity of) people to contribute ideas, but has attracted more people to the United States to contribute them. Philanthropy has played as important a role as copyright and patent protections in attracting intellectual resources to the United States. Inventors and creators of new ideas can do their work better and progress faster in this environment and earn better salaries. If ideas are the engine of an economy, I would argue that our best idea is the right to life, liberty, and the pursuit of happiness. This startling idea protects and liberates individuals to be as creative and productive as they choose to be.

In a knowledge-based economy, ideas beget new ideas, technologies engender newer technologies, and newer ideas and newer technologies build more of each. The whole process also creates lower prices as availability increases. Most people experience this personally as they purchase ever more powerful computers for less money every few years. Technological progress has put more computing capacity in the hands of third graders this year than was available to graduate students in engineering twenty years ago and at much less cost per unit.

In an idea-centered economy, sharing works better than hoarding. As the stories and data in this chapter show, generosity of spirit drives the mutuality that is a critical part of how we build relationships in our democracy and progress in our economy. As we will see, individual generous people like the Guggenheims, Alfred Loomis, and Mary Lasker—as well as all the people who contributed to the March of Dimes—delivered new ideas into our midst. Those new ideas helped drive our economy and shape the political consensus that motivates our decisions on how to spend our tax money.

IDEAS THAT CHANGED OUR WORLD

America's leading role in science at the start of the twenty-first century would probably surprise the American scientists and their patrons who struggled for credibility in the nineteenth and early twentieth centuries. In those years, Europe led the way. This was a golden age of European science, and patrons were plentiful, at least compared to an America preoccupied with civil war and westward expansion.

The first attempts to transform American science came from the top down. The pace of basic research had moved real scientific inquiry out of the realm of the generally educated person and into a growing specialization, one that generated public mistrust and forced scientists to seek private patrons rather than turn to the government. Although the federal government provided some money to science research during the late-nineteenth and early-twentieth centuries, this funding tended to focus on the immediately utilitarian, rather than on basic science, which had less predictable outcomes but more far-reaching potential.

As Howard Miller says in *Dollars for Research*:

> . . . qualitatively, in the nineteenth century, financing from the private sector did much to give tone and tempo to American scientific work. Federal and state agencies encouraged investigations that promised useful results. . . . But politicians were unimaginative, and frequently timid. . . . Individual philanthropists underwrote new and abstract researches . . . private benefactors were free to innovate, to experiment, to venture capital on the unknown.[4]

To compete with the Europeans without broad, popular support, American scientists and their private donor patrons began to develop new institutions, including universities, specialized scientific institutes, laboratories, and observatories. At the same time, they continued to support individual inventors, producers of intellectual capital. By the twentieth century, the research universities and foundations became the structures that scientists and major donors could rely on to facilitate their efforts. By the mid-twentieth century, their achievements began to exert pressure that eventually dramatically expanded the funding science received from the federal government.

Patrons, or philanthropists, funded sites and projects at institutions where invention and innovation are part of each year's annual reports: Rockefeller University, University of Chicago, Stanford, Carnegie (now Carnegie-Mellon), the Institute for Advanced Study in Princeton. These and many others became the sites from which the United States established its worldwide primacy in science, engineering, medicine, and technology.

That's the basic pattern. A primary example of how this worked would be aviation. The space program and commercial aviation were dreams of inventor Robert Goddard. He did not live until 1970 to see Armstrong land on the moon, but he saw it in his mind's eye at age seventeen in 1899. Years later he reported on the day he climbed a cherry tree to trim its branches and paused to look at the sky:

> . . . as I looked toward the fields at the east, I imagined how wonderful it would be to make some device which had even the possibility

> of ascending to Mars. . . . In any event, I was a very different boy when I descended the tree.[5]

Goddard remembered October 19 as Anniversary Day—and for the rest of his life he focused on making space flight a reality. On the other hand, most people at the time, and particularly the American government, had no interest in aeronautics, which was widely considered little more than "technological exhibitionism." The concept of commercial aviation had not attracted serious attention in the United States. So, although European scientists were pursuing research to advance the field, the U.S. government was putting no funding into it.

Goddard finished college and received a Ph.D. in solid-state physics at Clark University in 1911 before beginning teaching and what research he could fit into his schedule. As a young assistant professor, he had little time for the discovery work he wanted to do. Still, in 1915, he studied how rockets could be used to propel scientific instruments to the outer regions of the earth's atmosphere. During the war and after, he pursued his ideas about solid-state fuels.

The other crucial part of the intellectual capital equation was Harry Guggenheim. He had served as a naval pilot during World War I. Returning from the war, Guggenheim had become obsessed by the potential of aviation. He began to talk about his enthusiasm to his father, Daniel, multimillionaire businessman and philanthropist, and gradually Harry managed to turn his father's interests to this new field. "Airplanes," Harry wrote, "are the harbingers of peace, the instrumentality that will bring about a lasting sympathy among nations . . . closer communion between various communities. . . . The airplane will bind nations together through increased understanding."[6]

By 1925, Harry had induced his father to fund the nation's first school of aeronautics, with a gift to New York University of $500,000. After his own gifts were launched, Daniel approached his friend, President Calvin Coolidge, to try to infect him with an enthusiasm for this new industry. He succeeded. In early 1926, Coolidge approved the first government grant to the field, creating the Guggenheim Fund for the Promotion of Aviation. Coolidge eventually granted nearly $3 million to the fund, with the intent to "provide for aviation at a critical period of its infancy immediate, practical, and substantial assistance in its commercial, industrial, and scientific aspects."[7]

In the meantime, Charles Lindbergh, a national hero as a result of his remarkable transatlantic solo flight in a single-engine plane, met privately with Daniel Guggenheim and proposed that aviation did not go far enough. Jet propulsion and space travel posed the next challenge, and Robert Goddard was the man Guggenheim should back. Lindbergh described Goddard's experiments, such as the brief July 1929 launch of "Nell," the first liquid-fueled rocket. He recalled the inventor's exclamation to the press after the launch: "We could send a rocket to the moon if we had a million dollars, but where would we get a million dollars?" Within minutes, Guggenheim had decided to give Goddard the seed money he needed.[8]

The first payment became the first installment. Over an eleven-year period, Guggenheim provided Goddard with over $180,000. These funds provided his salary and research support and material for the first real steps into aeronautical engineering. Goddard could take extended leaves of absence from teaching and work full-time on jet propulsion. His research during this period became the basis for advances in jet propulsion as diverse as the bazooka and the multistage rocket that Armstrong rode to make the first steps on the moon. Although Goddard did eventually obtain a small grant from the Smithsonian and, during the war, had received a small grant from the Army Signal Corps, Guggenheim sustained his research during this critical period. Guggenheim was the one who was willing to invest before outcomes were certain. Goddard and Guggenheim made each other's dreams come true, inventor and investor in partnership that would eventually include government, and then would predominantly include government.

So what did the fund Guggenheim provided actually make happen? It established a lab to study fog flying, and, by late September 1929, Jimmy Doolittle flew the first flight entirely guided by instruments. It funded the research and development of the first gyroscope compass, a vastly improved model weather tracking and reporting service, the first commercial airline in America, and schools of aeronautical engineering at MIT, the California Institute of Technology, Stanford, Harvard, Georgia Tech, Syracuse, and the Universities of Michigan and Washington. It also funded Theodor Karman, who invented the wind tunnel and designed the DC-3. By the year 2000, the airline industry in the United States was a $92 billion industry. That's 1.4 percent of the gross national product of the country. Here is a summary of how one scholar describes the impact of Guggenheim's generosity:

> By mid-century, Harry, using funds from his father's foundation, had established the Daniel and Florence Guggenheim Aeronautical Laboratories and Jet Propulsion Centers at Princeton and Caltech . . . and had endowed Robert H. Goddard professorships at both institutions. By then virtually all of America's senior aerospace engineers were graduates of Guggenheim-sponsored schools.
>
> Foremost among those schools now is the partially Guggenheim-funded Jet Propulsion Laboratory at Caltech. . . . Explorer I, America's first unmanned satellite, utilized JPL-devised solid-fuel upper stages and JPL instrumentation. . . . JPL . . . supervised the development of the Ranger, Pioneer, Surveyor, and . . . in 1976 a JPL Viking . . . landed on Mars. . . . In 1977 the JPL-designed . . . Voyager I and II . . . were launched on missions that will take them past Jupiter and Saturn and ultimately out of the solar system on man's second probe. . . .[9]

Separately, the Guggenheims also funded visits to all corners of the country by famous aviators as a way of popularizing flying and capturing the imagination of the American public, helping to make air travel an industry. Harry sent the pilot who flew Commodore Richard Byrd over the North Pole on a tour of forty cities. He also sent Charles Lindbergh in his *Spirit of St. Louis* to forty-eight states to thunderous applause at each site. By 1930, the science and industry of aviation had jumped forward in the public mind, and government funding became more substantial. By 1946, the year after World War II ended, the federal government had begun to put billions into building airports. In 1992, Professor Paul Stephen Dempsey of the University of Denver estimated that the current replacement value of the U.S. commercial airport system, virtually all of it developed with federal grants and tax-free municipal bonds, would be $1 trillion.

As early as 1909, Robert Goddard realized that rockets would have to be fueled in stages and that fuel tanks would have to fall away as their propellant was consumed in order to achieve the required boost out of the earth's atmosphere. Today, all rockets and planes depend on some of Goddard's three hundred separate aeronautical inventions. Goddard's ideas would never have developed if Daniel and Harry Guggenheim had not shared his dream and funded his work.

The Guggenheims illustrate the power of private dollars in the change process. They enabled Goddard to do research, rather than fund-raising. They pulled other funders, including the federal government, into funding aviation through a carefully orchestrated campaign. They moved government funding forward faster than might have been the case in the absence of their pioneering efforts. Private funding such as this makes a huge impact on economic growth, though one difficult to measure. What if aviation and the commercial airline industry had not gotten the boost the Guggenheims gave it? What if aeronautical engineering and jet propulsion research had not been so strategically supported? These areas would have developed eventually, but with delays.

Huge as the impact of the Goddard/Guggenheim team was, they were far from alone in developing intellectual capital. Most of us probably think the government's commitment to research and development produced the scientific advance called radar. And we would be wrong. Alfred Loomis underwrote it with a very personal donation that combined Wall Street genius with a law degree and an amateur's love of science. In the mid 1930s, after having hugely augmented his fortune by foreseeing the stock market crash of 1929, he retired from the Street. At the age of forty-five, he bought a chic New York mansion and turned it into a state-of-the-art physics lab. He invited famous scientists, particularly physicists, to give and attend presentations of original research there. Over the years his guests included Albert Einstein, Werner Heisenburg, Niels Bohr, Enrico Fermi, and others.

Gathering these thinkers from around the world, picking them up at the dock in his Rolls-Royce, Loomis heard stories about research in Europe and especially efforts to build an atomic bomb in Germany. Franklin Roosevelt heard about Loomis's efforts and asked Vannevar Bush, head of the Carnegie Foundation, to help him bring the physics lab into the government service. Bush called on Loomis, and philanthropy was in the war effort before the United States was in the war. In the years before World War II, the American philanthropist and amateur scientist collaborated with America's and England's most illustrious scientists to develop technology that would change the outcome of the war. Jennet Conant's book, *Tuxedo Park: A Wall Street Tycoon and the Secret Palace of Science That Changed the Course of World War II,* tells this story of citizen Loomis's commitment to advancing intellectual capital.

In the months after Vannevar Bush's call, Loomis focused his research on developing microwave radar. "Contained in a small device called a cavity magnitron that could be held in one's hand, the radar invention sparked a concept in Loomis's mind that was to revolutionize warfare as we knew it," said Conant. "Because of his secret 18-month project, Loomis gave the Allies the single most important technology that helped win the war. Had it not been for that project, America would have been so far behind in its preparedness, that millions of lives would have been lost," she concluded in a recent interview at the Katonah Museum of Art.[10]

Once Loomis's team developed radar and the equipment was installed on Allied planes, the team was brought directly into the government's work on the bomb at Los Alamos.[11] Loomis personally funded weapons and defense research and development, inspiring the government to bring money to innovative high-technology projects.

Medicine, like physics, also benefited from the investment of private dollars and philanthropic leadership. Mary Lasker's support for the National Institutes of Health (NIH) saved hundreds of thousands, perhaps millions, of lives. Lasker put the prestige and significant funding of the Lasker Foundation to the task of inspiring the federal government to increase its funding commitment to the NIH. Mary Lasker worked for most of her very long life, from 1900 to 1994, as an organizer and lobbyist as well as a philanthropist to develop funding for medical research, starting with birth control in 1939. As she began her foundation in 1945, the government was funding NIH at barely $3 million per year. As the last vestiges of her immediate impact concluded in 1999, following her death in 1994, the federal government was giving NIH $15 billion per year. Mary Lasker's philanthropic dollars and her personal lobbying efforts created and enabled vast change.[12] For the last thirty years, the federal government has been providing significant and growing funding for medical and health-related research. Another case of a citizen nudging government engagement in important directions for the greater good.

THE ACCOMPLISHMENTS OF SMALL DONORS

I do not want to give the impression that only donors with vast sums at their disposal can help to develop intellectual capital. There have been many cases in the history of American generosity that reveal the power of masses of smaller donors. Part of America's great strength lies right there. In the spirit of democracy, Americans tend to believe that what we do matters. We start and join voluntary associations, as Tocqueville noticed, because we believe our efforts will pay off and make the world, our nation, our state, or our community a little bit more the way we think it should be. This is our entrepreneurial spirit. It strengthens our brand of capitalism and also puts muscle into our social fabric. Yes, voting is an important way to shape society. Our personal gifts are as well. A powerful example: there were 80 million supporters of Jonas Salk's research just in the specific year he developed the polio vaccine. These donors supported, sometimes with as little as a dime at a time, the National Foundation for Infantile Paralysis, better known as the March of Dimes.

It is difficult for people born after the 1950s to imagine the widespread danger of the disease called polio. At that time, about thirty thousand people, mostly children, contracted polio every year. Of those, sixteen thousand were paralyzed by the disease. Thousands ended up in leg braces or wheelchairs. Others were confined to "iron lungs," airtight cylindrical steel drums in which the patient lay, with only his or her head outside it. Pumps lowered and raised the air pressure inside the drum, thus contracting and expanding the patient's chest walls. With this artificial form of breathing, polio victims could be kept alive. To both parents and children in the 1940s and 1950s, the iron lung was a terrible sight. The early symptoms of the disease were sore throats, headaches, and fever. When any child complained of one of these symptoms, parents were struck by the fear that it might be polio. In addition to those who suffered paralysis, there were thousands who for the most part recovered but, in adulthood, suffered from postpolio syndrome. Indeed, many people still deal with the muscle and joint pains, fatigue, respiratory problems, and loss of muscle strength that characterize the syndrome.

Research into a vaccine was desperately needed. President Franklin D. Roosevelt had been stricken by the disease as an adult and negotiated his presidency with a wheelchair, leg braces, a cane, and, on ceremonial occasions, the strong right arm of his son. But Roosevelt knew that trying to get government funds in the quantity needed would simply take too long. Instead, he lent his name and his leadership to transforming a small, private organization, the Warm Springs Foundation, into the National Foundation for Infantile Paralysis.

The National Foundation for Infantile Paralysis began raising funds in 1938 to eradicate polio in America. Their approach, which turned out to be sheer genius, was to ask for dimes. Comedian Eddie Cantor coined the phrase "March of Dimes" (playing on the popular newsreel feature *The March of Time*) and called for his radio listeners to send their dimes directly to the White House. The March of Dimes captured the public's imagination. One group of teenagers laid a long strip of adhesive tape on the sidewalk and asked people to stick dimes on it. Small towns spread out canvases on their basketball courts at halftime, and people threw dimes. Disney Studios made a cartoon with the Disney characters marching to fight polio and singing the words, "Heigh-ho, heigh-ho,/We'll lick ol' polio,/With dimes and quarters/And our doll-aaars—/Ho, heigh-ho." The dimes rolled in. Soon, the March of Dimes was raising more money annually than any other health-related campaign.

Funds went to research to discover the secrets of the virus, but these funds also developed human capital and, through it, many more new ideas. Support went to fellowships for gifted young scientists interested in microbiology and virology. Some funds stayed in communities to help stricken children and their families, and other funds spread public information about the disease. In 1940, the foundation had an operating budget of $3 million, in 1953, more than $50 million. Nineteen fifty-three was also the first year the National Institutes of Health recognized microbiology on their list of supported fields, and that year the nonprofit National Foundation for Infantile Paralysis provided twenty-five times more funding for polio than NIH provided.

The foundation also had the strength to impose discipline on the spending of money collected, especially on the selection of research centers that would receive support. American donors agreed to keep giving even though their well-meaning local doctors and local scientists were not permitted to receive any of the locally collected funds for their research on polio. One impeccably qualified panel of specialists reviewed the candidates for foundation funding and assured that only the best researchers in the country were entrusted with funds to move the endeavor forward as efficiently as possible. After all, epidemics broke out every summer somewhere in the country. Every year children died or were left paralyzed. No time or money could be wasted. People respected the importance of expertise over the comfort of regionalism.

The March of Dimes Foundation, as it became in 1979, established a new and highly effective way to extend the power of any citizen to put his or her personal generosity to the service of improving the world. This was the first time that Americans had been asked to take direct action to benefit science. They were not really helping the children they saw on the posters, who were already sick. They were funding scientific development that might eventually eradicate the disease. Citizens' generosity was also helping the citizens themselves and those who might never contract polio if a vaccine could be found in time. So this first effort at engaging the public in contributing funds for scientific progress made a strong connection between the interests of the receivers for the funding—the scientific researchers—and the interests of the donors themselves. Both groups wanted a vaccine as soon as possible.

Seventeen years after its founding and well more than 4 billion dimes later, the foundation announced the discovery of the Salk vaccine on April 12, 1955. From 1938 to 1959, the foundation spent $315 million on direct support for the medical care and sustained rehabilitation of polio victims, $55 million on scientific research, and $33 million on fellowships and other education and training of medical and science researchers and practitioners. As traced by Richard Carter in *The Gentle Legions,* the impact of this funding on the professional science community was extensive: "In 1938 . . . the science of virology consisted of fewer than 40 individuals, few of whom had an interest in polio. The foundation helped train 372 researchers, 288 practicing physicians, 2,674 physical therapists, 778 medical social workers, 143 nurse supervisors, 62 physical and occupational therapy supervisors and 3,118 other persons whose skills were important not exclusively to polio but to the general state of American health."[13]

During the past sixty years, interested citizens have organized drives to raise funds for research for a wide range of diseases. It is now a part of American culture that people contribute to the advancement of new ideas in science. The process of conquering polio provided a model for how other diseases would and could gain the research and patient-support funds required to render them as rare as polio is today. Hundreds of support organizations now appeal for funds using the structures pioneered by the National Foundation for Infantile Paralysis.

What role do these organizations play in funding research in this country? According to the R & D Forecast, funding for research and development in science in the United States will reach about $302 billion in 2003. Of that, almost two-thirds ($194 billion) will be corporate funding. Another $89 billion will come from the federal government. (That is up more than 10 percent over 2002, but

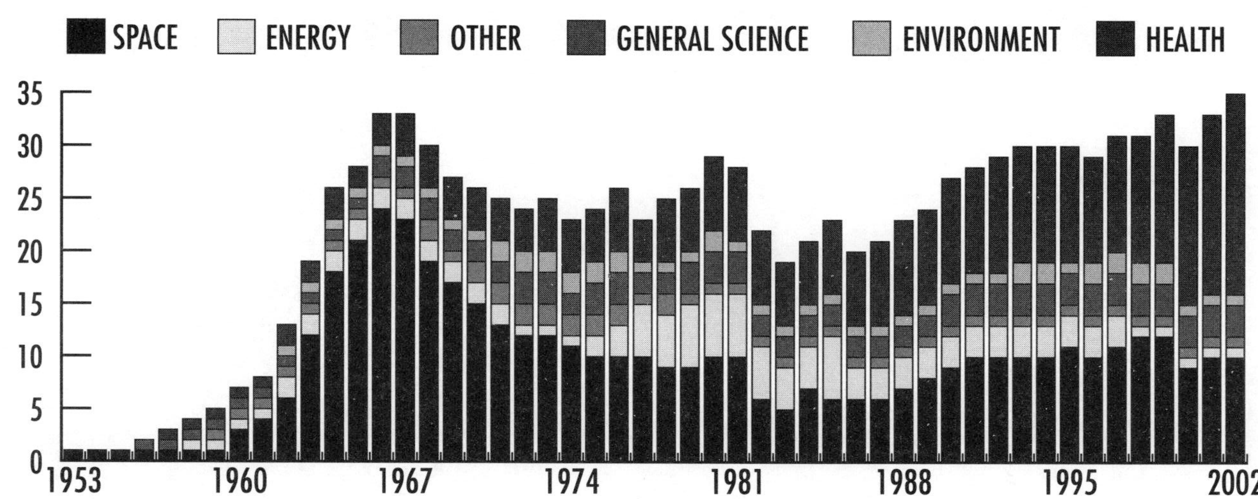

Source: AAAS, based on OMB Historical Tables in *Budget of the United States Government FY 2004*. Constant dollar conversions based on GDP deflators. FY 2004 is the President's request. Note: Some Energy programs shifted to General Science beginning in FY 1998. FEB. '03 © 2003 AAAS

almost all of that increase will go to military and bioterrorism research.) Universities and other nonprofit organizations are expected to spend about $18 billion on scientific research. In other words, the majority of scientific research done in this country is paid for and controlled by corporations. The federal government is a distant second, and more than half of its total is military spending. Another 10 percent goes to space exploration. In fact—and this is the remarkable part—*government spending on health and medical research is almost exactly equal to that of non-profits.*[14]

The National Foundation for Infantile Paralysis did not invent this model. As with so many good ideas, some credit must go to Benjamin Franklin:

> In the first place I advise you to apply to all those whom you know will give something; next, to those whom you are uncertain whether they will give anything or not, and show them the list of those who have given; and lastly, do not neglect those whom you are sure will give nothing, for in some of them you may be mistaken.[15]

SCIENTIFIC IDEAS ARE NOT THE ONLY ONES THAT PAY

Wherever you work or live in the United States, your life has been touched by the power of the U.S. stock market. Our understanding of that market derives from the contributions of Alfred Cowles, a wealthy businessman from Denver. Cowles, the head of his own investment-advising firm, established the Cowles Commission at the University of Chicago and supported the most quantitatively gifted economists of his day to launch the field of econometrics. World leaders and private citizens alike rely on the principles that have emerged from this field to manage the global economy and their own retirement funds. The commission moved to Yale in 1955 and is now known as the Cowles Foundation.

After 1929, Cowles had doubts about the worth of his own profession, which was offering investment advice. Instinctively, he felt that the best guesses of the professionals had little predictive value.

He and everyone else in his field needed much more precise information about securities and the significance of the fluctuations that affected their prices. He decided to discontinue his own advising business until he could do a better job, and he started to take an objective look at what was really happening. To do this, he needed some new tools of analysis. So he teamed up with a fledgling organization of economists from the United States and Europe who were interested in the same challenge: the application of mathematics and statistics to economics. The Econometric Society held its first meeting in Washington, D.C., in 1931, and a new field—econometrics—was born within the field of economic theory and methodology. The Econometric Society received its funding from Cowles and initiated its research journal, *Econometrica*. The society's motto was "science through measurement."

Cowles himself developed a lifelong commitment to working with the economists. He experimented with an index, the Cowles Index, that became the forerunner of the Standard and Poor's 500 Index. Accumulating massive amounts of data from the stock market, he showed how the random arrival of information about the market and individual stocks had significant effects on the rise and fall of stock prices, an insight known subsequently as the "random walk theory." Cowles eventually reviewed almost seven thousand market forecasts over a fifteen-and-a-half-year period and found that there was no evidence that market forecasters had been able successfully to predict the future of stocks or any other elements on which they worked. Cowles and econometrics undertook the task of improving the analytical tools available to economists and investors.

Even without Cowles's personal work in the field, the story could be told by simply listing some of the people who did their research at the Cowles Foundation. Nine Nobel Prize winners in economics did important work supported by Cowles's funds and the other sources that eventually joined him in assuring that the resource needs of econometricians would be met. Those other sources included such organizations as the Social Science Research Committee of the University of Chicago, the Rockefeller Foundation, the National Bureau of Economic Research, and the Guggenheim

Foundation. The best minds in the field came from all over the world and worked together to create and test some of the most important economic ideas of our century—ideas that reshaped the field of finance and investment.

A quick review of just some of the Cowles Fellows who eventually received the Nobel Prize in economics will confirm Cowles's importance to the American economy—actually, to the global economy. Harry Markowitz pursued his work at Cowles and came up with the idea that investors should be as concerned with the risks in their investments as they are with their rates of return. He developed an innovative and still practical theory, portfolio selection, first described in 1952 in an article of the same name. He received the Nobel in 1990 for this theory, and his work revolutionized the stock selection-investment process.

James Tobin solved another piece of the puzzle by laying out two steps in the allocation process. This involved dividing the portfolio into more and less risky investments—that is, stock on the one hand and bonds and cash on the other. Tobin received the Nobel in 1981.

Gerard Debreu and Kenneth Arrow, both Nobel laureates, in 1972 and 1983, respectively, who were funded by Cowles, provided the first formal proof of the existence of market clearing prices for the general equilibrium model of an economy. Debreu's joint work with Herb Scarf on the application of game theory to the model of equilibrium clarified the distributional consequences of equilibrium. Franco Modigliani, another Cowles Foundation Nobel laureate (1985), received the award for econometric research which showed that people plan their life spending based on their own assumptions about how long they will live or about how much they will earn. This idea is known as the "permanent income theory of consumption."

Lawrence Klein received his Nobel in 1980 for another kind of work: "econometric model building, forecasting, policy analysis, and study of business cycles." As a starting point, he used the work of both Jan Tinbergen and Ragnar Frisch, two other fellows at the Cowles Foundation who received their Nobels in 1969. Their initial work in developing and applying dynamic models for the analysis of economic processes put statistics at the service of economists. For instance, Tinbergen focused on developing models of economies with multiple equations and showed the relationship between economic targets and policy instruments deployed by government. Following these leads, Klein put the equations together into useful models of the United States so that they could be used to study the macroeconomics issues of post–World War II conversion. At the University of Michigan, Klein and Arthur Goldberger constructed the first version of the Michigan Model of the United States, which has served to forecast changes in the U.S. economy ever since the end of the Korean War.

The nine Nobels in economics who worked at Cowles in Chicago or in New Haven also included Paul Samuelson (1970), whose textbook is used in most college economics courses in the United States. They all did research that defined and advanced economics and related fields, either while they were in residence at Cowles or afterward. Since 1932, the connection between economics and mathematics and statistics has deepened and created some of the most important advances in modern economic theory. This work reshaped the practice of investment and is still dominating thinking today. All this innovation, this and the intellectual capital that has contributed to wealth building, is the result of an initial personal gift, the personal interest, and the nurturing of talent and resources of a generous citizen, Alfred Cowles, who made basic changes occur for the greater good. Major benefits accrue to millions of people today, to institutions raising and investing money, to the strength of the United States economy and, in fact, the global economy.

One major donor financed the Cowles Commission, which affected economic growth in a way that was clear and direct. There is another, more recent contribution, that, like the March of Dimes, came from many smaller donors and the concerns of an entire country about a problem that was affecting our health, our economy, and our very lives. This grassroots movement began with the anger and grief of two women.

The new idea was that driving drunk is an actionable illegal activity. "Friends don't let friends drive drunk." "I'll have a soft drink. Tonight I am the designated driver." No one in 1970 had ever heard these words. Americans accepted the idea that being drunk excused a person who caused an accident, even a fatal accident. Many felt frustrated by the level of ambivalence surrounding such irresponsible behavior, but what could anyone do?

Cindi Lamb and Candy Lightener decided they would do something. Cindi's daughter was paralyzed and Candy's daughter was killed in separate accidents a year apart, by drunk drivers who had multiple prior arrests for driving while intoxicated but were driving legally when the accidents happened. Lamb and Lightener marshaled the generosity of Americans to change both public opinion and the laws of the land.

Laura Lamb was five months old in 1979 when she and her mother were in a head-on collision with a drunk driver who was traveling at 120 mph. The driver was a repeat drunk-driving offender who had kept his license under Maryland's lax drunk-driving laws. As a result of the crash, Laura became a quadriplegic. The man who killed Cari Lightener in 1980 was driving on a valid California driver's license. He had just been released on bail after being charged in a hit-and-run drunk-driving accident. He had three prior arrests for drunk driving, two of which had resulted in convictions. The third had been plea-bargained to "reckless accident."

At a dinner after Cari's death, Candy and her friends decided to start an organization that would fight against the laws allowing the driver who killed her daughter to get behind the wheel of a car. They named their new group Mothers Against Drunk Drivers, known today as Mothers Against Drunk Driving (MADD). Within the first two years of its existence, MADD joined with a similar group founded by Cindi Lamb in Maryland. The new organization enlisted the help of congressional representatives and established eleven chapters in four states. It had also received a small grant of $65,000 from the National Highway Traffic Safety Administration (NHTSA).

MADD has been a powerful force in changing America's mind around drinking and driving. It has attracted a large group of donors, for many reasons. One reason is that the women leading the organization were charismatic and passionate and had riveting and heart-wrenching stories to tell. In 1983, a television movie about Candy Lightener captured the public's and the politicians' hearts. Another reason is that drunk driving affected thousands of Americans directly and personally. They responded to an organization that catalyzed change on a scale and at a pace that surpassed the usual business of law making.

In addition, along with the thousands of smaller gifts, some wealthy individuals secured the future of MADD. Bob Plunk, corporate leader at Preferred Risk Insurance Company (now GuideOne), paid for office space for the fledgling MADD and also supported its early publications. Plunk's brother-in-law and his wife were both killed by a drunk driver. Dorothy Leavy lost a daughter to a drunk driver and decided to support the changes in the law that MADD was seeking. Leavy secured hundreds of thousands of dollars from her husband's insurance company, Farmers Insurance Foundation. Plunk and Leavy responded with funds at a pioneering moment, well before more general support had begun to gather. Their personal losses inspired these financial commitments.[16] Today, MADD has more than six hundred chapters in all fifty states and in countries around the world. It is one of the largest crime victims' assistance organizations in existence. Thirty percent of its revenues come from membership and special events.

Since MADD was formed, more than twenty-three hundred laws have been passed in the United States regarding drunk driving.[17] In 1984, MADD activism led to the federal law requiring states to adopt a minimum drinking age of twenty-one or lose their highway funding. The organization was also behind the powerful "designated driver" idea, now so widely used across the country. A new social and political consensus formed around encouraging harsh penalties for drunk driving, something unheard of before the efforts of MADD and its contributors—large and small.

Has this new idea and new institution had an economic impact? Let's look at the effect on human capital. In 1983, a report to a House of Representatives subcommittee stated that "Each year, highway accidents involving alcohol create economic losses of over $20 billion, and incalculable losses in terms of human suffering, wasted potential, social dislocation, and death."[18] The report also noted that, at that point, twenty-five thousand people died annually as a result of drunk drivers and that a disproportionately high number of such drivers were young people. And what has happened since the founding of MADD? "Tougher laws and stepped-up enforcement brought a 41 percent decrease in alcohol-related traffic deaths between 1980 and 1994, with a flattening out of the numbers since then," according to the *American Bar Association Journal,* which credited the change to MADD.[19]

The government wasn't doing it well enough or fast enough. Private investment in our society in this one area now saves us thousands of lives and billions of dollars every year.

The environmental movement, like the anti–drunk-driving effort, is an even more powerful example of intellectual capital initiated by citizen insights and donations. It has changed our society to the great improvement of our collective health and spawned new industries to the great improvement of our economy. It resulted from citizen giving that followed the inspiration of a few moral and social entrepreneurs. This movement created a need for new ideas for waste disposal, reuse of waste plastics and other materials, and redesign of biodegradable materials for packaging and other uses. If we are looking for the influence of citizen generosity and willingness to invest in untried new ideas, let's look at the precursor of one of the movement's core organizations, the Environmental Defense Fund (EDF), now called Environmental Defense.

When Bellport High School teacher Arthur Cooley was asked by the students in his adult biology class what they could do to save the local wetlands, he helped them found the Brookhaven Town Natural Resources Committee. The committee comprised Cooley's students, concerned housewives, and researchers and professors from Brookhaven National Laboratory and the State University of New York at Stony Brook (SUNY). Charles Wurster, who eventually became a founder of EDF, was an associate professor at SUNY at the time. The fledgling organization began working on the concerns expressed in an earlier lawsuit brought in Long Island in 1957 against the spraying of DDT.

Then, an unlikely set of coincidences in 1966 led to the establishment of the first activities of what would become the Environmental Defense effort. Initially, a Patchogue attorney, Victor J. Yannacone, brought a suit to stop the spraying of DDT in the local marshlands, because his wife had prevailed upon him to do something about a fish kill that had happened recently. The Brookhaven Town Natural Resources Committee had sounded another alarm at almost the same time. They were noticing a die-off of birds, crabs, and butterflies. These distinct events seemed to suggest that something was definitely wrong in the Long Island environment. Scientists and lawyers put their heads together, and class-action suits resulted. Suffolk County was the first in the country to ban DDT. The scientists wrote, "Continuing to use DDT against mosquitoes in Suffolk County would be like using atomic weapons to control criminals in New York City."[20]

In 1967, the leadership of the Brookhaven group created the Environmental Defense Fund in order to expand their scope. When the Environmental Defense Fund first started, it operated out of one room in the attic of the post office in Stony Brook. The founders were scientists and volunteer conservationists. They raised money to finance their efforts and went to court to save the osprey, bald eagle, and peregrine falcon living on Long Island. In 1977, the Environmental Defense Fund moved to New York City. In addition to contributions from the public, its early funding came in the form of grants from the Ford Foundation and the Rachel Carson Fund of the National Audubon Society. The fund's efforts initiated the field of environmental law and led eventually to many new laws and a new public consciousness about the environment. The intellectual capital generated by these funds and efforts ushered in a whole new way of thinking and launched a generation of new ideas. New businesses, new materials, new services, and new processes and devices became part of the last thirty years of the twentieth century. By 1998, environmental products and services constituted a $181 billion industry. In 1996, that industry employed more than 1.3 million Americans, more than were employed in chemicals and allied products, paper and allied products, aerospace, even motor vehicles and car bodies.[21]

Publicity from the success of the litigation against the use of DDT led to EDF's growth. Effective advertising and direct-mail campaigns also helped. In 1971, its membership was twenty thousand. In 1975, it was over fifty-six thousand. Regional offices were opened in Washington, D.C., and Berkeley, California (1970), then in New York City (1971), and Denver, Colorado (1973). In 2002, the organization had over three hundred thousand members and its fiscal 2001 operating support and revenue equaled $42.8 million. The funding profile reflects the mix of sources that often develop in the mature stages of organizations initiated with citizen contributions. The three hundred thousand members provide for 59 percent of its budget ($25.1 million). Over 150 foundations count for 31 percent of the budget ($13.1 million), and bequests for 4 percent of its budget ($1.5 million). Programs are 81 percent of its expenses, fund-raising 12 percent, management and administration 5 percent, acquisition of new members 2 percent. It currently employs more than two hundred scientists, lawyers, economists, and "other professionals" in eight offices across the United States.[22]

Environmental Defense has been involved in numerous legal cases and direct actions over the years. In 1970, its activism led to placing all hunted whales on the U.S. endangered species list. In 1972, it won a permanent nationwide ban on DDT. In 1990, it convinced the McDonald's Corporation to discontinue use of foam containers, which ultimately led to 150,000 tons less packaging waste per year. In 1994, it won a Supreme Court case against exemptions for hazardous waste in incinerator ash. More recently, Environmental Defense developed the Safe Harbor programs. To date, landowners have enrolled about 2 million acres in the program. The organization has also been involved in successful efforts to phase out lead in gasoline and to develop the Montreal Protocol, which was written to phase out the use of ozone-destroying CFC gases.[23]

Business leaders and environmentalists began as enemies and are increasingly on the same side of a number of issues, though certainly not all. *People* magazine noted the emergence of a cooperative spirit when reviewing the work of Environmental Defense president Fred Krupp.

> A decade ago Krupp's willingness to cooperate with corporate America rather than simply confront it would have been considered heresy by many environmentalists. Today he is the point man in an EDF strategy called Third Wave Environmentalism, in which

> science and economics are used to persuade business that environmentally oriented decisions can be good for the bottom line. "Fred is comfortable discussing environmental issues in cost-benefit terms," says Denis Hayes, organizer of the 1970 and 1990 Earth Days and director of Green Seal Inc., a new group that is certifying environmentally sound products. "He is effective because he understands that the business world is more responsive to consumers than to regulators."[24]

Environmental Defense's mission no longer sounds radical. Every state now has its own office of Environmental Protection, and the office in the federal government is at Cabinet level. Virtually all cities and towns have recycling efforts, and, in most parts of the country, environmental-impact statements must be developed before new construction can be approved. Those of us who are over forty-five have watched a new way of looking at the world emerge daily before our eyes—brought to us by the connections scientists and citizens made as they insisted we could all do a better job of living on the land and water. The connections included knowledge and funding. The osprey, the peregrine falcon, and the bald eagle, among other birds, are now off the endangered species list. The Hudson River—unswimmable, unfishable, and desperately polluted only twenty years ago—is now a lively, healthy waterway. The list could go on for pages. Is our economy better off now? Unequivocally yes. How did this happen? Citizen generosity from major and small donors.

One more story. It's a great one, because it is so little known and is such a dramatic illustration of the economic benefits to the many from the generosity of a few (in this case, one single sponsor). Interestingly, many of the people I have just talked about—physicist Robert Goddard, EDF founder Charles Wurster, polio researcher Jonas Salk, the engineers at Cal Tech, and Bellport high school science teacher Arthur Cooley—have something in common. They all received their pensions through Teachers Insurance and Annuity Association (TIAA).

In the era before Social Security, the very low pay of college teachers meant that many retired to the poorhouse. This fate discouraged many gifted people from spending their days in laboratories and in classrooms developing the next generation of educated citizens. Fortunately, Andrew Carnegie considered teachers very important people to the future of the country. In 1905, he made a gift of $10 million to create an endowment for a free pension program for college and university faculty. By 1918, he saw that the fund would need to grow faster than his own gift could support alone, so he made another gift of $1 million to found the Teachers Insurance and Annuity Association. This fund managed the contributions of the teachers themselves and those of their employers, the colleges and universities.

The full story of this new kind of institution, the college teachers pension fund, shows the power of entrepreneurial generosity. Not only did Carnegie's gift address a pressing need, but he insisted that teachers and their employers contribute to the fund, building on his principle of self-help. Furthermore, he arranged to shelter the fledgling project. During the first twenty years of its existence, the fund received free office space and had all its other expenses paid by the Carnegie Corporation. The whole fund grew dramatically. By 1937, it had grown so large that Carnegie created a new nonprofit TIAA to hold the shares of the fund and then, through a special act of the New York legislature, incorporated the new company and turned the ownership of the pension fund over to it. Eventually, other non-profits such as community foundations, major public foundations, and think tanks and their employees were accepted as well.

In 2001, TIAA-CREF had grown to hold $300 billion in assets under management—all from a good idea and an initial personal gift of $1 million. With secure pensions, teaching became a profession that could attract and sustain bright and able people. As teachers have retired over the last sixty years, they have had more spendable income for purchases and travel during their later years and more assets to bequeath to their families. The economic energy created by this single gift and the initiative it sparked has transformed thousands of lives.

This chapter has been about intellectual capital, about ideas. Generosity is a good partner for ideas. Requiring no financial return, donors can support the speculative, the leap into the future. Of course, they hope for progress in the field they are supporting. They also anticipate that benefits will spread from the wider use of the asset they have financed, but they are able to bet on mere possibility. So, when an idea is promising but cannot attract investment, even venture funding, a donor can make a personal gift and perhaps jump-start the future. Or, before a full consensus on a social change has emerged, contributions from one or more donors can invent an organization or an institution. Eventually, if it works, it leaves its mark on society. When an invention or an idea proves itself with donated funds, its long-term funding can be assured, and something will be added to our society and economy. Success breeds new entrepreneurial activity and new economic assets. Combined with American ingenuity and entrepreneurship, personal generosity has assured that, over the centuries, new and better ideas have developed in a timely way and built our social fabric and our economy. As a result, both capitalism and democracy get stronger.

6

GENEROSITY AND THE FUTURE OF DEMOCRATIC CAPITALISM

Yet the true friend of the people should see that they be not too poor, for extreme poverty lowers the character of the democracy; measures therefore should be taken which will give them lasting prosperity; and as this is equally the interest of all classes, the proceeds of the public revenues should be accumulated and distributed among its poor, if possible, in such quantities as may enable them to purchase a little farm, or, at any rate, make a beginning in trade or husbandry.

—ARISTOTLE, *Politics*

A man of humanity is one who, in seeking to establish himself, finds a foothold for others and who, desiring attainment for himself, helps others to attain.

—CONFUCIUS, SIXTH CENTURY B.C.E.

The previous chapters, with their examples of investments in human capital, physical capital, and intellectual capital, show the power of personal initiative and generosity, the power of social entrepreneurialism to improve our society and our economy in America. They also offer compelling testimony to the potential long-term health of American democratic capitalism. By most metrics, the United States is now the most successful and prosperous country in the world. The majority of our citizens enjoy a higher standard of living and per capita income and the nation enjoys a higher sustained rate of economic growth than any other country with this level of diversity in the population. Moreover, the United States has led the world in technological innovation and the creation of intellectual property, particularly in quality-of-life fields such as software development, biotechnology, materials science, and pharmaceuticals. Moreover, we accomplished these things *because* we have been able to utilize the most diverse and mobile population in the world. The question we face together is whether we can sustain and grow our philanthropic spirit in the face of increasing material wealth and personal well-being. Will we fall away from the commitments to philanthropy that have strengthened our social and economic health?

Many challenges confront us, both domestic and international. I will focus on the domestic ones because the problems in the two arenas are closely related and addressing them first at home will make changes we undertake overseas more believable at home and abroad. In the coming pages, I will delineate the role that generosity must play in their successful resolution.

But in order to understand what really matters for success in the future, we need to reflect a bit more on the lessons to be learned from the preceding chapters. First, the development of human, physical, and intellectual capital via philanthropic investments sustains our belief in *upward mobility as a democratic imperative*. Second, that development relies on *the commitment of Americans to the pursuit of happiness*. I want to draw your attention to these two fundamental factors because they define our success as a nation some 230 years after our founding. These inseparable drivers of personal and collective growth distinguish our economic, social, and political ambitions from those of other nations and can serve, in my judgment, as the best guides for our economic and social health going forward. Each is tied to generosity and must be understood if our democracy and our brand of capitalism are to endure successfully for the next century. To achieve that longevity, our society will have to deal imaginatively with the economic and social problems that face our nation in the first decades of the twenty-first century. The second part of this chapter describes these challenges and reviews how a dramatic increase in philanthropy can enable the country to make important progress just as it has at other critical moments in U.S. history.

UPWARD MOBILITY

Upward mobility is an excellent measure of the dynamism of the relationship between democracy and capitalism. It quantifies how well the idealistic promises of democracy are actually working for those in the weakest position in the economy. The rate at which people move up through the income-distribution categories vividly shows how well the economy is building human capital and whether it is enabling wealth building in the very groups that need investment before they can achieve economic progress.

For generations of newcomers who have chosen to immigrate to American shores, the U.S. economy and its education, health, and social services—despite significant flaws—have generally rewarded hard work with economic and social progress. The stories of countless millions of immigrant families attest to the truth of this statement. Our society opens opportunities and rewards highly competitive, dedicated efforts, if not always immediately in the first generation, then in the second and third generations resident here. Democracy offers justice and equality of opportunity to each citizen. It grants the promise of, in short, upward mobility. This has worked dramatically better for whites than for people of color, but consciousness of this issue has created significant progress over the decades since the beginning of the civil rights movement.

How robust is upward mobility today? For instance, what percentage of the people who were once in the bottom quintile of the income distribution in the United States are still stuck there fifteen or twenty years later? Pause and take a guess at the answer to this question. It's likely to surprise you.

The Dallas Federal Reserve Bank asked almost the same question in 1995. The Fed used the University of Michigan's Longitudinal Panel Study, which has collected information from the same people every year since 1968 to document their status for social science researchers.[1] Looking at the people in the bottom 20 percent of the income bracket, the Fed report states:

> The conventional view leads us to think they were worse off in the 1990s. Nothing could be further from the truth. In the University of Michigan sample, *only 5 percent of those in the bottom quintile in 1975 were still there in 1991* [author's italics]. Even more important, a majority of these people had made it to the top 60 percent of the income distribution, middle class or better, over that 16 year span. Almost 29 percent of them rose to the top quintile.[2]

The story is almost as good for other income brackets. More than 70 percent of the people who were in the second-poorest quintile in 1975 moved to a higher quintile by the end of the study in 1991. Twenty-six percent got right into the wealthiest quintile. Those in the middle fifth also did well, with almost half of them moving to the second or first quintile. More than 30 percent of those in the second-highest quintile in 1975 moved up to the top category by 1991. This kind of movement characterizes upward mobility and wealth-building opportunities for those at the bottom. Some smaller percentage fall back each year, and, of course, new arrivals and new families, often new single-parent households, refill the bottom quintile.[3] Only 5 percent of the people who were in the bottom quintile in 1975 were still stuck there in 1991!

If you guessed wrong about this, you are not alone. When I interviewed colleagues on Wall Street and a number of faculty members from different universities, they guessed, on average, in the 60 percent range. Some even guessed that as many as 85 to 90 percent of those in the bottom quintile in 1975 were still there in 1991. Few people, even those in financial services or higher education, realize how powerfully our economy works for an individual.

Moreover, people in this country generally *believe* that they can move upward. They have faith in the American economic and social system as a vehicle for their own personal advancement. Critics of capitalism have long argued that lower-income groups will, over time in a competitive market economy, become chronically discouraged and angered and, finally, will rise up, riot, and take down the system. Is this kind of anger and dissatisfaction apparent in the United States? Harvard economists Alberto Alesina and Rafael Di Tella and Robert MacCulloch of the London School of Economics focused an investigation on this question: How does income inequality affect the happiness of Americans as compared to Europeans? Are Americans, particularly those in the lowest-income levels, happy with our income distribution, or do we teeter constantly on the verge of revolution? Using surveys of 123,668 answers from people in the United States and twelve European countries over a twenty-three-year period (1972–1994), the researchers found that the poor in the United States are as content about income inequality as the other quintiles in this country. The group of people with the least money did not express unhappiness about the fact that incomes are unequal in this country. In fact, most people in the United States *and* in those twelve European countries said that they were not unhappy about income inequality. The only groups who *were* significantly unhappy about income inequality in their own countries were the poor in European countries and the wealthy in the United States. And this data was collected at a time when income disparity was actually widening in the United States![4]

These results show that, in general, Americans seem to be less affected by income inequality than Europeans. Further investigation of the results across income levels and ideological groups indicates that the wealthy and the right-wingers in European countries express very low concern about income inequality, while the European poor and its leftists express strong negative attitudes to it. On the contrary, in the United States neither the poor nor the left-wingers feel strongly about income inequality. Only the wealthy reflect somewhat negatively on it.

The researchers worked to interpret these outcomes and asked, "Do differences of opinion simply reflect different preferences about the merits of equality on the two sides of the Atlantic? . . . Is a preference for equality just a matter of "taste," or does it reflect something else in society, such as the level of social mobility?"[5] They surmised that if objections to inequality were a matter of

HAPPINESS IN THE UNITED STATES: 1975–94

REPORTED HAPPINESS	ALL	UNEMPLOYED	MARITAL STATUS	
			MARRIED	DIVORCED
Very happy	32.17	17.85	39.24	20.02
Pretty happy	56.37	52.72	53.14	62.06
Not too happy	11.45	29.43	7.62	17.92

REPORTED LIFE SATISFACTION	PARTISAN SUPPORT		INCOME QUARTILES			
	LEFT	RIGHT	1ST (LOWEST)	2ND	3RD	4TH (HIGHEST)
Very happy	29.93	36.62	24.28	28.73	33.91	41.71
Pretty happy	57.26	54.89	57.43	58.07	57.53	52.48
Not too happy	12.81	8.49	18.28	13.20	8.56	5.81

Note: Based on 24,333 observations. All numbers are expressed as a percentage.

taste, then the wealthy in various countries would be likely, perhaps, to have the same views of it—for instance, seeing equality as a luxury good or even a normal good for which demand rises as income increases. This is clearly not the case, because the rich in America and those in Europe have exactly opposite views of inequality. So, the researchers conclude, "A more reasonable interpretation is that opportunities for mobility are (or are perceived to be) higher in the United States than in Europe."[6]

Americans' belief in social mobility could logically account for the tolerance of inequality by all but the rich because all other categories, given their belief, have room to move up while the rich in a mobile society see that they can only move down. Europeans, without confidence or much experience in upward mobility, could be predicted to rank exactly as they do in the survey. The rich, who are already at the top in a society where mobility is not significant, are content with where they are and are likely to stay. The poor, con-

LIFE SATISFACTION IN EUROPE: 1975–92

REPORTED LIFE SATISFACTION	ALL	UNEMPLOYED	MARITAL STATUS	
			MARRIED	DIVORCED
Very satisfied	26.46	15.21	28.79	18.61
Fairly satisfied	53.96	44.21	54.04	51.00
Not very / Not at all satisfied	19.59	40.59	17.17	30.39

REPORTED LIFE SATISFACTION	PARTISAN SUPPORT		INCOME QUARTILES			
	LEFT	RIGHT	1ST (LOWEST)	2ND	3RD	4TH (HIGHEST)
Very satisfied	21.98	34.88	21.90	24.36	26.81	32.58
Pretty satisfied	54.15	50.97	49.52	54.54	56.71	54.96
Not very / Not at all satisfied	23.87	14.16	28.58	21.10	16.48	12.47

Note: Based on 103,773 observations. All numbers are expressed as a percentage.

versely, are stuck in a bad place from which they have little hope of emerging, hence their higher levels of discontent with inequality.

This hypothesis is supported by large amounts of poll data published by Everett Ladd and Karlyn Bowman in 1998.[7] They report that Americans are tolerant of inequality as long as they see that, generally, wealth is the result of personal output and that everyone can make it if enough talent and hard work are devoted to the task. Of course, not everyone believes this, but extensive polling of Americans indicates that the more people who believe that opportunities for wealth remain reasonably open to everyone, the more tolerance Americans show for inequality.

This is a critical point and a major asset to our society that I believe we must sustain. Our belief in upward mobility provides the foundation for wide-reaching prosperity without creating crippling class animosity, disruptions, or, worse, class-based violence.

As we have seen in previous chapters, this upward mobility did not happen by accident. Upward mobility for the great majority of people is not what might be expected from a free-market economy. Capitalism works as a great wealth concentrator and a weaker wealth distributor. This means that in capitalism, wealth builds wealth. People with some money can invest it in new projects and can often make even more money. So wealth tends to build where it is already in place. Capitalism tends not to distribute or redistribute wealth into the population.

Our current success is, in part, the fruit of extraordinary generosity and outstanding persistence to ensure that tax and other laws continue to advance upward mobility. It represents the willingness of all kinds of citizens to work hard and to move on and move up and then care for those who cannot do so for themselves as yet (or for some, maybe, never). It takes money and vigilance to ensure that our competitive capitalist system supports real economic progress, not just borderline subsistence, for people at lower levels. This is where the constitutional guarantee of the pursuit of happiness comes in.

THE PURSUIT OF HAPPINESS

The individual dimension of the pursuit of happiness is the one most commonly thought of today. We tend to think of this idea as the right to pursue our own vision of happiness without interference from fellow citizens or the government. The government is to do no harm. It may not arbitrarily threaten the lives, decisions, or the security of citizens, nor restrict their personal freedoms to speak, associate, practice religion, or pursue personal ideals and goals so long as they fit within the framework of the rule of law and the common good. The right to pursue happiness is an invitation to self-expression, to make each individual's efforts an asset to the individual and to the rest of society.

However, to the founding fathers, the concept of the "pursuit of happiness" was social as well as individual. They affirmed "that the happiness of the society is the first law of every government."[8] David McCullough quotes John Adams on the reason for the very existence of government: "The purpose of government, he had said in his *Thoughts on Government,* was the 'greatest quantity of human happiness.' "[9] The greatest quantity of human happiness, quite reasonably, translates as the greatest *number of people* enjoying the most happiness. In addition to ensuring the individual the right to pursue happiness, in other words, the founders were also voting to protect what to us would seem to be the virtue of generosity. The rights to life and liberty set the framework of personal well-being. The right to the pursuit of happiness connects the individual to the collective good. It expresses collective confidence in the value of each citizen as one whose ideas and actions could contribute to the economic success of the nation through self-sufficiency and personal motivation.

The enumeration of what the founders called "unalienable rights" was very carefully considered. Jefferson and his fellow drafters discussed and ultimately rejected embracing the rights to life, liberty, and *property* as fundamental to democracy. Property, or one's fortune, one's wealth, was certainly connected to life and liberty as a right that all citizens deserved. The material things people owned assured that they could be free to determine their own fate. Without the right to own property, people could be forced to comply with the demands of others. If they did not have the assured right to own their own land, they would be more like slaves or indentured servants. Consequently, many deliberators thought that the best way to support the common good was to protect the individual citizen and the right to property. Property created independence through ownership, which like life and liberty, some argued, had to be unalienable rights. Locke's ideas on the natural rights of man and his notions about the social contract between the government and the governed made a strong case for the importance of private property, with the individual right to overthrow any government that infringed on this domain.

But Jefferson's preference ultimately favored a concept more complex and more important even than private property—the right to pursue happiness. Happiness is both an individual and a collective concept. Some actions involve the pursuit of highly personal, individualistic aspirations. But others, often thought of as "generous actions," are destined to contribute to collective happiness or greater good, to the sum of well-being across the population. Scottish Enlightenment leader John Hutcheson, a clear influence on Jefferson, believed that generosity was the main cause of happiness: "The surest way to promote . . . private happiness [is] to do publicly useful actions. . . . The action is best which procures the greatest happiness of the greatest numbers. . . . The general happiness is the supreme end of all political union."[10]

This was a very ancient idea. Economist Seymour Martin Lipset has described what he dubs the Aristotle hypothesis, which points to the importance of economics to politics:

> From Aristotle down to the present, men have argued that only in a wealthy society in which relatively few citizens lived in real poverty could a situation exist in which the mass of the population could intelligently participate in politics and could develop the self-restraint necessary to avoid succumbing to the appeals of irresponsible demagogues.[11]

The Aristotle hypothesis proposes that it is logical that we are all better off if the least well off are quite well off. They become stronger assets to the democracy and also to the economy. Therefore, "self-interest rightly understood" makes the case for capitalism at all levels to support redistribution in ways that respect the dignity of citizens and their capacity to build wealth and/or live in a state of well-being. This concept has had enormous consequences for our democracy.

There is another aspect, as well, to this philosophy of maximizing happiness. According to this belief, generosity increases happiness, not only for the person who receives it and for the society as a whole, but for the donor. Happiness is not self-indulgence at the expense of others. As the founding fathers thought of it, it is the result of virtuous behavior, the good life, well and honorably lived. McCullough again notes John Adams's views on the subject: ". . . all 'sober inquirers after truth' agreed that happiness derived from virtue, that form of government with virtue as its foundation was more likely than any other to promote the general happiness."[12] So, the individual in American democracy has the right—and indeed the obligation—to pursue happiness as a consequence of virtue. This connection to virtue means that happiness derives, in part, from contributing to the success of others.

There is an individual benefit to the virtuous approach to the pursuit of happiness, of course, and that is the personal happiness derived from generous behavior. The strength of this force for personal generosity is only now being appreciated in economic terms. Rather than a *homo economicus* who is self-maximizing at every turn, Matthew Rabin and a set of behavioral economists are defining a new creature. They are carving out a new area of research in economics that studies how people actually make decisions, and they do not always make rationalizing, self-optimizing decisions, as economists have generally assumed. We are motivated in many decisions by what Rabin calls " 'other-regarding' goals such as fairness, reciprocal altruism . . ."[13]

All the research indicates that once basic needs have been met, getting more things for oneself apparently has less effect on personal happiness than might be imagined. For example, beyond the basic studies showing that significant increases in wealth had only a marginal increase in the person's happiness, Rabin goes on to quote the work of three researchers who interviewed winners of lotteries and a control group. The winners showed no increase in happiness over non-winners, for which the researchers offer two explanations. "First, mundane experiences become less satisfying by contrast to the 'peak' experience of winning the lottery. Second, we become habituated to our circumstances."[14]

Beyond levels of basic comfort, more wealth does not correlate with more happiness, more giving does. Givers develop the advantages of companionship, sense of accomplishment, and relationships that, research affirms, are fundamental to both personal well-being and social cohesion. Recent researchers note, "happy persons' desire to increase equity in the world and share their good fortune."[15] After reaching a standard level of well-being, then getting more things for ourselves apparently does not make us happy for long. But generosity toward others is associated with higher levels of happiness—the kind that is connected with self-esteem, feelings of purposiveness and meaning in one's life, and relief from sadness at injustice.

Altruism—that is, voluntary actions intentionally directed to help others and expecting no personal reward—is a force with which to be reckoned.[16] The personal gain here is not monetary. But human motivations are usually mixed to some degree. Consequently, the idea that a person could gain the respect and admiration of others for generosity and other altruistic behaviors does not negate the power of the altruism nor does it reduce the happiness a giver feels. In fact, there is evidence that the more people who believe that others are also generous or altruistic, the more generous they themselves are. The more a society advances the culture of generosity, the more upward mobility and social health improve. The more a society advances the culture of generosity, the more its citizens are likely to experience longer-lasting happiness and in turn be motivated to continue increasing equity and good fortune for others.

I saw examples of these results of generosity often among scholarship students and their donors when they met at annual luncheons at Connecticut College. I remember one year vividly when Saja Mohammed, freshman and valedictorian of her Hartford, Connecticut, high school, met members of the well-to-do Boston family that had endowed, in the 1930s, the scholarship Saja was holding.[17] The two donor women, a mother and her adult daughter who came to the lunch to represent their family, are white, well-to-do, Christian, and second- and third-generation college-educated. Saja is black, Muslim, from a low-income background, and the first person in her family to go to college. None of these distinctions seemed to matter. Saja and the donors shared their personal stories. The donors were fascinated with Saja's descriptions of her course work, her study-abroad experience in Vietnam, and her aspirations. Saja in turn wanted to know about the donors' families and how the college was when they were students there many decades earlier. As I listened to their conversation I could see that Saja felt valued as an interesting person with talents and relieved that she was not simply regarded as a needy case. The Bostonians reflected pride in this new daughter whose future their gifts were enhancing.

As she takes her first job and then goes on to graduate school, Saja will be following in a great American tradition—moving up in American society. She will also be more likely to continue her donors' tradition of philanthropy. Saja's scholarship donors continued the family's three generations of gift giving to build their endowment because it gave them happiness. Each year, the luncheon confirmed their sense of the connection between giving and their own happiness. Each generation inculcated these values in the next one and also in the scholarship recipient.

In fact, after thanking their donors', most students expressed their intention to try to give a scholarship themselves someday. Each person influenced the others. The young people from low-income families of all races and ethnicities absorbed the philanthropic values of the traditional donors. The donor families saw how these gifted young people, many from recent Asian, African, and Latin American immigrant families, would be assets to the country. I doubt that anyone thought of the event as marking upward mobility and improving our social health and collective happiness, but it was.

THE CURRENT STATE OF SOCIAL HEALTH IN AMERICA

So, how are we doing in America today with regard to our unalienable rights? Simply put, we're losing ground. Over the past thirty years, losses in opportunity have occurred. They are not yet at a widely observable level, but as they become more obvious they will rankle, especially for those in the lower-income levels. America's poorest quintile does not yet report feeling dissatisfied or unhappy, angry or resentful about the disparity between their incomes and quality of life and those of the highest-paid quintile. We can surmise, because of the Ladd and Bowman polls, that this is in part because economic opportunity still seems to exist.

Our country developed a progressive income tax system in part to address this issue, but the drive in the past three decades has been in the direction of reducing tax rates and kinds of taxes, such as inheritance taxes. Furthermore, we are limiting social services, reducing time on welfare, and expecting larger numbers of formerly dependent citizens to work to support themselves. Carefully monitored for intractable problems, these changes may offer some of the most powerful improvements in our society since, ironically enough, the New Deal. The jury is still out. Meanwhile, our future is at stake. The problems arise when discrimination excludes some people from entering the game, or when disaster strikes and destabilizes one or more of the players, or when personal ability curtails a citizen's potential to enter a competitive economy, and always when children are simply left behind in this great country.

Look at some statistics and consider whether we are content to let current directions continue over the next twenty years. Currently, the richest 20 percent of the population gets 46.8 percent of all the family income earned in the United States. The poorest 20 percent gets 4.2 percent of it. But, in 1970, that top quintile earned 40.9 percent and the poorest 5.4 percent, so over thirty years, in constant dollars, the gap has widened. More problematic, the income share of the middle three groups of 20 percent each (the middle 60 percent of our population) has also declined. This means 60 percent of the U.S. population earn a smaller income share than they did thirty years ago. In fact, the top 20 percent actually receives only 2.1 percent less than the entire middle 60 percent of the U.S. population. Now, even though the full size of the national income is a larger sum of money, the allocation of income shares across groups is not remaining stable. It is tipping significantly toward favoring the very wealthy. This is the normal tendency of capitalism's drive to concentrate income where capital already sits.

As a nation we have generally been able to depend on a positive correlation between economic progress and social progress; wealth production has led to social progress for decades. Since the early 1970s, this relationship has shown signs of breaking down. From 1973 to 1998, we have seen our economy improve and social well-being in our democracy decline significantly. I believe that our growing disequilibrium is poised to cause havoc in the next thirty-five to fifty years.[18] Measures taken annually by the Fordham Institute for Innovation in Social Policy indicate that, since 1970, the following indicators of social health have worsened: child abuse, child poverty, teen suicide, average weekly earnings, health insurance coverage, out-of-pocket health costs among those aged sixty-five and over, food stamp coverage, access to affordable housing, and the gap between rich and poor. Child poverty has risen 23 percent from 1970 to 1998. Average weekly earnings have dropped by 10 percent, while health insurance coverage dropped by 50 percent and teenage suicide increased by 51 percent.[19] The size of these increases and declines is such that, taken together, they outweigh the improvements in other areas and amount together to an overall decline of 38 percent in Americans' "social health."[20]

Social health indicators show significant improvement in seven areas: infant mortality, drug abuse, high school dropouts, unemployment, poverty among those sixty-five and over, homicides, and alcohol-related traffic fatalities. Infant mortality dropped from 20 deaths per 1,000 live births to 7.3 deaths. Yet, significant differences persist by race and economic status. In fact, the CDC (Centers for Disease Control) established that babies born into families below the poverty level (13.3 percent of the population) had a 60 percent higher chance of dying before age one than other babies. In this area, the United States compares very poorly with other industrialized nations, ranking twenty-third out of the twenty-three modern industrial economies.

The percentage of high school students who dropped out of school from 1970 through 1996 declined from 17.3 percent to 12.8 percent, but the United States ranks dead last in graduation rates among the top seventeen industrialized economies. While white and black students achieved near parity in staying in school, Hispanics have had far less success with only 65.5 percent of students graduating in 1996. The consequences for our future economic progress are highly significant.[21] All of these fundamentally affect our ability to sustain a healthy worker base, the human capital that drives so much of the economy.

Studies by economist Edward N. Wolff and others confirm the

bad news in a couple of these key categories: earnings and the income gap. Between 1947 and 1973, American families in every income category achieved growth in average income. Unfortunately, this record ended around 1973. In fact, from 1947 to 1973, the poorest families in the United States had the highest average rate of income growth, but from 1973 to 2001, average income for the bottom two quintiles remained almost stagnant (after inflation adjustments). In 1973, the upper-income limit defining the lowest quintile was $15,247. In 1994, it was only $15,863. It rose slightly after that, but only to $17,970 in 2001. In 1974, the income defining the second quintile was $28,965. In 1994, it was $29,773, and in 2001, it had gone up to only $33,314. During the same period, income for the top 5 percent went from $98,388 to $150,499. Robust growth in real income occurred for only the top quarter of the population measured by income distribution.[22] Measuring average wealth, as opposed to average income, the picture remains as bleak for the bottom 40 percent. Including their bank accounts, stocks and bonds, and housing, but excluding durable goods and pension wealth, this group had less average wealth in 1998 than in 1983.[23] Meanwhile, the fast growth of the 1990s increased the number of households worth $1 million or more by nearly 60 percent, while the number of $10 million households quadrupled.[24]

Interestingly, the United States has made real progress in the poverty levels of elderly citizens, with the skilled support of volunteer citizens contributing their energy and funds to bringing change. The elderly poor were our most neglected group in society until relatively recently. The poverty rate has declined from 24.6 percent of those over sixty-five in 1970 to 10.8 percent in 1996. This progress has moved those over sixty-five from three times the poverty rates of other adults to a slightly lower poverty rate for the elderly than for other adults. A decision was made to change the well-being of the elderly poor by adjusting Social Security and Medicare because it seemed undemocratic that those who had given the most for the longest would slip into retirement in desperation. The powerful American Association of Retired Persons (AARP) has created the kind of advocacy group—with a paid staff of eighteen hundred and 160,000 volunteers in fifty states and thirty-five hundred local chapters—that is as powerful as the American Legion was on behalf of the GI Bill fifty years ago. Thousands of support groups working for the elderly have also supported their cause. So the programs were developed, and they succeeded over less than fifty years. Again, they followed the pattern of citizen leadership, with the government only later lending critically important support. This means change can be made.

Sadly, children have no advocacy group with the power of the AARP, and children do not vote or write their congressional representatives. Even with our general progress in many areas, we are not yet at the levels of well-being for children that has been attained by other industrialized nations. This progress with the elderly notwithstanding, if the United States continues on its current path, our middle class is likely to become disaffected as its income distribution becomes even more severely skewed. The lowest 20 percent could become angriest. Given our history, this will not happen quickly or easily. People have faith, and while unemployment is low we manage, but in a protracted economic recession or period of stagnant growth, with increasing layoffs, reduced health insurance coverage, and dwindling opportunities to believe the next generation can move up, our intergroup civic trust—the heart of democracy—will be eroded.

I am convinced that we don't want major disappointment in our democracy to occur and break the great social asset we enjoy from the commonly shared belief in upward mobility. I am also convinced that just as citizen generosity has led to highly significant advances in our past, we can do it again. The current disorientation of the market strengthens the case for a faster-paced effort to increase philanthropic focus on these problems—before anger and hopelessness set in.

The U.S. aversion to the kind of high tax rate that is easily tolerated in Europe demands a higher commitment from all citizens to make philanthropic investments in human, physical, and intellectual capital, all for the greater good. If our brand of capitalism requires lower tax rates, then we need remarkably higher levels of generosity, philanthropy that is designed to enable people to build wealth not dependency. This is the generosity we should understand and adopt in order to continue to strengthen both our democracy and our economy. This is the kind of philanthropy that has built our country. It establishes precedents for subsequent government funding and builds the political consensus that we can afford the required changes. It is the kind of philanthropy that is the subject of the rest of this book.

THE CURRENT STATE OF HAPPINESS IN AMERICA

Our success ties back to qualities of the American spirit: generosity fueled by optimism and the encouragement of the founding fathers to pursue happiness. Unfortunately, something else besides social health has begun to break down in the last thirty years. Perhaps this problem is best captured by Robert Lane, who has recently published an important book with a fateful title, *The Loss of Happiness in Market Democracies*. Lane researches the malaise that has befallen us despite our increasingly successful market economy: "what I see as a growing (and unhealthy) tension between our individualistic, self-actualization mentality of the '90s and the pursuit of happiness as our Founding Fathers intended."[25]

The founding fathers did not have studies on happiness. But current research indicates that growing wealth or property increases a person's happiness only to a point. Human beings seem to adjust quickly to creature comforts. Lane tells this story: "Something has gone wrong. The economy that made Americans both rich and happy at one point in history is misleading them, is offering more money, which does not make them happy, instead of more companionship, which probably would."[26]

Lane believes that the weakening of family and community relationships over the past twenty-five years has played a major role in the loss of happiness people report and that income cannot supplant that loss. We are evidently not unhappy, as the Alesina and Di Tella study shows, about income inequality, but we are registering a lower sense of personal well-being for other reasons. The statistics Lane provides suggest that economic security and political freedom are important but insufficient assets in the production of self-reported happiness. We need to remind more citizens of the limits of satisfaction when one pursues happiness for the self alone. Lane keeps returning to the role of companionship and personal engagement as the sources of happiness of which we have begun to lose track. As we care for and engage with others, we manage to overcome the isolation of the human condition and experience personal satisfaction.

In his energetically discussed and disputed *Bowling Alone,* Robert Putnam reviews data from a variety of sources that confirm the problem of weaker civic engagement, less social time face-to-face among fellow citizens, fewer voters, and no observable surge in giving, despite a surge in wealth accumulation. Unfortunately, this coincides with highly significant failures in moral leadership among public figures at the highest levels. We have been through a time that has shattered faith in institutional leadership of all kinds. Scandals have embroiled corporate leaders, presidents of non-profits, and academic and religious leaders. Government leaders at all levels, not only the presidency, have wracked the nation with ethical falls of every variety. Financial ruin and loss of investor confidence have resulted from failures of integrity, from the savings and loan scandals of the 1980s to the recent spate of accounting and insider trading scams and scandals affecting some of America's largest and best-known corporations. Most distressing, perhaps, we have dealt with failures in the spiritual sector, especially the Catholic Church's handling of clergy who have abused the trust of their parishioners.

The loss of general feelings of well-being or happiness and the loss of trust in leaders at all levels weaken the nation's capacity to attend energetically to economic and social problems. With both leadership and happiness under fire, we need, more than ever, new resolve in a majority of citizens and the opportunity to turn to innovative private leaders.

The virtuous cycle that develops when individuals in significant numbers commit acts of generosity has profound implications for our economy and our society. The freedom to act entrepreneurially has created many fortunes, large and small, and great economic dynamism over centuries. Remarkably, without undue intervention from a third party, the natural limits to this pathway to happiness seem to have operated fairly often. We have certainly produced our share of robber barons who gave six-hour banquets at which hundred-dollar bills were used as napkins and guests arrived in gold-inlaid suits of armor. From the grotesque waste of the Gilded Age to the conspicuous consumption of dot-com multimillionaires, we have produced people whose wealth was exceeded only by their selfishness. But we have also seen, time and again, people who have turned to helping others as the ultimate pathway to the pursuit of happiness. In so doing, they have invested in the upward mobility of their fellow citizens.

Acts of generosity, or the pursuit of happiness *for others,* constitute one example of what Tocqueville called "self interest, rightly understood." The catalytic interaction between acts of generosity, higher levels of happiness in society, and more robust economic activity defines America. Very significant increases in our generosity and our application of our financial support to improve social health would offer us one approach to reversing the unhappiness in our market economy that Lane and Putnam report. In this situation, there is simply no substitute for clear-sighted, ethical leadership. We have seen the impact of such selfless commitment to the common good throughout the stories in the first half of this book.

CONCLUSION

We need to understand and begin correcting the problems that should not be part of America's landscape for her citizens, and we need to do this before these problems become collectively obvious and damaging to a broadly shared spirit of continuing commitment to the greater good. Without a vigorous new dedication to enabling the lowest two quintiles in our income distribution to make significant progress in wealth accumulation, many citizens may begin to doubt the reality of upward mobility. At that point, people in our upper-income brackets will be hurt by a negative change in our social environment and will end up having to deal with the costs of fixing what will be much more expensive financially and more damaging socially.

We have the time now to create the plans that will address the major problems and even push on toward sustainable approaches to well-being and wealth building for all. Our other choice remains to do nothing more than we have been doing, let our giving remain at the current levels, continue to drop tax rates, and ignore these issues for a decade or two. A further deterioration of our problems will cause a great negative impact on our society and our economy. If those of us who can afford to give at higher levels refuse to do so, we are agreeing to a more precarious future for our own children who will inherit a different America from the one our parents prepared for us. I believe it is in the best interests of all Americans and the American economy to increase our generosity. The suggestions in the rest of this book are a progrowth, not just a feel-good, approach to the future.

Investing now in a higher quality of life for all is the wiser choice for several reasons. We can avoid having socially disabling bitterness and cynicism capture the minds of a significant portion of our citizenry, and not just of those in the lowest quintile of the income distribution. We can avoid the much higher cost of fixing problems later, after they have had time to worsen. On the way we will be shortcircuiting many problems, particularly if we attend to challenges involving children in America. We can sustain the sense that in America the people know how to build a fair and prosperous society. We are blessed that so many of our people still basically believe this.

Recently, our economy sustained one of the longest and strongest bull markets in history, creating stunning wealth and expanding dramatically the economic resources of millions of Americans. We engaged in the fastest set of positive changes for women and minorities our nation (and perhaps any other nation) has ever seen. Most professional schools have achieved close to equal enrollment and graduation rates for men and women. Most of our postsecondary educational institutions have done an admirable job integrating and educating first-generation college students from every race and both genders. Blacks have achieved higher levels of economic progress than ever before in our history. Many closed doors and glass ceilings have slowly yielded to women, minorities, gays, and disabled citizens, as well as to a larger number of immigrants from increasingly diverse backgrounds. The United States has profited from involving these new economic players in many ways. We have led the world in the creation of intellectual property—in the design and application of technology, whether in telecommunications, biotechnology, agriculture, or pharmaceuticals.

The economic success of these past three decades has brought millions to middle-class status and fed upward mobility. Those who have benefited, even if we have also experienced some losses in the recent downturn, have a duty to share some of the privileges, not by a handout but by a hand up.

Neither democracy nor long-term success in capital markets can occur if the individual pursues happiness at the expense of others. These words close the Declaration of Independence: ". . . we pledge each other our lives, our fortunes and our sacred honor." American citizens assure mutually their rights and their well-being. Consequently, the individual or group that routinely neglects fellow citizens in the pursuit of their personal happiness violates the social contract in our democracy. Narcissism, greed, and civic disengagement sustain neither democracies nor markets. For all the benefits people get, we owe generosity and engagement in some personally appropriate way to the advancement of opportunities of our fellow citizens.

Philanthropy, America's unique approach to investment in upward mobility, has made a major contribution to our distinctive brand of successful capitalism. In the previous chapters we have seen how generous Americans have fostered a more fair and robust economy by being entrepreneurial and inclusive. We can apply this solution, with significantly more power now, even in view of the market bust in the early part of the decade. As we have seen, generosity has often ushered the government to building what needs to be built, investing where investment was needed, and preparing to change laws; only later have the government, and eventually the for-profit private sector, taken up responsibility for funding "innovation."

Remember that it was Abolitionists and Freedman's Societies that brought attention to the evil of slavery. Suffragettes saw to women's rights. During the Progressive Era, thousands of citizens fought for decent jobs, working conditions and salaries, health care, urban development, children's needs, and, later, for widely available college education (in the GI Bill). The civil rights movement was supported by citizen generosity as were penalties for drunk driving and environmental pollution, among other new ideas.

The generosity citizens practiced in the pursuit of their individual happiness and their personal sense of satisfaction has helped change the laws and improve the balance between democracy and capitalism. The result has made our market economy a success and our social progress hard-won but steady. The engine for this generosity was certainly the rule of law and the material wealth available in our capital markets, along with our democratic tax structure that permits people to keep a significant portion of their earnings and wealth. But the energy and inventiveness hard-wired into our culture also helped put the emphasis on fairness and the pursuit of happiness.

In chapters 7 through 11, I make the case that, over the next thirty years, we need a new American revolution, this time to improve our capitalist democracy by expanding generosity as an economic and social force. We need to reinvigorate philanthropy in order to keep democracy alive, to continue to make capitalism more just and more effective, and to right the negative directions that have emerged during the last thirty years.

And just what do we want to achieve in our democracy, especially over the next twenty to thirty years? What should the country look like in 2030? What needs fixing? Many features of our society need to be fixed, regardless of our stunning successes. Some Americans will want to close economic gaps, such as differences in wealth accumulation resulting from the discrimination African Americans have faced when trying to buy homes in areas that appreciate in value. Others will want to address early childhood education or health gaps contributing to unacceptable and increasing rates of child poverty. Still others may attack opportunity gaps, such as the generally poor K–12 education in poor communities. Investing in human capital, in building physical capital, and in advancing intellectual capital over the next ten years will enable the promises of democracy and capitalism to come closer to the lives of more and more Americans. That, it seems to me, is the job for all of us.

7

THE CHALLENGE OF AMERICA'S WEALTH AND THE COMING WEALTH TRANSFER

> *In the long run men hit only what they aim at. Therefore, though they should fail immediately, they had better aim at something high.*
>
> —HENRY DAVID THOREAU, *Walden*

For the future of a healthy democracy and market economy, the wealth the country has built in the last thirty years stands as both an opportunity and a threat. We need to aim high and assure that we create an opportunity.

In 2001, Ben Wattenberg, author and fellow at the American Enterprise Institute, interviewed Professor Paul Schervish of Boston College for his public television series, *Think Tank*. Schervish is director of the college's Social Welfare Research Institute (SWRI), and he and his colleagues have been researching wealth and philanthropy. The deep breath Wattenberg took to begin his comments signaled that he and his guest were about to say something they considered momentous:

> The big story is what may be called the emergence of the mass affluent class. You can look at millionaires, for example. In 1980, there were approximately 700,000 families, about three million

> people, who lived in a millionaire household. A household with a net worth of $1 million or more. Today, [there are] five million families, 20 million people. . . . [W]ealth, which was once the preserve of a sort of aristocratic few, has now become a mass phenomenon."[1]

Paul Schervish and his colleague John Havens have been doing research on the impending mass accumulation of wealth for over a decade. Their research confirms that during the period from 1998 to 2052, the United States will see between $31 and $41 *trillion* in private, intergenerational wealth transfer create some 10.1 million new millionaires (counting their wealth in constant, inflation-adjusted dollars).[2] Right behind them in the income distribution will be the "merely affluent" and pensioners whose assets have acquired significant additional value during the past twenty years. Even with a flattening of the growth rate in the United States economy (GDP) to 2 percent per year for the whole fifty years, the wealth transfer will achieve *at least* this predicted level. The number could go much higher.

How did this happen? There are several factors. First, it's been fifty years since there's been a depression or major recession in this country. That's fifty years for property values to appreciate and for sound investments to pay off. Second, net worth—the combined value of all the houses and other property, all the stocks and bonds—has increased hugely. The total net worth of Americans has increased from $7 trillion in 1950 to $38 trillion in 2000. Third, there are the baby boomers. It has been this largest population cohort in history that benefited from the bull markets of the last half of the twentieth century. Their investments grew at an unprecedented rate, and even the recent leveling off has not totally unraveled the fortunes made. The boomers will die and pass those fortunes to their children, who will do likewise in due time—voilà, the intergenerational wealth transfer. Assuming they use it and invest it even moderately wisely, this inheritance will serve each generation lavishly and will increase, providing more to pass on to the next generation.

Schervish and Havens wrote their initial report on this wealth transfer in 1999 and, after many questions calling for a new analysis in view of the downturn in the stock market and the effects of September 11, 2001, they revisited the phenomenon and prepared a new report that shows that the forecast for a $41 trillion wealth transfer has not changed. Their estimate has been adopted by the Council of Economic Advisors, reviewed positively by the Bureau of Labor Statistics, and used in analyses done by the Congressional Budget Office. The researchers affirm that "the relevant question is not whether $41 trillion will be transferred, but how much more than $41 trillion will be transferred." They project that in 2052, "we will be able to look back and say that two-thirds of the transfer came from only 7 percent of estates—the very wealthiest."

The researchers further clarified that wealth transfer is not simply inheritance. Only $25 trillion of the $41 trillion will move to heirs; at least $6 trillion is expected to go directly to philanthropy; the rest will go to estate taxes and legal expenses for settling estates. And while $25 trillion will be inherited, several generations will benefit. Boomers will receive only about $7.3 trillion of the money and their progeny will receive the rest. Boomers will be benefactors more than beneficiaries of this wealth transfer.

Schervish and Havens's estimate assumes only a 2 percent real rate of annual growth in the $32 trillion of wealth held by individuals and their foundations in 1998—not the high growth rates attained in the late 1990s. This rate is lower than historic trends. Furthermore, the Federal Reserve Flow of Funds Accounts estimates that total household wealth equaled at least $32 trillion by 1998, and the number was higher after 1998.

The report takes into account the fact that Americans are living—and therefore spending—longer and can be expected to continue this trend in the future; that people spend down their assets after retirement; and that trends in annuitization and in spending by baby boomers do not reduce the estimated transfer amount.

Is this $41 trillion good news? Of course it is. But it has a dark side. This wealth accumulation will occur *even if the average American at the same time loses earning and buying power.* It is the already affluent who will become rich, and there could be an income-distribution problem of the first order. Upward mobility for those in the lower quintiles will be a matter not of climbing the ladder of success, but of leaping desperately across the chasm of wealth. In the meantime, a large proportion of the wealthy population may lose touch with the experience of need and drop its commitment to those in the bottom quintile of the income distribution. In a situation of mass affluence, parents would have to make special efforts to expose themselves and their children to disadvantaged families and to avoid overindulging their own offspring. That would take a special consciousness that we have rarely witnessed among the majority of the wealthy. Our political leaders will likely come from the wealth stratum as well and our government policies could well be guided by their experience of the world.

This wealth transfer will deepen an already wide division between rich and poor in this country. Research confirms what many of us suspect: that wealth is highly concentrated, rather than well distributed, in the United States. This is one of the characteristics of robust capitalism. Thirty-two percent of the nation's wealth is held by the top 1 percent of Americans. This is also the case in England, but other countries show very different distributions. Our 32 percent compares to 16 percent of the wealth in the hands of the top 1 percent in Sweden, the top 1 percent holding just 19 percent of the wealth in France, and the same group holding 20 percent in Canada.[3]

This is true because wealth depends not just on income but on assets. There are two different components to "rich." Income is earned annually and is usually the sum on which annual federal and state taxes are levied. Wealth is the full accumulation of financial assets less any indebtedness. It includes home equity, income from dividends on stocks and bonds, interest on savings accounts, cars, land, and any other significant valuables. Gifts and inheritances add to wealth. Both income and wealth are measures of well-being. Wealth, in contrast to income, brings greater security because it assures owners that their standard of living is secure regardless of variations in jobs, salaries, and short-term calamities.

At this moment in history, it is still possible for low- and middle-income households in the United States to acquire significant assets over a lifetime. The average wealth of American households in

1962 was $81,333; in 1989, it was $244,000; in 1998, $270,000. Fifty-six percent of households headed by a person over forty-five years old reported net assets (wealth) of at least $100,000 in 1998. (Interestingly, a survey of Americans indicates that most people think less than a third of American households have this level of wealth.) According to a survey by the Opinion Research Corporation of America International, commissioned by Providian and the Consumer Federation of America, 26 percent of American households with incomes between $10,000 and $25,000 have assets above $100,000. Thirty-eight percent of those with incomes between $25,000 and $50,000 reach the same level of assets. In general, households headed by older people tend to be better off. They have had more time to build equity, savings, and other assets. These statistics matter because they help define America's track record of upward mobility.

For less-than-wealthy households, the impact of home ownership on wealth accumulation is significant. Most American households report that the major source of their wealth is their home equity. For households whose net assets fall between $100,000 and $250,000, 43 percent of their wealth results from home equity, 17 percent from retirement accounts, and 6 percent from investments.[4] Only 34 percent of the wealth of the affluent derives from their home equity, 17 percent from retirement accounts, and 11 percent from investments like stocks, bonds, and mutual funds. Besides larger incomes and significant contributions by their employers to retirement funds, the wealthy accumulate wealth faster over time because they hold more of the tools of wealth building.

However—and this is the crucial point—there is a large proportion of Americans who have virtually no wealth. They do not own homes, much less stocks and bonds. About 31 percent of American households have no or negative financial assets, according to Melvin Oliver and Thomas Shapiro in *Black Wealth/White Wealth*. That includes 60 percent of African American households, 54 percent of Hispanic American households, and 62 percent of single-parent households. What's more, half of all Americans have less than $1,000 in investable assets. Another way to look at it is that 10 percent of America's families control two-thirds of the wealth.[5]

When polled, 27 percent of Americans who were asked what their best chance was of acquiring $500,000 responded that *the lottery* was their best chance.[6] Is this a redefinition of the American Dream, not achievement by hard work and savings but by winning the lottery? Is this a sign that faith in upward mobility by the usual means is flagging? More than a quarter of our citizens are evidently not convinced that home equity and investments in businesses, retirement funds, stocks, and bonds can actually enable them to acquire wealth over their lifetimes, or perhaps more sadly, they do not believe that these asset builders are within their reach. Not surprisingly, people with primary confidence in lotteries are not prevalent among those in higher wealth brackets.

IS PHILANTHROPY KEEPING UP WITH THE WEALTH TRANSFER?

Traditionally, Americans are generous. We've seen that. Are they generous enough to keep up with the wealth transfer, generous enough to counteract the effects it may have on our social health, the right to the pursuit of happiness, our belief in upward mobility, indeed the soundness of our democracy itself?

The future leverage of generosity will clearly pass into the hands of the generations receiving the wealth transfer. Although 89 percent of all Americans make donations, the wealthy are the major givers, for the simple reason that they have more to give. Indeed, 46 percent of individual contributions to charity come from families worth more than $1 million. An additional 25 percent of gifts comes from families worth between $200,000 and $1 million. As those rich families become wealthier, more money in absolute dollars is expected to go to charity.[7] The question is will they give a larger percentage of this wealth.

Wattenberg's graph underlines the facts: The population with more than $200,000 annual income gives 71 percent of the nation's contributions. This group represents 4 percent of the U.S. population. Households in the group whose annual income is between $100,000 and $200,000 per year comprise 11 percent of the population and give 13 percent of the total. This means 15 percent of the population

Total Contributions to Charity by Household Net Worth

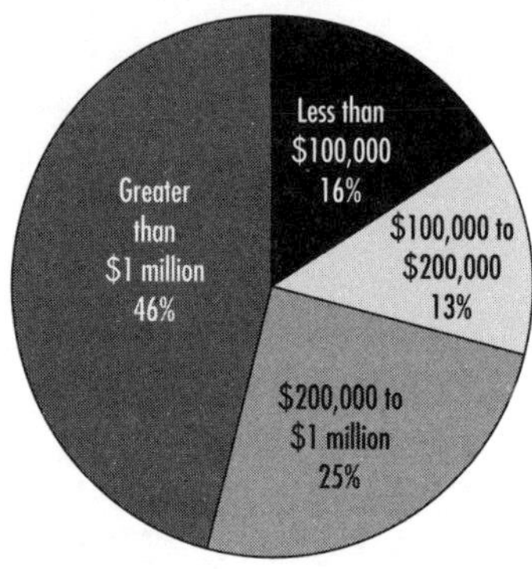

Source: Social Welfare Research Institute, Boston College

gives 84 percent of the money. Interestingly, their rate of giving is less than that of those with an annual income under $100,000. There are, of course, many more people in this lowest earning group. In fact, those with net worth less than $100,000 comprise 85 percent of the population. The important fact in this set of statistics rests in the insight that Americans at all economic levels give. Obviously, individuals in lower income groups *simply do not have the financial capacity* to match the dollar amounts given by the wealthy.

The real problem I want us to think hard about is the trend in generosity. While we have been getting richer, and therefore getting and giving more dollars, our actual generosity—that is, the percentage of our income and wealth we donate—has been relatively flat for thirty years. Personal generosity has ranged from 1.9 percent of personal income in 1970, to a thirty-year low of 1.5 percent in 1995, and back up to 1.8 percent in 2000. For thirty years, it remained close to 2 percent of the nation's GDP.

As more of us are better able every year to satisfy our wants and needs, we are not sharing a larger percentage of our income and wealth. We are retaining it in savings or spending it on ourselves and our families. Yet some segments of the population, as we have just seen, are experiencing reductions in their well-being, notably children. This, it seems to me, is intolerable. We must mobilize both governmental policy tools and America's secret weapon—philanthropy—to attend to the needs we have described and to set some new directions.

CAN PHILANTHROPY MEET THE CHALLENGE?

The philanthropy I'm encouraging is not just a fallback for a government that is failing to put its money where the need is. We have experienced a significant loss of confidence in the specific forms of aid that the government has given to low-income families. The economic downturn of 2001–2002 has begun to show changes in research data. Surveys indicate that over one-third of Americans view themselves as "have-nots," compared to just 17 percent in 1988. Two-thirds of the public now believe that something needs to be done about the income gap between wealthy and other Americans.[8] Vast numbers of Americans no longer believe that welfare is a way out of poverty. We are disillusioned by the inefficiency and, in far too many cases, the built-in problems of a system that, at its best, didn't work all that well. But we simply cannot abandon the poor. If government services aren't working, we need to try something else. That's where philanthropy comes in.

In the process of attending to these needs as private citizens, we will develop new strategies that can become part of public policy. Philanthropy has, in the past, been quicker than government to imagine, test, and implement innovative methods for solving social problems. If we can do it again over the next twenty years, the country may reconsider our tax structure and how best to direct tax money to address social health problems that challenge our way of life. This is the process that has worked in earlier generations. It seems to offer decent chances of success in the current environment.

So, let's look at what could happen, if generosity does *not* fail, if the current slump in giving is *no more* than a short slump, if the wealth transfer does *not* corrode compassion among upper-income families and increase the gated-community, "I've got mine" mentality.

First, Americans have given more than $2 trillion to charity over the past twenty years. That includes money left from estates. Schervish estimates that, in the next twenty years, our giving will grow to $6 trillion. Three times as much! A great deal could be done with $6 trillion. But Shervish and his colleagues have a further projection. If giving continues at the rate of the past twenty years, $34 trillion could go to charity in the next fifty years!

That is really generous, and it's just maintaining the status quo of current giving. But will we? The critical question is, As the affluent and their children become even wealthier, will they remain as committed to sharing as in the past and then give even more to keep wealth building and wealth sharing in balance? *What will motivate them to do this?*

Will it be fellow feeling? Empathy? Eventually, no one alive will remember living through the Great Depression. Those who lived through that time had empathy with the poor and have had a spe-

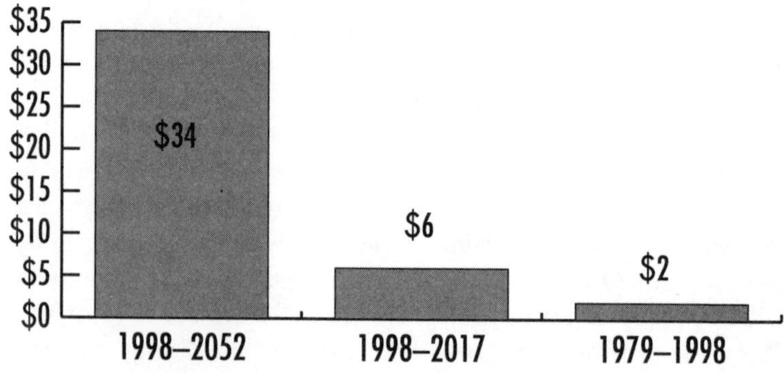

Source: Social Welfare Research Institute, Boston College

cial gratitude for the kind of material well-being that today most other middle-quintile people take completely for granted. If current trends continue, most of the wealth-controlling group will prefer to live and vacation in gated communities.[9] Their children will attend private and increasingly elite schools. The airport delays after the terrorist attacks in September 2001 have also been inducing this same group to use private planes rather than commercial airlines. Other, similar methods of isolation are likely to develop in the years to come. These very wealthy people may be living seriously detached from regular people in a way that their parents did not. So, no. Not empathy.

Will it be religious values? If so, no signs have yet appeared. The Institute for Social Research at the University of Michigan periodically conducts the "World Values Survey." It polls a statistically valid sample of adults from sixty nations. Their 1995–1997 survey showed that fifteen of nineteen industrialized countries, including the United States, have had a significant decline in church attendance in recent years. And the single most reliable indicator of an individual's level of charitable giving is church attendance. A 1994 poll conducted by the American Association of Fund-Raising Counsel's (AAFRC) Trust for Philanthropy showed that donors who attend church give an average of 2.2 percent of their income to charity, and those who do not average only 1.4 percent. Those who go to church every week give 3.3 percent. These people extend their giving to all kinds of non-profits, not just their own churches. As church attendance drops, giving drops. So we probably can't rely on religion.

Will it be social pressure? Given current mores, the wealthy may be attached to their material things in a way that was more common in the Gilded Age than in the twentieth century. They may also be much more ostentatious about their wealth than the puritan heritage allowed Rockefeller and those of his generation to be. This is, after all, the land of the SUV, which represents 25 percent of new-vehicle sales in spite of the fact that it gets seventeen miles to the gallon and is significantly more dangerous on the road than a car, especially to other drivers.[10] It's the land of the minimansion, with its conspicuous crystal chandelier shining through a window obviously placed to display it. It's the country that consumes 25 percent of the world's production of goods.

Will it be the centuries-long tradition of generosity in this country? Possibly. But only if we cultivate an understanding of just how important that tradition has been to us. I'm afraid future generations may be likely to miss the positive impact of our history of generosity on social cohesion and economic growth. That, of course, is why I'm writing this book.

In the future, this country will need to continue mitigating the flaws of capitalism, assuring social connectedness, and sustaining an environment favorable to the values and work ethic of a capital-market democracy. The economy must sustain upward mobility and hope for those struggling to achieve, in addition to sustaining the wealth that well-endowed families expect to hand down to their children. While numbers of dot-com millionaires started social-venture philanthropies through which they gave their own money and their personal involvement, will they continue now that the times have changed and their fortunes are diminished? We all lose if the gap between rich and poor widens beyond bridging.

If thirty or fifty years from now the country is confronting increasing discord among the income groups, more conflict, and less productivity, the breakdown in social cohesion and trust will have eroded the confidence in the market, with global as well as domestic implications. Our economic system is built on investor confidence in the likelihood of return on invested funds over long stretches of time. Likewise, parents' and children's willingness to make sacrifices and practice self-discipline and postponement of pleasure on behalf of a strong education rests on their confidence that these efforts will pay off in a better life for the child in the future. If that confidence, like investors' confidence, is shattered, both kinds of personal investments will fall off. This would occur to the great detriment of the republic as a whole and of citizens as individuals.

The country needs to plan carefully so that twenty years from now we are pleased with the results of the wealth we have acquired. We should by then be proud of the rate at which the bottom quintile and the middle classes have attained a larger share of the nation's well-being and of the strengthening of our democratic values. This recent wealth accumulation should be a great asset to our ability to help other nations, especially if we can use voluntarily contributed portions of it to address our own most unacceptable social health challenges—such as child poverty—and do so in a way that leads to new political consensus and better government expenditures. This will require focus and discipline akin to our wartime efforts to combat invaders or terrorists. What we do now will define the future. As the next chapter will indicate, despite some real pitfalls possible in generosity, there are currently a significant number of excellent ideas already moving around the country, awaiting scaling up and out. If these and other ideas succeed, history may one day say that this wealth accumulation was a world-class opportunity that Americans knew how to exploit for the common good.

8

THE CHALLENGE OF DIVERSITY

Give me your tired, your poor, your huddled masses . . .

EMMA LAZARUS, "THE NEW COLOSSUS"

America has always been diverse. When the first Europeans set foot here, the land was already settled by hundreds of different Native American cultures and governments. As immigration to the colonies of the New World increased, the diversity of the population increased. Before 1790, about 300,000 people came here from England. Another 300,000 came, unwillingly, from Africa. Germany contributed about 100,000 and, according to the Ellis Island Foundation, about 175,000 Scottish and Scotch-Irish joined the mix.[1] In the West and Southwest, Spanish and, later, Mexican immigrants predominated.

The European and African immigrants arrived in a land with a strong and already established tradition of generosity. In the words of Luther Standing Bear, an Oglala Lakota chief: "Out of the Indian approach to life there came a great freedom—an intense and absorbing love for nature; a respect for life; enriching faith in a Supreme Power; and principles of truth, honesty, *generosity,* equity, and brotherhood as a guide to mundane relations" (author's italics). The Pacific Northwest potlatch is an example of a First American giving tradition. Among the groups that practiced this tradition were the Nuu-chch-nulth, the Coast Salish, the Kwakiutl, the Haida, and the Tlingit. A potlatch was a social event held to mark the host's social position. Sometimes it commemorated a special occasion such as the birth of a child or a daughter's first menses. If the host was very wealthy, he might invite guests from surrounding communities as well as his own.

According to an exhibition of the Peabody Museum of Archaeology and Ethnology, "Potlatches were also the venue in which ownership of economic and ceremonial privileges was asserted, displayed, and formally transferred to heirs." At a potlatch, the host distributed gifts to all the guests. The gifts served to display his wealth and importance and, when the guests were witnesses to important economic or spiritual transactions, to make the events memorable to them. This was crucial in all cultures without written records. Memory trainer Jon Keith cites an occasion from the Middle Ages in which a nobleman made a gift of land to a monastery. To make sure his son would remember the transaction and therefore honor it, he threw the boy, fully clothed, into a pond. The boy was fished out, dripping wet, and remembered the day for the rest of his life. A potlatch guest who took home a canoe or a goat-hair blanket would, by the same token, remember the potlatch and the fact that it commemorated, for example, the transfer of an important piece of property.

Those who study earlier cultures now say that the potlatch was an important way to redistribute wealth in the community, and it is only one of many generosity traditions among First Americans. But these traditions were very different from the generosity understood by Europeans, and they were often abused as a result. Europeans mistook the joint ownership of land, traditions of open-handed hospitality, and other aspects of Native American life as evidence of a simple-minded, primitive culture. This misinterpretation cost America enormously.

European Americans have also tried to interpret the lives and actions of African Americans through their own value filter. Among the key features of African American generosity are the concepts of fictive kin and the "covenant of care." When black families were torn apart by sale or death under slavery, they were re-formed in accordance with African traditions. Parentless children were taken immediately into other homes. Young adults without spouses became fictive kin to established family units. Women mothered the children of their brothers and sisters. This kind of generosity has continued to this day and is certainly as profound as funding a scholarship, but European Americans have failed to recognize it. When they did, they often saw it as evidence of dysfunction in the black family.

The covenant of care is another aspect of African American values. In black towns and in the black neighborhoods of cities, sociologists have identified this feature of black life. William J. McAuley described the covenants in an article on their importance in the black towns of rural Oklahoma:

> The covenants of care have much in common with the relationship convoys that are the central concept of the convoy model developed by Antonucci and Akiyama (1987) and Kahn and Antonucci (1980). The convoy model proposes that individuals move through life with convoys of people who are meaningful to them and who have important positive or negative impacts on them. These social convoys change in size, composition, and function over the course of the lifespan.
>
> One difference between the concept of social convoys and covenants of care—or perhaps, it is an extension of the original conceptualization—is that the covenants of care tend to be highly situated within and focused upon the towns themselves. Thus, they transcend friendship and family social support systems (although these systems certainly thrive in the all-black towns) and encourage support for town residents.[2]

In other words, whole towns and communities offer the kind of care to each individual that white Americans expect only from their family and close friends. That care ranges from repairing one another's homes and hanging one another's curtains to community Christmas parties at which all the town's children receive gifts together. Unfortunately, white Americans often look at low-income black communities and see only boarded-up windows and leaning porches, missing the profound traditions of generosity and interdependence. Again, this misunderstanding has cost the country.[3]

We are facing that danger again. Today, Americans of European descent make up the majority in this once Indian land. Their traditions shaped the country's ideas and institutions around generosity as around so many other things. Indeed, immigration laws long prevented non-Europeans from entering the country in numbers large enough to endanger European dominance.

In 1924, U.S. immigration laws were changed in response to the huge influx of people, primarily from Europe, in the late nineteenth and early twentieth centuries. Immigration, even of Europeans, closed down to a trickle. But in 1965, Congress reopened our borders, and since then, almost 1 million people have immigrated legally into the United States each year. This is more immigrants than all the other countries in the world *combined* accept annually. There were 33.1 million immigrants living in the United States in 2002. We have never seen such numbers before. In a *Brookings Review* of the 2000 census, Ken Prewitt noted that 10 percent of the U.S. citizenry is now foreign-born and 90 percent are born in the United States. The foreign-born percentage of the population was actually higher in the first few decades of the 1900s, reaching 14.7 percent of the total U.S. population in 1910, but the 1930 census was the last time the percentage of immigrants was as high as it is today. And now we are seeing immigration that is not primarily European. Since 1965, more than 4 million immigrants have come from Mexico and almost 1.5 million from the Philippines. Korea, the Dominican Republic, India, Cuba, and Vietnam have each contributed about three quarters of a million.

Americans who live by European-inspired values have a second chance here. Instead of misunderstanding, abusing, or ignoring the values of these new cultures, Americans have the opportunity to learn about and learn from these diverse peoples. Diversity has the potential to threaten the delicate balance of capitalism and democracy, but it also offers rich opportunities for reinvigorating generosity as the broker between democracy and capitalism.

WHAT ARE THE CHALLENGES?

In 1890, nine out of ten foreign-born Americans came from Europe; in 1960, three out of four did. Today, the foreign-born population is 50 percent Latin American and 25 percent Asian, while a smaller but significant additional number emigrate from Africa and the Middle East.[4] Only 14 percent come from Europe.[5] As a result, in large cities and small towns, native-born Americans are now connected to a substantial number of people they don't know very much about.

The problems that result are legion. Work styles, use of time, importance of family, dress, and speech, among other daily issues, create new experiences, ones that are challenging and sometimes frustrating for all. Signs of friendship and courtesy are wildly divergent, and well-meaning people, newcomers among them, make mistakes in connecting to one another gracefully. Americans cannot easily distinguish among Eritreans, Somalis, Ethiopians, and Senegalese, or among many of the Asian peoples. Language problems develop in schools, and they are challenging and sometimes expensive to handle. Students in English as a second language (ESL) often have no *first* language in common. Holidays and holy days occur at what may seem at first to be a baffling rate. Systems at schools, colleges, banks, and other institutions require patience from everyone involved.

Some parts of this situation resemble those in the earlier phase of heavy immigration from Ireland, Germany, Italy, Eastern European states, and Russia. Both earlier and post-1965 immigrants faced different work environments and neighborhood communities. There were usually language problems. Both began immediately to construct micro-communities of their own ethnicities. Now many of the first arrivals following the 1965 change in the laws have assimilated into the mainstream of American life, just as those earlier immigrants did. They are doctors in our hospitals and teachers in our schools. They are running businesses of all sizes. Indeed, they have virtually the same rate of entrepreneurship as natives: one in ten is self-employed. Thirty percent are college graduates. They belong to the chamber of commerce and Kiwanis. In 2002, almost 40 percent of immigrants who were eighteen and older were citizens. They represented 6 percent of all eligible voters.[6]

Some aspects of their situation are quite different, however. For the most part, though not always, of course, those earlier immigrants came from climates and geographies similar to those they found in the United States. Often, our more recent immigrants do not. There are adjustments to be made in everything from farming to clothing. Race is having an even more profound impact. For most of the first fifty years of the twentieth century, the minority population remained at a stable 13 percent of the population and almost all of it (90 percent) was African American, with a long and commonly shared history in the United States. Now our minority population stands at 25 percent of our total population, and only half of it is African American. From 1950 until 1998, the minority population tripled, as new waves of immigrants arrived and started families. Just from 1980 until 1998, the minority population grew 63 percent, compared to an 8 percent growth rate in the non-Hispanic white population. The U.S. Census predicts that by 2005, Hispanics will outnumber non-Hispanic blacks, and Asians will comprise 13 percent of the population. We have never tried to assimilate anything like that many people who are physically identifiable—and whose children will be identifiable—as "not American" by a great many native-born, white Americans. Given our track record with race, that is likely to present problems for generations.

The very large immigration from a contiguous country, Mexico, also makes the new integration of immigrants different from earlier times. Mexican Hispanics can visit back and forth, maintaining a strong connection to their original culture. Families spend vacations visiting their Mexican relatives. The proximity of family in Mexico can be a strong temptation for parents whose teenagers are, in U.S. urban areas, increasingly exposed to dangers from gang violence. Anecdotal evidence suggests that adolescents are often sent back to Mexico for safety while parents and younger children remain in the United States. Moreover, for many socially conservative families, the local American culture their children will absorb does not respect age or family ties, and has what one academic called "Beavis and Butt-head" values, something Hispanic parents do not favor. Many traditional European families had similar objections, but sending their children back to the old country for a few years was not an option. No such extreme separation as that required of earlier European immigrants is now required of Mexican Americans.

Consequently, more tension exists now than in earlier times, when more of a consensus existed among new arrivals about the importance of English, the strength of U.S. culture, and the desire to assimilate, and when native-born, white Americans could believe that the new immigrants would someday become "just like" them. In some communities, these new arrivals are revitalizing sections of cities by starting businesses, and native-born Americans are generally not vocal about their concerns over nonassimilation into the melting pot. In areas where the new arrivals are putting a strain on tax rolls because they need services, frustrations tend to surface.

The black population is becoming more diverse as immigrants from the Caribbean islands and Africa join African Americans, whose history in this country goes back centuries. The mix of different cultural, religious, linguistic, and ethnic traditions brings great change inside African American communities, a change that white Americans often seem unable to comprehend. (The absurdity of thinking that a person whose family has lived in this country for two hundred years would have the same culture and values as one who had just arrived from Nigeria reflects the power of racial myth in this country.) Just to convey the dimensions of this change, note that in 1970 about sixty thousand people born in Africa immigrated to the United States. In 1990, a quarter million new immigrants came from Africa, and in 1998, over half a million. Some come from North Africa and bring their Muslim religion and North African culture with them. Many more come from Nigeria and Ethiopia, Ghana and Kenya and bring very distinctive sub-Saharan cultures with them. The communities may share skin color, but often they share little else. They create distinct communities where they settle, as earlier white immigrants from different countries and cultures did. These groups belong to different religious assemblies.

They have different views on cultural values such as education, gender, and family, and they have distinct needs and contributions to bring to the larger American communities they enter. None of this is news. It is everyday life all over the country where, for instance, Ethiopian, Ghanaian, and Senegalese groups have settled in large enough numbers to define themselves in local schools and civic institutions.

The exploding Hispanic population is just as diverse, with at least three major, culturally distinct groups in the United States—Mexicans (18.7 million), Cubans (1.3 million), and Puerto Ricans (3.1 million living on the U.S. mainland). The remaining 14 percent of the Hispanic population includes large numbers of Salvadorans, Colombians, and Dominicans. Asians include thirteen different groups, and Pacific Islanders include six different subgroups (Chinese, Filipino, Vietnamese, Asian Indian, Korean, Japanese, making up 84 percent of the Asian population).[7]

Our religious diversity is increasing as well. Since philanthropy is deeply connected to religious traditions in the United States, a major influx of new religious traditions is significant to the maintenance of our long-standing values. Seventy percent of the U.S. population belonged to a religious denomination in 1998, an increase from 41 percent in the early 1900s. Immigration from Italy and Poland and later from Latin America has increased the ranks of Catholics from 13 percent of the population in 1900 to 23 percent in 1998. Arrivals from Eastern Europe brought the Orthodox population (Greek, Russian, Serbian, and Bulgarian) to 4 million by 1998. The Jewish population more than tripled from 1.5 million in 1900 to 5.5 million in 1998.[8]

Yet, the most remarkable growth occurred among Buddhists and Muslims, with Buddhists increasing their American population tenfold (between 3 and 4 million in the mid-1990s).[9] Muslims, who were too few to count in 1950, increased to more than 6 million by 1998, establishing this group as the fastest-growing religion in the United States at the turn of the twenty-first century.[10] Hindus have increased rapidly as well, numbering over a million people residing in the United States in the late 1990s.[11]

I've spent this much time recounting the statistics of our growing cultural diversity because our shifting cultural identity as Americans has profound repercussions. As we enter the twenty-first century, we live in a world that is, paradoxically, more interconnected and more fragmented than ever before. Even before the attack on the World Trade Center in September 2001, porous international borders, the growth in world trade and investment, unimaginably powerful weapon systems, the awesome power of a single individual with suicide and mass destruction in mind, digitized information zapped around the globe—all these phenomena have made us more vulnerable to one another. Václav Havel, philosopher-playwright and past president of the Czech Republic, has pointed out that, for the first time in history, we have what can be called a world civilization. At the same time, individuals, groups, and nations are reacting to the global trend by emphasizing very specific and, at times, separate cultural identities. In this country, gated communities are one manifestation of the discomfort some Americans feel when confronted by great numbers of new and different members of society. Concentrated in California, Florida, and Texas—three of the states with the largest immigrant populations—the collections of privates homes and estates tucked behind guarded gates have grown rapidly in number over the past twenty years. There are now more than twenty thousand such communities, housing 8 million Americans, and people have various reasons for moving into them. Some want to escape crime, gangs, and drugs, but others simply want a certain kind of life in their immediate community, one they can control. Interestingly, it is working- and middle-class people that give fear of crime as their major reason for moving to gated communities. In *Fortress America,* authors Edward Blakeley and Mary Ann Snyder affirm that there is little emphasis on security in the gated communities in the United States, unlike those in Russia or Venezuela.[12] There has been a growing tendency, however, for the residents to begin making appeals to be relieved of paying taxes for services they do not use in the towns where they reside. In our democracy, this purposeful removal of citizens from the commonweal seems dangerous. Where people do not share cost of trash removal, road maintenance, and security, they may care less and less about fellow citizens and the greater good. The separation that gated communities represent weakens the physical and imaginative sense of common ground in locales.

But we have some strong drivers for commonality and interdependence. Most of our new arrivals have come to improve life for their children and to taste the fruits of upward mobility and the pursuit of happiness, not so different from the reasons earlier Americans came here. Poverty is most pronounced among the most recent immigrants, who tend to be younger and have less education and work experience than those who have been in the United States longer, according to the census. However, the economic status of immigrants who arrived before 1970 more closely resembles that of the native-born U.S. population. This statistic indicates that the majority of the immigrants achieve the economic profile of the native-born population in just one generation. Also, a bit of homework reveals that the religious and cultural traditions of these recent immigrants, as different as they are from Judeo-Christian traditions, also emphasize the common good and generosity, defined as charity but also as economic progress through access to capital.

The people of this country must not make the same mistakes with our new immigrant population that we have made with Native Americans and African Americans. We can no more separate ourselves from one another than we can separate ourselves from the rest of the world.

TOWARD A NEW UNDERSTANDING OF GENEROSITY

As American society and individual American families become ever more heterogeneous, the values of many more cultures will influence the future of generosity in this country, where, since 1630, European Judeo-Christian traditions have dominated. Learning about the ways widely influential global cultures define and practice generosity has the potential to teach Americans new ways to be innovative in their philanthropy and to reach more Americans as we develop human, physical, and intellectual capital in this way. To cope with the inherent tensions of modern democratic life, we must, as Václav Havel says, "reveal and identify that which unites us rather than that which divides us. . . . It is perhaps the only way of awakening or reviving a sense of responsibility that transcends the personal, the kind of responsibility that could avert [threats to humanity] . . . such as the impact of population explosion, environmental degradation, or the deepening gulf between the rich and the poor."[13]

In the United States, the wisdom of philanthropy has provided an underlying social consensus for our highly successful political and economic systems. American traditions of obligation to share and show compassion derive from the tradition of the second great commandment—love thy neighbor as thyself—and from Maimonides' teachings on Tsedakah. Tsedakah is generosity inspired by the dignity of the other person, a child of God. We are instructed to put the other on a par with ourselves. The justice/equality aspirations expressed in our founding documents, the substantial progress we have made over the course of our history toward realizing those aspirations, and our strong history of civil society are all based on the sacred and civic wisdom texts and the traditions they have shaped. If, as I hope, we will rededicate ourselves to higher levels of well-directed generosity, we need to learn our own history and values, as well as those of other cultures.

One way involves learning how all of these religious groups growing in the United States bring with them some tradition of generosity designed to sustain others. The Jewish concept of Tsedakah; the Islamic concept of giving alms, Zakat; the Christian parable of the Good Samaritan; the Buddhist story of Vessantara; the Hindu concept of *ahimsa* or sharing good fortune—each conveys the links between justice and prosperity. Islam encourages sharing financial resources to achieve a stronger society by linking the spiritual improvement of the rich with the material improvement of the poor. Hinduism resembles Aristotle's teachings on generosity, the Vedic hymns of Hinduism citing the changing nature of fortune and the importance of charity as a way to create security for the future. The Vedic hymns, indeed the whole complex ritual of the Vedic period, state simply that giving ensures prosperity. In Buddhism, compassion, generosity, and living in the spirit of interdependence draw believers to behaviors that renounce social injustice and all notions of inequality among people. In fact, as told in the story of Prince Vessantara, generosity is the last of the virtues to be polished before reaching nirvana. In Confucianism, generosity is not an action that human beings commit; it is who we are, the generic word for man also actually being the same word for benevolence. And since it focuses on reciprocal nurturing, generosity sustains the workings of society and assures the advanced cultivation of individual human beings. Similar wisdom is carried in Native American folktales and West African stories about the Yoruban god, Ogun.

The new cultures converging in the United States bring with them some practical economic support and development structures that communities of non-European immigrants have evolved over hundreds of years and, in some cases, have adapted to work with capitalism. Many are grounded in philanthropy that is characterized as partnerships, matching gifts, or even no-interest loans rather than outright gifts. These structures tend to widen responsibilities for the economic well-being of financially diverse community members without imposing taxes, penalties, and bureaucracies. Many of these structures are called "ROSCAs," "rotating savings and credit associations." They include the *kye* in Korea, the *hui* in Taiwan, *chit* funds in India, and the *tontines* in Senegal and Cameroon, and they use spiritual values to create financial security and economic opportunities for people in local settings.

The Korean *kye* is a form of ROSCA used to purchase things that cannot be owned jointly and that cost more than a single person can purchase at one time. Suppose that ten people want to start businesses that will cost $50,000 each to initiate. Each one can save only $5,000 per year. They form a *kye,* and the members each give $5,000 each year for ten years. Each year the group produces $50,000 for one of the members, starting that member in business. The funds are put to full investment use immediately. Three economics researchers, Tim Beasley, Stephen Coate, and Glenn Lowry, present the characteristics that make *kye*s successful.[14] They found that it is necessary that individuals keep their commitment to pay into the *kye* after they have met their own needs. This may appear problematic since *kye* members are often not able to borrow in conventional credit markets precisely because they lack a credit history, have weak financial profiles, and cannot be presumed to repay such loans. ROSCAs in general circumvent such default problems by exploiting individuals' social connectedness. This is borne out in the anthropological literature, which reveals how the incentive to defect from a ROSCA is curbed by social constraints. ROSCAs are thus typically formed among individuals whose circumstances and characteristics are well known to one another.[15] Defaulters are shunned, experiencing social exile as well as being prevented from any further ROSCA participation. This lending system, unlike commercial lending, does not depend on documents but on personal characteristics, on relationships, and on family ties. These ties enable the system to substitute interpersonal relationships for the credit histories and documentation that regular commercial banks employ in order to improve the chances of loan repayment and to control inappropriately high levels of loans to high-risk borrowers.

These funding groups date back many hundreds of years and support the accumulation of capital in settings where the lack of credit history, collateral, or banking relationships would normally hamper new arrivals into the community. In the early stages of the ROSCAs, the new members typically work for the more senior members, and the new members can show their work habits and have a chance to gain the confidence of community members based on their dependability and likely acceptability as financial and business partners.

While not precisely gift giving as we know it, ROSCAs belong as part of our discussion of how the new diversity can help us advance the American dream, because individual citizens will be needed to create a strong financial base for the ROSCAs. This base will make it more likely that banks and credit unions will participate. As businesses show profits, children complete college, and homes are bought with the benefit of ROSCAs and the private partnerships that secure them, society may begin to see some improvement in social health, some drop in dependency on government subsidies, and some healthier life outcomes.

The *tontine,* used in Cameroon and Senegal, is very like the *kye.* In West Cameroon, experiments are under way to combine the traditional advantages of the *tontines* with more significant commitment to the advantages of modern banking. Researchers are tracking the work of the Caisse Populaire de Banéghang, a savings and loan cooperative in the West Cameroon village of Bansoa. Since 1999, this bank has been developing a new type of loan system that links the traditional interpersonal relationship-based *tontine* with the classic loan structure of a semiformal finance institution. The bank intends to blend the advantages of the proven *tontine* system—flexibility, solidarity, self-responsibility, and group drive—with the modern terms of the more formalized bank loan cooperative, the most significant features of which are its capacity to offer longer terms of loans and at more favorable rates.[16]

These structures combine traditional generosity with banking and investment structures designed to make capital available to those who need it, grow economic strength in the community for the greater good, and, through dependable repayments, assure a functioning structure for the future. Americans could learn a lot from such experiments applied in our own needy areas, where credit risks have typically made access to capital impossible. In local communities in much of the nation, low-income and recently arrived working-class people still do not have opportunities to become independent, with no access to capital through the usual paths at banks and credit unions.

Islamic sacred texts advocate an economic system whose ultimate objective is the maximization of social benefits by creating healthier financial institutions that serve the advancement of the masses. Islamic law (Shariah) outlines certain conditions that must be met for contracts to be legitimate. One of the essential conditions is the rejection of interest, which Mohammed classifies as usury. Islam allows profit and loss to be negotiated so that the greater investment or higher productivity or additional services of one party can be appropriately and fairly compensated for. The Shariah does not ban fees for services rendered, for instance, by banks. The Islamic system is equity-based, not debt-based. The kind of lending and profit sharing taught by Islamic law is actually a partnership much like that Maimonides would have advocated.

This approach was taught in a two-day seminar at the Agriculture University in Peshawar, Pakistan, in November 2000. For years there had been tensions between the clergy and development workers. Development workers had begun to see that a major proportion of the poor would rather remain so than break Islamic law. The seminar's focus was on how to incorporate the theories and practical implementation of Shariah into finance and business. Specialists from business, banking, and finance met with leaders of nongovernmental organizations (NGOs), academics, journalists, and students, as well as members of the clergy. They all worked together to create practical programs that, while following Islamic law, were also in financial forms that could be realistically implemented. During the workshop, eminent speakers from the International Institute of Islamic Economics and Al-Baraka Bank explained Islamic lending concepts and shared their experiences. The participants applied these concepts and principles to real-life situations. As a result, lending models for livestock, agricultural inputs and trading, shop keeping and machinery loans were developed.[17]

As Americans learn about these structures, we can examine how their features help people to grow economic and social strength in small communities. We can consider what pitfalls American communities would find if they adapted them. Some blended structures are already being scaled up. One example is Grameen banking, known as micro-lending, which now shapes the way some 40 percent of USAID funds are distributed. Mohammed Yunis developed this model. It is a kind of micro-financing, from an amalgamation of Bangladeshi and American structures for generosity, trust building, and economic development. The Grameen model has assisted millions of poor people in developing countries. It is being studied for clear suggestions for export to other settings. In a recent article David Gibbons remarks in summary:

> International replication and adaptation of Grameen Banking has been a process of identifying, through analysis and practice, the "essential grameen," that is, the interrelated set of activities and procedures that are necessary for its successful implementation in

> any context. At the most general level, these have been found to be three: 1) cost-effective identification of the poor, exclusive focus on them and priority for the poorest women; 2) delivery of financial services to them by trained field staff in such a way as to facilitate their successful participation and timely repayment of their loans; and 3) quickest possible attainment of institutional efficiency and financial self-sufficiency, that is consistent with the overriding goal of poverty-reduction.[18]

However, the idea of self-sufficiency of the poor can be threatening to those whose lives are devoted to attending to the needs of the poor. Grameen strategies are uniquely successful because they aim to liberate the poor from the people and organizations that have helped them but have also inadvertently held them in place as poor people.

All the ROSCAs share this characteristic of the Grameen Bank. They work because they are based on mutual trust, the solidarity developed through long-term relationships, and a commitment to reduce poverty and dependence. Their disadvantage resides in their relatively short-term loan-repayment timing, making them less useful for larger capital projects that demand larger sums over longer periods of time.

Americans have a powerful history of generosity, but we also have a lot to learn. Our new and broader cultural diversity can be, with the new financial wealth, our greatest asset. If we learn to adapt and adopt new ways and we also communicate our ways to the newcomers, this respectful integration could go a long way toward moving us to more productive ways of making generosity fulfill its prosperity-building role. If we let the cultural diversity in our midst nudge us into more isolated subunits, it could also hasten the development of ethnic tensions and the "clash of civilizations" right here in America, which Sam Huntington forecast in his book of that name.[19] I do not expect that outcome. These relatively new economic approaches to releasing the poor from their conditions may well rival the social service approaches that have for so long held a primary place in U.S. public policy.

We are experts at assimilation, perhaps with struggle, but we get there. Willingness to learn from other cultures has always characterized U.S. society. If history is an example, the wish to assimilate will certainly guide some new arrivals to model aspects of their lives on what they see long-standing Americans doing. In areas of family life such as food, child rearing, and family and gender relations, a blend of cultures is more likely. In areas such as community generosity, we can only speculate. In our diversity, we will surely need a set of shared ideals for the future. Personal generosity, clearly a part of a global wisdom tradition, offers such a possibility.

BEGINNING THE PROCESS

Our common task should be to strengthen the culture we share. To do that we all need to understand the role of philanthropy and to explore a wider range of ways to make it work in the emerging cultural mix. How can generosity be utilized and expanded to fit our changing demographics? If the mainstream culture wants to assure that new arrivals take generosity by individual citizens as seriously as those here for generations, what can we do? We certainly can learn about the cultures of generosity of the newly arrived and connect some of our approaches to some of theirs. We can use culturally appropriate ways to ask the new arrivals to teach us how they sustain needs and build opportunities for others in their homelands. We can prepare to incorporate these new ideas into the culture of giving locally, with banks and credit unions cooperating. Eastern religions that focus on self-enlightenment can help to highlight the benefits to personal happiness and inspiration that result from great generosity. Other elements of Eastern religious values focus on the embrace of the other and all civilization through the gift to any single person. This orientation may also liberate some Americans to new thinking for new levels of generosity.

These new citizens are new wealth, new human capital, often with new and better ways to address problems. In the not-so-distant future, we will have access to even more stunning sums of money, while still attempting to balance the assets and liabilities of the capital market system and the pressures it places on democratic principles. The abundance of diversity, newly and rapidly arriving, assures a rich and enriching basis for new developments in our economy, but only if the environment that sustained a highly competitive market economy remains softened by the imaginative, entrepreneurial energy of citizen generosity binding our future success together.

9

DANGEROUS DONATIONS

Instead of exhorting you to augment your charity, I will rather utter an exhortation that you may not abuse your charity by misapplying it.

COTTON MATHER, 1698

Women know the true damnation of charity because the habit of civilization has always been to throw them cheap alms rather than give them good wages.

REBECCA WEST, 1912

In the garden of good and evil, nothing, not even generosity, is one-sided. Over and over again, generosity has provided the resources for the virtuous cycle of upward mobility, the pursuit of happiness, and society-wide growth. But it is difficult to give well. So, now that we have seen some excellent examples of beneficial generosity, let's be clear on the pitfalls.

I've said I don't really care what motivations people have for philanthropy, so long as they accomplish good things, and that's true. However, the wrong motivations can make good accomplishments difficult or impossible. They can affect the decisions made by the donor, the administration of funds, and the feelings of those being helped. As you take up this chapter and its ideas, remember that giving is full of economic and social power. It can transform the giver and the recipient, or it can create new problems in society. Philanthropy serves our economy best when it strengthens democracy and equality, rather than indulges individual egos. Donations can be dangerous, but perhaps we can learn from the mistakes of the past—and avoid creating twenty-first-century versions of them.[1]

GENEROSITY POISONED BY EGO

Major industrialists such as George Pullman made very dangerous donations for the most common reason that donations prove dangerous—the pride and self-absorption of the giver. Pullman's gifts to his own workers felt paternalistic and dictatorial to the recipients. He had little connection to the needs they expressed. He gave them what he knew was good for them, confident they would eventually see his wisdom.

In 1864, Pullman, with a friend, designed and built a train car for sleeping and two years later decked out a dining car. He began the Pullman Palace Car Company. His entrepreneurial spirit saw an important opportunity to offer one of his sleeping cars to carry the fallen Abraham Lincoln back to Washington. So many saw this sad and magnificent procession that, overnight, the market for his cars surged. By 1880, he had designed and built a small town near Chicago called Pullman, just for his employees to have a good place to live and raise their families. It was a planned community with theaters, a library, and a hotel. Pullman decided what would be included, and Pullman provided it. His employees had no say in the environment that was being provided for them. To Pullman's surprise, their gratitude was greatly tempered with resentment.

In 1894, Pullman cut wages 25 percent without also cutting rents and other costs. He then fired the workers who had come as a delegation to discuss their concerns with him. The strike and riot that followed demonstrated the absence of trust and mutual respect inherent in Pullman's "generosity." Pullman may have meant well, but he gave what he believed was good for the recipients, ignoring their requests and suggestions. Jane Addams said it succinctly: "In so far as philanthropists are 'good to people' rather than 'with them' they are bound to accomplish a large amount of harm."[2]

GENEROSITY CRIPPLED BY RACIAL IGNORANCE

Some dangerous donations have funded activities that break the law or undermine the values of the Constitution. These are clearly dangerous and frequently done secretly to hide their origins. Neo-Nazi causes and the Ku Klux Klan jump to mind, but we also have the sad example of well-intentioned contributions by northern philanthropists in the post–Civil War era. The cause was education of formerly enslaved people. The contributions worked well when northern philanthropists and black leaders remained in charge. Gradually, and very naively, however, the wealthy, well-meaning northerners ceded more and more power on the Southern Education Board to white southern leadership. That leadership turned out, unsurprisingly, to be white supremacist, with a very different idea about what the future should look like for black Americans. Their focus was the balance of power between the races, not the hand up that the board had initially intended.

Another example of the toxic effect of ignorance and racism was a two-page segment of the landmark Flexner Report suggesting that funds be withdrawn from black medical schools. Abraham Flexner was a former high school principal whose brother, a physician, recommended him to the Carnegie Foundation as the right person to do an investigation of American medical education. The foundation sent him out to visit and evaluate medical schools around the country. He began in January 1909 and finished in April 1910. Considering the state of travel in the country at that time, one can imagine the degree of thoroughness he was able to achieve in his review of each school. At one point, he visited sixty-nine schools in ninety days. Seldom did he have more than a day at any school. He had never been inside a medical school before. He knew nothing about medicine or any of its attendant sciences. And yet, he was an intelligent man with good intentions. He was also caustic and was criticized for writing his report with "pure, unadulterated cussedness, raw malice, and percolated venom."[3] But the major problem was that he was culture-bound. He was part of a culture in which elitism was accepted and valued. Worse, that culture did not value people of color.

An official of the American Medical Association (AMA), which had very strong opinions about what constituted good medicine and a good physician, accompanied Flexner. At the time, of course, the AMA was an all-white organization. In the words of historian Darlene Clark Hine, "The AMA was specifically concerned with the proliferation of medical schools, the over-production of physicians, and the absence of coherent regulatory and accreditation legislation. If the overall status of the profession was to be elevated, and medical education and care improved, white medical leaders determined that the profession needed to reduce the numbers of schools and limit access to the profession to elite, or middle-class, college educated, white males."[4] Flexner also received considerable input from the Carnegie Foundation itself and Rockefeller's General Education Board, both of whom had similar definitions of professionalism at the time.

In the report's ninth chapter, which was all of two pages long, Flexner reported on the seven black medical schools that existed at the time. There were more than 8 million African Americans in this country in 1910 and their treatment was, to say the least, not a priority for white physicians. And yet Flexner recommended that five of the seven schools where black physicians could be trained be closed. He did not suggest that more money might be given in order to enable these or other schools to meet higher standards. He made no reference to the possibility that black students should be allowed into white medical schools but suggested that any money donors wished to give to the education of black doctors be given to the remaining two schools, Howard University College of Medicine and Meharry Medical College. This almost certainly seemed to him to be a very reasonable solution to the problem. There is no doubt that the five smaller schools, like most small medical schools at the time, were inadequate to the task they had set themselves, but Flexner also asserted that they were sending out undisciplined men. He had too little information to come to these conclusions. He did not interview or investigate the physicians who graduated from these schools and went on to practice in black communities around the country. As we know, he probably spent no more than a day at the school itself. Flexner's report, whatever else it may have done for American medicine, hugely limited the number of African American doctors in this country for generations to come. With the laudable intention of improving American medicine—and some significant success in doing so—the foundation that funded Flexner was guilty of making a donation that proved extremely dangerous for black Americans.

Racial ignorance raises its head again in the story of some well-intentioned people who failed the "expectations" test. They were supporters of a local woman of color whose dream was to develop and head an after-school program for low-income children in her neighborhood. These good people agreed to serve on the board of the learning center and to make significant cash contributions to provide books and snacks. They worked to connect the facility to local college student volunteers. These young people helped the children with their homework and with the practice they needed on their reading and writing skills. An elderly woman donated a house to the Center, but no funds for upkeep, and the finances were never adequate to repair the facility properly. More important, no one supervised the college students to assure they were properly trained to help the children. No assessment of the impact of the program on the children's skills was ever undertaken. The children kept coming, and the director and board felt the need was urgent to continue supporting their project. They did not press too hard for what they began to call "unrealistic standards."[5]

Gradually, public school officials began to question the quality of the program. The program's director felt insulted by the negative review and thought that perhaps it was motivated by racial prejudice. She reiterated that her board and her financial backers had never questioned the quality of her program.

Of course, she and the school officials were both right. The board was wrong. They had not held the director to the same standards of quality and evaluation as their other nonprofit efforts, especially not those led by whites. The truth is they did not believe the director had the capacity to meet the same standards as others in the community. These well-meaning people were funding the director from a base of prejudice—low expectations. They communicated their value judgment to the director, who then rejected honest, professional assessments from others. Moral of the story: Honesty is crucial to generosity.

GENEROSITY THAT ISN'T

Sometimes self-interest comes disguised as generosity. For example, some colleges have begun to make dangerous donations, using their scholarship funds—important engines of upward mobility—to fill beds and attract full-pay families. In the last ten years, many colleges have given "merit" scholarships to children of well-to-do families. These students are not any stronger academically than others in their class, but colleges are able to obtain financial data that predicts the receptivity of these families to a monetary inducement in making their decision about the college the student will attend.

Private colleges and universities are doing these merit scholarships to attract families who can pay the rest of the tuition as well as contribute to the school's "annual fund" and perhaps make a larger contribution to celebrate their child's graduation. A $25,000 full scholarship intended for one needy student goes much farther if it is divided into five $5,000 merit awards to well-to-do students. Five beds are filled, families each pay the balance of $20,000, and additional donations are gravy. Good business thinking—for the short term—and bad news for expanding upward mobility. This is a distortion of the way generosity used to work. Current leaders in academe need to recall our historic commitments to educating low-income citizens.

Contributors of support to college professorships occasionally insist on determining who will fill the "chair" they have funded and even the curriculum that will be taught. A major giver to a well-known art museum wished to curate a show funded by her gift. The donor had no expertise as a curator, although she was a fine connoisseur. One is tempted to ask whether she would have wished to perform in the operating room had her gift been to a hospital. Generosity, in short, must not disguise efforts to buy inappropriate influence.

In these examples, generosity is meant to achieve a goal other than the direct aim of the gift. These donations are dangerous because they increase cynicism among observers and pollute the idea of philanthropy. Philip Morris received unwanted attention for just this kind of gift to the people in Kosovo who were facing starvation after the war in Yugoslavia. The headline in the *Wall Street Journal* said it all: "Philip Morris's Ad on Macaroni and Peace—Kosovo Tale Narrows Gap Between Philanthropy, Publicity."[6]

The ad rather transparently sought to rehabilitate the company's badly sullied image after the tobacco trials. The details were a true embarrassment: the company ended up spending more to stage the ad than to feed the Kosovars. The sixty-second ad was shot in the Czech Republic with an actress flown in from Atlanta to perform on a "war-torn" set, what the *Journal* called "one of the most lavish re-creations ever attempted for a TV commercial." It featured a perky passenger named Molly energetically deplaning as she explains that she is from Philip Morris. The cargo doors fly open, revealing crates marked "Kraft" inside. The food delivered was valued at $125,000. The epic ad cost well over a million dollars. Bad enough for the thousands of Kosovars, who could have been fed by the million dollars in production expenditures, but worse for generosity itself. Generosity can thrive only in an environment where candor breathes free.

DELAYED DONATIONS

Timing can also be an important issue in philanthropy, just as it is for families that try to balance their budgets from week to week and month to month. When a need or an opportunity exists this week, money that comes in next week can be useless or greatly reduced in value. In a small city in the Midwest with many low-income families, a group of citizens created a non-profit to deal with urban problems. They approached an individual for funds to buy and renovate a set of houses available at very good prices. A local corporation in the midst of a major building project was willing to join the partnership and engage their own construction company to offer some pro bono work on the house renovations. All parties agreed.

However, the donor's family began to raise questions about how exactly their donation would be used. Deliberations and negotiations went on for fourteen months and finally concluded happily with the gift made. Unfortunately, the corporation's building was approaching completion, and the workers and equipment needed for the collaboration had moved on. The lack of focus and fear of risk taking by the donor's family scuttled a fine partnership that could have created a dozen renovated residences for low-income families. Timing, as they say, is everything.

GENEROSITY MITIGATED BY LOVE

Perhaps the saddest of the dangerous donations in this chapter are the ones parents of wealth make to their children. The story is instructive for parents at all income levels. Most parents want to be generous to their children, whatever their income level. For wealthy parents, great generosity becomes a dangerous donation. This is not a new phenomenon. Horace Mann, born as the nineteenth century began, thought it was a terrible idea for the wealthy to share too much of their fortune with their children. The result, he said, would drain "the muscles out of the limbs, the brain out of the head, and virtue out of the heart." Many of his contemporaries agreed. Many current advisers to wealthy families, psychologists, and yes, college presidents agree, too, but it is not easy to challenge people with the news that indulging children adds to their problems growing up. After all, Horace Mann no longer needs to collect fees or secure annual and capital gifts from the very parents his words address.

Many children of overindulgence have traveled extensively, had school vacations extended to suit their families' plans, seen their parents intervene forcefully on their side when their poor self-discipline caused problems at school. They have often received extensive coaching to assure success at whatever they undertook. They have had the best clothing and equipment for anything they decided to do. Typically, they have not slogged through a boring, or physically demanding, low-paying summer job—not a job lifeguarding and working on a tan at the club, but a really demanding job like waiting tables in a luncheonette or working on a construction crew. They have had their time and talents optimized and have gained a feeling of entitlement. With all due respect to the good intentions of the parents, this approach creates children of *wealthfare*, whose social profile resembles the children of welfare.[7] Both groups often exhibit low ambition and low expectations that what they will do in life will matter. They have less focus and less sense of purpose than the offspring of parents who are not poor but cannot take money for granted. When some parents have nothing extra to share with children and others can give a child almost anything the child wants—both represent extremes—the result is the same: the undermining of the child's belief that his or her personal effort will make things different. Psychologists call it "anomie."

Welfare parents have few options, but the wealthy ones do. Instead of making dangerous donations to their children, they can take the funds they would have shared with their children and put them in an account that they and their children distribute after careful consideration. Families with foundations are beginning to take this kind of work very seriously, teaching philanthropy to their children in the course of their development. But even families that give only modest gifts, perhaps just their annual contribution to United Way, can make the decisions with their children. They can also make sure that the sum represents some sacrifice, some effort by the children, perhaps by earning part of the gift or by delaying some personal want and putting additional dollars into the gift.

CONCLUSION

These stories show that donations become dangerous when they encourage dependence or entitlement, when they engender deep bitterness, or when the donor's courage or good judgment fails and politics and ideology are permitted to transform the gift into an embarrassment or a burden. Some donations are destructive because of the causes they fund, campaigns against the very democracy and equality that we need to balance capitalism.

Bad timing and a low tolerance of risk in the giver can rob the gift of its power. If individuals have taken too long to decide, the moment passes when the gift can do its work. If donors are not willing enough to shoulder risk with their gifts, they fund too little, too late. Other funding is, if not dangerous, then foolhardy, including gifts for frivolous hobbies when poverty is especially severe and also especially poorly funded. In other cases, gifts that come with strings that bind a recipient create donations that do more harm than good.

Are there lessons to be learned? Absolutely. Among them: Generosity is a complicated business.

10

WORKING SOLUTIONS

What I gave, I have; what I spent, I had; what I kept, I lost.

—OLD EPITAPH

We know what the challenge is. Because of the wealth transfer and the danger of losing our delicate balance between capitalism and democracy, we need to try to ensure that generosity will continue and grow. The way I see it, that involves four important undertakings. First, we need to involve and inspire givers, not just in our generation but in the generations to follow us. Second, we need to make meaningful partnerships between the wealthy and others in our local communities. Third, we need to expand generosity into targeted investment rather than charity. Finally, we need to increase our personal and institutional giving.

Fortunately, there are models for success in all four of these undertakings. America is already benefiting from new institutions and ideas that are using generosity in new ways to fix what is broken. These need to be scaled up and scaled out.

REACHING YOUNG PEOPLE

Because the second half of *The Greater Good* is focused on the future, we do well to begin this chapter with young people. Their views and commitments will heavily influence the future. If this next generation is to engage in fixing what is not functioning well in our society, they will need firsthand knowledge. One way to involve young people is by showing them close up some of the problems and possible solutions. That has already begun.

Service Learning

There has been a remarkable increase, over the last ten years, in the number of hours that students in America's schools and colleges spend in volunteer community service. Millions of young people now see poverty, human dislocation, and dysfunction firsthand week after week in broken urban schools, in shelters, and in housing projects. They are exploring what these systems need to work better. Special courses in all fields now combine regular class work with reading and writing assignments and weekly volunteer-service hours.

Service learning courses are a very sound, and not entirely new, educational method. As early as 1938, John Dewey outlined the basic principles. First, students learn from observing their own environment better than from simply listening to facts and theories in a classroom. Second, when students address themselves to the welfare of others, they expand their horizons and learn responsibility for their fellows. Those remain the guiding concepts of service learning today. Sixteen years ago a project called Campus Compact began. It currently involves more than 750 of the nation's three thousand colleges and universities, including community colleges and historically black colleges. The presidents of these schools are convinced that community service is a vital part of education in a democracy. The institutions typically organize large community service programs and teach a significant number of service-learning courses across the academic disciplines. Currently 28 percent of the students in member institutions are involved in service projects.

The services these students provide often have an immediate economic impact. Economist Kim Marie McGoldrick described a service-learning project in the Department of Economics at the University of Richmond in 1998. As part of the Women and Gender Issues in Economics course, students volunteered time at a temporary shelter for homeless women and their children. "Students participated in a number of activities during their 15 volunteer hours," said McGoldrick, "but spent most of their time identifying resources, such as employment and educational opportunities and long-term child care, for particular shelter occupants. Whereas some of these activities did not have a direct impact on the economic status of women being serviced by these agencies, the cumulative services offered by the Emergency Shelter have a significant economic impact."[1] While they were learning, the students were investing time in human capital.

In addition, students are making connections to the world outside the institution as future problem solvers. College graduates are generally the ones who end up running corporations, filling public office, and teaching the next generations. They need to know firsthand about the lives they will be influencing. But students are also forming their own ideas during their years in college. If we want the very best possible intellectual capital, students must be connected to the raw material of social and economic creativity during their formative years.

These students are also crossing boundaries. Service learning is at the opposite end of the spectrum from gated communities when it comes to dealing with diversity. And finally, they are learning about the efficacy of generosity. They are seeing what can and cannot be accomplished by this third contributor to our economy. They are seeing what works and what doesn't.

A nationally funded project called Americorps now offers thousands of young people a chance to volunteer in disadvantaged settings as a kind of domestic Peace Corps. Americorps offers a small stipend and support for the volunteer's subsequent college education. Other projects, like Teach for America, offer a transition from pure volunteerism at school or college to the world of work, but at salaries far below what these young people could achieve in the market. This is not a trivial change for the lives of the current college-age generation. One result I have seen already is that many more students are asking harder questions of their faculty and administrators and of politicians and policy makers. They want to know why, for instance, we are not making the improvements in these disadvantaged settings that we seem to make in our own environments. We have not yet seen the full impact of the experiences that this younger generation has had as volunteers because this phonomenon is only a decade old. Fostering this service generosity among the young will likely encourage greater philanthropy from these individuals as they join the workforce and their local communities.

Family Foundations

Family foundations offer great advantages to a wealthy family intending to draw its members together in a common enterprise. Foundation work may even provide an excellent second career for senior family members. Family foundations certainly provide important exposure for younger family members while participating in the deliberations of the foundation. As they learn to deploy the family's wealth to advance the well-being of other people, they become more directly knowledgeable about the lives of others and see their own lives in a broader context. These experiences can instill a sense of the responsibilities that accompany an inheritance. Through their involvement in the foundation's governance and the investment of the foundation's endowment, they learn how to manage wealth, how to manage and hire people who will help them in this work, and how to exercise leadership skills.

Family foundations are tax-exempt trusts or corporations holding funds contributed by a single donor or family. These trusts are often controlled by family members and make charitable donations. Family foundations have gained in popularity because they allow the entire family to be involved in philanthropy while also providing significant tax benefits. Some two-thirds of all larger family foundations have been formed in the past twenty years.

In 1998, the Foundation Center counted more than eighteen

thousand family foundations. They are a subset of independent foundations, and although individually most are small, they represent two out of five U.S. foundations. Taken together, they gave a larger portion of all foundation donations than corporate, community, or operating foundations combined. In fact, almost half of all foundation giving came from family foundations. Two-thirds of all family foundations distributed less than $100,000 in the latest year, while the top 1 percent—characterized as the family foundations distributing over $5 million—gave half of all the family foundation grant dollars distributed. Understandably, the bulk of this giving remained in the local or regional area where the money was made. Only one in thirteen family foundations offered grants on a national or international scale. All tended to fund arts and culture, the environment, science, and religion. They did not fund health care as extensively as independent foundations, although they funded education more frequently.[2]

Family foundations may incur costs, including part-time and full-time employees, that are necessary to operate the trust. These employees can be family members. Foundation employees are entitled to reasonable compensation for services performed for the foundation and may be required to attend periodic foundation meetings.[3] Professional advisers are sometimes engaged by foundations to provide guidance on these, as well as financial, issues. The foundation is less likely to succeed if the members, especially the leaders, neglect to allow for a diversity of opinions and interests. The family members need to feel respected for their individuality.

One of the major challenges in family foundations is remaining committed to the goals of the founder while engaging the changing needs of the community. One sterling success is the James Ford Bell Foundation. Its founder became president of General Mills in 1932 and served with the company until 1947. He established his family foundation in 1955. His interests were the Minnesota historical society, the University of Minnesota (in particular its museum of natural history and its library), the arts, and rare books, among others. Under the able leadership of his son, Dr. Ford Bell, and the foundation's director, Diane Neimann, the foundation not only continues to support the founder's interests, but also supports neighborhood development. The Central Neighborhood Improvement Association and the Summit Academy OIC/Southside Neighborhood Housing Initiative are numbered among its many engagements with the needs of inner-city communities. The foundation advances many local leaders of color into the ranks of Minneapolis city leadership, increasing the diversity of that group.

Some family foundations begin in great wealth, but not all. The Helen Bader Foundation, named for a quiet philanthropic woman from Milwaukee, has had a profound effect on the city she loved. With her husband she started and ran a chemical company from the 1950s to the 1970s. After her divorce she pursued a master's degree in social work at the University of Wisconsin in Milwaukee. The school is now named in her honor. She worked on Legal Aid and on better treatment for Alzheimer's patients. This foundation supports Bader's interests and also works on the housing projects and economic development of inner-city neighborhoods in Milwaukee. Like Bader, the foundation tries to inspire more generosity from other givers.

These stories are typical of many family foundations whose commitments to their towns create an ongoing source of asset building in people, facilities, and new ideas. More family foundations would make America even stronger.

MAKING MEANINGFUL PARTNERSHIPS

Robert Putnam may be right that more of us are "bowling alone" and fewer of us are going to Elks and Lions Club meetings, but some of us are organizing our charitable efforts and getting personally involved with the recipients of our giving. This is one of the best ways to avoid the pitfalls of dangerous donations. It also enriches the lives of the donors while they invest in the human, intellectual, and physical capital of their communities.

Community Foundations

Community foundations, first developed by Frederick Goff of Cleveland, Ohio, in 1914, appealed to attorneys and community leaders and caught on quickly all over the country. They are as simple as most truly brilliant ideas are. In essence, individuals and corporations within a community give money into one fund. Out of that, money is expended to improve the life of the community. A knowledgeable staff is employed to administer the money and to advise donor members about its uses.

After the 1969 Tax Reform Act, community foundations expanded their numbers rapidly, in part because they could offer tax advantages that were not extended to private foundations. The tax law changes worked positively in the field because they benefited charitable giving at all economic levels, allowing many people to become philanthropists who had never expected to qualify for the title. More than three hundred community foundations were founded between 1975 and 1985 alone. Over the past thirty years, community foundations have increased their rate of giving faster than either individuals or corporate foundations. They typically invest funds in scholarships, housing, community leadership, and job training.

For the past twenty years, many large funders—the Ford, the Mott, the Wallace–Readers Digest Funds, the James Irvine, the W. K. Kellogg, the John S. and James L. Knight, the Kresge, and the David and Lucile Packard foundations; the Lilly and California endowments; and others—have given millions of dollars to spur the establishment and growth of community foundations. But the unique character of the community foundation is its local nature, its focus on local people and local issues, and its funding by former and current members of that same community. Indeed, the boards of these foundations comprise local citizens, offering an important opportunity for leadership and engagement in improving the quality of life, particularly economic well-being, in their local communities.

A November 2000 survey of 582 U.S. community foundations reported that their combined assets were $29.9 billion in 1999, up $4.6 billion from the year before. The study, conducted by the Columbus Foundation, showed that sixty-one community foundations reported more than $100 million in assets, compared with twelve in 1988.[4] They made grants exceeding $1.9 billion in 1999, an increase of 26 percent from 1998. The grants went to everything from day-care centers to symphony orchestras. They funded community gardens and shelters for abused women. They improved life in 582 communities.

Community foundations offer donors, many of whom have modest assets, a way to contribute to their communities and also to maximize tax benefits to their estates. Donors can set up donor-advised funds and take a 50 percent deduction, instead of the 30 percent of adjusted gross income permitted donors to private foundations. In addition to having this extra 20 percent to put to work for philanthropy, those who contribute to community foundations are spared all the accounting, reporting, and bookkeeping of managing their own foundations. They may remain anonymous and the foundation will manage distributions or it will name and involve donors as they prefer. Moreover, those who set up funds in their community foundation know and love their communities and have often been active contributors. They get great satisfaction out of establishing significant ways to direct their wealth to assure that these communities will be benefited by them during their lives and after their deaths.

Those with community foundations should make sure they are connected not just to the wealthiest part of the community, but also to neighboring towns where more low-income people may be able to benefit as part of the community and also to donate to the effort.[5] Rosenwald taught an important lesson by his commitment to invest where local and lower-income people made contributions and also helped decide where the funds should go.

Since their fastest period of growth has been relatively recent, I include the community foundations here to encourage any community without one to consider developing one.

Community Development Corporations

Community development corporations (CDCs) are local nonprofit organizations that work toward the economic, physical, and social revitalization of local communities. They often include partnerships with for-profit companies and with state governments. They typically seek to bring in new businesses and industries to create jobs and enhance the tax base. Projects may include affordable single-family housing and renovation of existing housing that increases both home ownership and the tax base.

Some CDCs are led by religious organizations, others by colleges, and still others by citizen groups. There are currently more than thirty-six hundred CDCs nationwide. Fifty-two percent of these are in urban centers, while 26 percent serve rural areas. More than one hundred thousand Americans are involved in working with CDCs as volunteers and as paid professionals. CDCs work with banks and with community development financial institutions (CDFI) to fund their efforts.[6] They represent a vivid example of citizen generosity toward their own local communities in the ideas, funding, and time that people give to make improvements.

The CDCs apply for federal funds for improved housing and home ownership, for small-business development, for job training, and other needs for which the government may have funding opportunities. State and federal government agencies are not set up to enter a town with problems and establish new directions. In our democracy, the government staff at these levels must usually await applications by towns for available funds. Unfortunately, many poor communities lack leadership and sufficient experience and resources on their city staffs or among volunteer mayors and councilmen even to apply for these funds, so without outside help, they do not get the financial support they desperately need to improve their circumstances. Local CDCs often attract funds from local community foundations as well. Despite many frustrations it is possible to make substantial change in local settings, as I discovered in leading the CDC my colleagues and I put together in New London, Connecticut.

CDCs can be started by any person or group. For a very compelling story, let me introduce the Reverend Johnny Ray Youngblood, pastor of St. Paul's Community Baptist Church, in East Brooklyn, New York, and chair of the East Brooklyn Congregations (EBC). The Reverend Youngblood built this church from a group of a few hundred families to several thousand congregants. They were compelled by his vision that spiritually involved people should address social problems in their community. They gathered worshipers from other churches and decided to pool their resources, their talents, and their anger at local conditions.[7]

This group has succeeded in building twenty-three hundred affordable, single-family, owner-occupied homes as part of their Nehemiah I project. Nehemiah II involves health care, a medical center, and a partnership with the New York City schools to set up two alternative public high schools with small enrollments and an innovative public-service-oriented curriculum.

St. Paul's congregation gives $100,000 of their own money each year to projects that build their community. In fact, more than half of them tithe!

Local Initiative Support Corporation (LISC) is a bridge organization dedicated to helping resident-led community development corporations (CDCs) transform distressed communities and neighborhoods into healthy ones.[8] Like the Enterprise Foundation, LISC acts as an intermediary between the local collaborative group of citizens and major sources of capital at the state or national level. LISC marshals private sector resources for use by CDCs in local settings and extends financial and technical support to CDCs. It enables residents to set their own priorities and shape the process of community renewal. LISC believes that CDCs are the best vehicles for achieving lasting, positive change in predominately low- and moderate-income communities. These groups are accountable to local residents and engage in a wide range of economic and human development activities. By supporting the development of affordable housing and essential commercial, industrial, and community facilities through CDCs, LISC helps citizens change their own communities. Moreover, these redevelopment efforts go well beyond visible improvements: local leadership develops; outside investment increases; and productive alliances form among residents, local government, and the business and philanthropic communities. With support from over twenty-two hundred foundations, corporations, and individuals, LISC has invested nearly $4 billion in low-income communities. That investment has leveraged an additional $7 billion in private and public sector investment, helping CDCs in more than three hundred communities across America build over

110,000 affordable homes and over 14 million square feet of commercial, industrial and community space, and create over forty thousand jobs.[9]

Robert Rubin said recently in a presentation to LISC leaders:

> Persuading political leaders of both parties to substantially increase such support [to economic development through CDCs] will be an immense political challenge. We all will have to do a much better job in persuading the public of its stake in these issues. And we will have to do better demonstrating that there are programs that work—including the LISC model that avoids undue central bureaucracy, and direction, and harnesses the power of private capital and local leadership to further community development in distressed communities.[10]

This CDC movement has been instrumental in redeveloping a large number of distressed communities. It has made use of the normal structures of for-profit development and involved many people who are rarely engaged in creating human capacity in their communities.

CDCs are chartered to develop significant improvements in the tax base of poor cities. This then improves the funding available to poor urban schools, as well as to low-income home-ownership efforts and the like. An example of a productive early public/private partnership, the Office of Economic Opportunity, launched community development corporations to work in both urban and rural poor communities. The successes of many of these early CDCs laid the foundation for today's Community Development Financial Institutions (CDFI).

GENEROUS INVESTMENT

Community Development Financial Institutions

CDFIs are high-social-impact investment vehicles through which investors can put their funds into collectively planned community development, affordable housing, small-business development, and other activities to bring credit and capital to historically underserved communities. The term CDFI is relatively new, really an outgrowth of the War on Poverty in the 1960s and 1970s, but the concept isn't. It is part of a rich history in the United States of self-help credit. Beginning with immigrant guilds of New York City's Lower East Side and the Prairie Populists of the late 1800s, and continuing to African American communities forming the first community development credit unions in the 1930s, local communities have developed ways for local citizens to achieve self-help credit. These entities resemble the *tontines, kye, chit,* and the other credit vehicles used by people of other countries.

Currently more than six hundred CDFIs are functioning throughout the nation. Their mission is to build the capital base of their communities through private-sector financial structures. There are six basic types of CDFIs: community development banks, community development loan funds, community development credit unions, microenterprise funds, community development corporation-based lenders and investors, and community development venture funds. All are locally controlled and market-driven.

While the CDFI concept grew slowly through the 1970s and 1980s, the idea expanded rapidly through the 1990s. The CDFI Fund was created by the federal government in 1994, and bank investments in CDFIs began to qualify as tax-privileged Community Reinvestment Act activity in 1995. These changes attracted more funds to CDFIs and increased their impact on economic development nationwide.

CDFIs have rebuilt businesses, housing, voluntary organizations, and services central to revitalizing our nation's poor and working-class neighborhoods. They often offer nonconforming mortgages or loans and make accounts available to customers with limited or nonexistent credit ratings or histories. They provide education about finance and banking to people who may have little or no experience with this industry. They also accept unconventional collateral, provide equity, and offer management expertise where it is needed to help assure success.

Basically, investors willing to put their money in CDFIs take higher credit risks and support the individuals receiving funds with additional personal and financial support so as to improve the chances that the risk will be successfully mitigated. Their commitment is to enable hardworking entrepreneurs to act successfully in their own economic self-interest. Once successful, people helped by CDFIs can graduate to conventional financial institutions. CDFIs are complex partnerships with individual giving playing only one role. Government, religious organizations, and conventional financial institutions all invest and provide ancillary support to what is, essentially, community development and individual wealth building.

Individual investors, having pooled their money with funds from the other partners, can choose among several financial vehicles to make their investment and can expect a return generally at the same level of reliability as a standard investment. A deposit, for instance, could go to a community development credit union or community development bank; investors might choose to lend money through a nonprofit community development loan fund that relends to businesses, or invest in a for-profit community development venture capital fund.

Community Social Investment Funds

A number of social investment mutual funds have developed over the past decades. Among the very first was the Calvert Social Investment Fund, devoted to the premise that people could do well by investing in activities that "did good." In 1990, Calvert introduced, and shareholders overwhelmingly approved, an innovative program within the fund. The High Social Impact Investments program would invest up to one percent of the fund's dollars in "high social impact" companies. This translated to direct investments in communities that need more access to capital. To date, investments have climbed to approximately $9 million. These investments impact eighty-eight community organizations, including particular social and regional examples of micro-credit programs. Combining philanthropy with capitalism in a hybrid activity, the fund invested in three types of CDFIs: low-income housing funds, community development loan funds, and micro-enterprise loan funds.

The low-income housing funds go to local organizations providing financial support, affordable housing, and innovative social services to disadvantaged families. One such project among the many undertaken is the Housing Assistance Fund, which finances self-help housing programs in economically depressed areas such as the Mississippi Delta and the "maquiladora" region near the Texas-Mexico border. These programs involve families in a partnership with professional builders and other neighbors to build their own homes.

Community development loan funds support organizations that offer skill training and jobs to low-income residents of poor communities. One recipient of these funds has been Self-Help Ventures Fund of Durham, North Carolina. Created in 1984 with $77 raised from a bake sale, Self-Help has since then made over one thousand small loans to local residents and created over four thousand jobs and two thousand new child-care opportunities.

Micro-enterprise loan funds provide capital to people who are trying to start their own businesses and, as we have seen in other similar ventures, take risks and provide advice and expertise so the entrepreneur is more likely to be successful. One example of an organization receiving Calvert funds for micro-enterprise loans is Opportunity International. It provides opportunities for people in chronic poverty to establish viable businesses and transform their lives. Over twenty-five years, Opportunity International has loaned more than $125 million to four hundred thousand of the poorest families in the world and created more than a half million jobs.[11]

ShoreBank: A Lively Example of Hybrid Capitalization at Work

Here is a story of one entity built at the grassroots level and the impact that it has had. Using the CDC and public-private partnerships we have just reviewed, ShoreBank has created wealth-building and community-building assets.

Picture a black urban community of eighty thousand in which crime, drug abuse, and unemployment have reached such levels that landlords are deserting their buildings rather than trying to sell them. Now picture the same neighborhood fifteen years later, with $160 million in new investments, 350 large apartment buildings rehabilitated, and property values rising 5 to 7 percent a year. Hundreds of businesses have started, and thousands of people have received remedial education, job training, and job placement. The community is stable, crime is down, and the crack epidemic hasn't taken root. Yet none of this has been accomplished through gentrification. The community is still 99 percent black. Rents are still fairly low. People on welfare can still afford to move in.[12]

Executives at ShoreBank, a for-profit neighborhood development corporation, accomplished this on the south side of Chicago. How was this change achieved? By refusing to gentrify or do downtown renewal if that meant turning away poor and local people. That is the short answer. What did they rely on? Local businesspeople and current residents rather than developers and government. The bank turned members of the community into entrepreneurs, using their sweat equity and personal commitments. It sought local investors who would create a partnership in a unique structure, committed to the dual purposes of simultaneous development and profitability. The new bank aimed at status as a model, recognized nationally, for economic renewal of distressed neighborhoods through effective use of public and private partnerships and a clear focus on both urban and rural communities. The founders, once the theory and objectives were stated, set out to raise $4 million in capital. With the backing of an extraordinary initial investor group of eleven corporate, foundation, church, and individual shareholders—true pioneers of socially responsible investing—they raised $800,000 in capital, borrowed $2.4 million more, incorporated ShoreBank in 1972, and selected South Shore as both the bank and the neighborhood in which to test their idea.

Today ShoreBank Corporation has assets that approach $175 million. Its affiliates, both bank and nonbank, have together made almost the same amount of direct capital investments in a minority neighborhood that most people had written off. South Shore Bank alone has extended over $110 million of market-rate, unsubsidized credit to over sixty-five hundred local businesspeople and residents, more than half of whom had never borrowed from a bank before and all of whom have contributed to the bank's stunning cumulative repayment rate of 98.5 percent on the whole $110 million of "development loans" extended.[13] Urban renewal involves displacing residents; community development involves engaging them, raising their credit ratings, and utilizing their entrepreneurial energies to build their neighborhoods. ShoreBank now operates in four distressed Chicago neighborhoods, participates in the management of Southern Development Bancorporation in Arkansas, and directs a development banking consulting firm with an international client base.

This is a model that could be adapted all over the country. It involves "patient," generous capital investment in human resources, facilities, and new ideas—the three areas in which generosity utilizing market strategies increases economic growth. Policy analyst David Osborne notes:

> The ShoreBank Corporation . . . represents a conceptual breakthrough in the fight against poverty. [It] is among the first development vehicles ever created in this country . . . truly appropriate to the needs . . . in poor communities. . . . ShoreBank does not exist to make a profit; [it] exists to solve social problems. . . . [It] uses the methodology of the private sector to achieve public goals. . . . It is the creative tension between [its] social goals and the bottom line that makes [it] so effective.[14]

PLANS THAT GROW GIVING

Besides wealth, what else increases giving? Volunteering does. Households in which individuals volunteered gave twice as much as those that did not volunteer. Two other factors affecting the amounts individuals give include at least twice-monthly attendance at religious ceremonies and being asked to give. Both of these factors had a significant positive impact on the size of gifts made by individuals.[15] We therefore need to engage more people in volunteer activities and to recognize that spirituality seems to inspire Americans' sense of generosity. Institutions also need to deploy their board members and volunteers as well as paid staff in soliciting contributions if a significant increase is to occur. People must be asked. There are also some new ways to think about giving, ways to increase the generosity of individual donors.

The next two new programs address the issue of how to dramatically increase giving by people who already give. When we examine all the good laws and the great generosity in the land, and then focus on the great needs that are becoming more prominent with each year over the past thirty years, I believe that the best solution is to increase giving and to direct this increase in ways that build and leverage capital over time. That is, we need to use capitalism's best features to increase the resources available to relieve needs and build human, physical, and intellectual capital. Let us look at these very hopeful signs that this work is not only possible, it is under way, being accomplished by generous citizens leading the rest of us and the government and private sector—as is our tradition.

1 Percent Clubs

A mark of the new landscape is the 1 percent clubs developing in cities across the country. The "club" involves a voluntary annual commitment of 1 percent or more of a person's net worth or 5 percent of his or her yearly income, whichever is more, to worthy causes of their choice. In the fall of 1997, a small group met in Minneapolis on Thanksgiving weekend to affirm their intention to start giving 1 percent of their net worth (that is, their full accumulated wealth) each year. About thirty of those present were willing to have their names published in the *Star Herald* that weekend.

The group set up speaking engagements to spread their idea around the city. They created a newsletter and a brochure explaining their club. Then they drafted plans for a forum on philanthropy. The group brought in Bill Gates Sr. as a speaker, and members celebrated Give Back Day on the day when clocks were turned back to end daylight savings time. Give Back Day was set up specifically to target younger givers and move them to give significant gifts to their communities. The club celebrated fifty thousand hits to its website in the first three months it was functioning. These hits suggested a high level of interest in the idea of 1 percent giving.

By the end of 1999, the club estimated that the 250 1 Percent Club members had increased their giving by approximately $7 million. By 2000, the membership was up to 360, and their average gift had increased from $185,000 in 1999 to $234,000 in 2000. These individual increases created a net increase of $17,640,000 to the community of Greater Minneapolis–St. Paul for the year. The club increases membership by networking and ignores all relationships to political parties and other affinity groups, focusing solely on the commitment to give 1 percent of assets. As more of the wealthy live the 1 percent life, they show each other that life goes on relatively unchanged: children go to college and second homes are bought while significantly more money is given away to strengthen the community.

It is too tempting to imagine the change in giving in the United States if most big cities had one half of 1 percent of their urban/suburban populations giving 1 percent of their full wealth annually to improve their communities.

Capping the Wealth

In a capitalist society, the driving force in the lives of most productive leaders of industry is to accumulate more wealth. Is there ever enough? Do they ever stop and see wealth differently? Not usually. In fact, 2002 witnessed unusual greed among a small number of corporate leaders whose companies gave them loans for fifteen-thousand-square-foot homes in Florida and then forgave the loan and afforded the CEO's family a $6,000 shower curtain. Ken Dayton is not a usual leader of industry or a usual philanthropist. Ken is the former CEO of Dayton-Hudson Corporation. He and his wife, Judy, have committed to capping their wealth as they enter their eighth decade of life. The way they see their wealth is worth some of our time.

Few people give planning to reduce wealth the same care as planning to increase wealth. Ken Dayton is a great planner on both counts. He really understands the need for strategies to make appropriate progress in each area and is living out the nine stages he and Judy have outlined in their "Capping the Wealth" scenario. Ken sees the first stage of giving as a measured response to the person who asks us for a donation. He calls it the "Minimal Response." Someone asks you to buy a box of Girl Scout cookies and you do.

You and the asker feel fine after the interaction; "Responsive Giving" is what happened. The second stage is involvement and interest. In this stage, you get committed to an organization. For Ken and Judy, it was the Minneapolis Orchestra and the Walker Art Center. As they committed time and money to both enterprises, they wanted to give what they were asked to give . . . and more. Ken describes stage three as giving as much as possible. He describes the enthusiasm he remembers feeling after he realized he had given more than anyone expected, but just the right amount to assure the success of the campaign the organization had initiated. He calls stage three "As Much as Possible." This kind of giving requires planning so that it can happen while other obligations are respected and provided for.

In the fourth stage of Capping the Wealth, the Daytons moved to "Maximum Allowable." The law permits people to give as much as they want but permits them to deduct only a certain amount of the cash they give, a smaller percentage of the stock they give, and an even smaller percentage of the money they donate to personal foundations. In 1986, Congress instituted the alternative minimum tax (AMT), which further restricted the allowable deductions. For thirty years, the Daytons used the maximum allowable deductible as a guide for their annual philanthropic budget. Ultimately, they felt restricted by the AMT's impact on the maximum allowable and decided to push beyond it. If the number exceeded what they could deduct—they gave anyway.

They list this next phase as "Beyond the Max." Ken describes the freedom he felt in giving what he wished, unconstrained by federal allowances for deductibility. He felt able to give according to the needs of the organizations he and Judy wanted to advance and not according to some arbitrary number. They soon built up far more carry-over than the law would allow them to use in deductions over the five-year grace period. It was sad to see the deductions disappear, but so satisfying to feel free to give what they wanted and could afford. They had, however, lost their benchmark—the maximum allowable they had always used as a guideline.

In stage six, they moved away from measuring their giving against their income (or tax deductibility) and used their total wealth as the measuring stick for their giving budget. Ken reports high satisfaction with this tool: "If one invests wisely and doesn't overspend on personal consumption, there is money left over both to give generously and to reinvest for further wealth accumulation. The trick is to determine the right percent-to-wealth standard for giving. Until we started to measure our giving against our wealth, we did not fully realize how much we could give away and still live very comfortably and well."[16]

This kind of thinking promotes another train of thought. Giving a percentage of wealth each year induces a person to think about the relative importance of increasing giving and increasing wealth. Which is most important when? Eventually, Ken Dayton began to ponder how much he needed to live and to grow wealth. This led to the realization that he could give away everything beyond that number. This approach permitted him to live well, provide well for his future needs, and give very generously. The Daytons are sharing their wealth and seeing it make a difference while they are still alive. They are reveling in their planning sessions on where to make their gifts and how to help those gifts make the most significant difference.

As they take the steps to cap the wealth, they confess to hoping they have calculated correctly and are beginning to consider the eighth stage—reducing the cap on their wealth. Moving this topic out into the open has made their estate planning a more vigorous and less gruesome adventure.

The ninth stage of giving described by the Daytons is bequests. Long ago they transferred assets to their heirs. As a result, they now feel free to leave almost all their estate to the giving programs they have been working on for most of their lives.

Noting how giving has become a lively part of their lives, with stages that mark the progress in their thinking and their giving, the Daytons can catalog their generosity as a human activity that has provided deep meaning to their lives and made their wealth a spiritual and psychological asset. This is not often the case with many wealthy people. The stability of the Daytons' lives and their children's lives stands as a testimony to the fact that well-managed wealth can add rather than subtract well-being from the lives of rich people. The horror stories that move around are not inevitable to wealth, only to wealth poorly tended. What if more of us tended wealth as Ken and Judy Dayton have? They have been advancing many causes—not the least of which is our democracy and our market society.

CONCLUSION

It should be clear how impossible it would be to outline all the ways generous citizens are continuing a great American tradition. The stories are important so we don't begin to believe we have ceased to be concerned about the same issues that concerned our forebears. Most of the wealthy people I know believe we can do much more and that it would help if we all had a clearer sense of where the major problems were and where the significantly effective solutions are emerging. Along with the stories warning of the likeliest abuses of generosity, and a review of the strengths, weaknesses, threats, and opportunities in the newest programs, we can, I think, proceed to a call to change and renew our idealism in specific and productive ways, so a generosity revolution, a new American revolution, could begin.

11

A PHILANTHROPIC REVOLUTION

We are responsible for the world in which we find ourselves, if only because we are the only sentient force which can change it.

—James Baldwin, *No Name in the Street*

Over the past hundred years, one "big idea" has shaped the way American society has attended to the needs of the fifth quintile in the income distribution—that is, those with the least material wealth and well-being in our society. That idea was spawned by Jane Addams and those who worked with her to establish the hundreds of settlement houses where the poor received services—services that helped them live better and to join the workforce more prepared to succeed. So, from the last decades of the nineteenth century on, philanthropists and reformers such as Mrs. Russell Sage and Jane Addams pooled their resources, did studies, made personal visits, and funded and developed new approaches to improving the well-being of the poor. How? By providing services they needed and lacked. The work of these generous and imaginative citizens responded to the needs they witnessed and to their analysis of what the poor lacked that middle-income and upper-income people had already attained in our society. Settlement houses offered bathing facilities to the poor living in tenements. They offered English classes, job training, and after-school care for children, including music lessons. This big idea, services for the poor, is a model that worked and it was adapted by federal, state, and local governments. Eventually tax money was allocated to attend to the needs of these poor citizens. The country has been working from that services for the poor model ever since.

Today in America, more than a hundred years later, we are following this same model. Our outreach to the poor largely, although not exclusively, provides human or social services to them. This human services model, which for one hundred years has fostered upward mobility and was initially supported by citizen generosity, is now primarily government funded. Human services is still an area where very significant private donations arrive. This support should absolutely continue, both from the government and from philanthropy. However, I firmly believe that the need for social service generosity can be significantly reduced if we add to this another model, a model suggested by the economic progress we have made in the last century.

If the lives of poor people have changed over one hundred years because of the scaling up and out of Jane Addams's settlement house model, what about the other groups, the middle- and upper-income people? How have their lives changed in a hundred years? What have they acquired in our society over the past century that the poor don't have? One hundred years ago, 37 percent of the population had mortgages or owned their own homes. Today 84 percent of whites do, 48 percent of blacks, and, overall, 67 percent of Americans are home owners. This means, by the way, that they had access to enough accumulated capital so they could make a down payment. It also means that they acquired equity—wealth that accumulated as their property appreciated in this healthy economy. A century ago, only 1 percent of all Americans owned stock. Today 52 percent of Americans own stock—a huge increase.[1] However, in 1998, the top 10 percent of Americans accounted for nearly 80 percent of the total ownership in stocks, mutual funds, and retirement accounts.[2] Likewise, in 1900, very few Americans benefited from private pensions, but then most Americans did not survive much past what we would now consider retirement age. (Life expectancy in 1900 was 47.3 years. For a child born in 2000, life expectancy is 76.9 years.)[3] Today, 75 percent of Americans will benefit from a private pension plan, thanks in part to Andrew Carnegie and his gifts that set up TIAA-CREF.[4]

Mortgages, stock, savings accounts, and pensions represent some of the ways that wealth building became available to the middle class in America over the past one hundred years. As Ben Wattenberg and Paul Schervish showed us earlier, we are now dealing with mass affluence in the United States. Comparing the lifestyles of the top four quintiles of the income distribution one hundred years ago with those of the same group today reveals startling changes. From life expectancy and health to the number of meals consumed in fine restaurants per month and the quality of vacations and clothing, the vast majority of these four groups live like wealthy people lived a hundred years ago. Wealth building, not just incomes, made the difference.

Citizen generosity inspired and initially funded this first big idea. It became a system and then a cabinet office, Health and Human Services, to improve the lot of the poor. I want to propose that we add a new big idea. In fact, a number of the programs described in the previous chapter do illustrate a new big idea of the size of settlement houses. In addition to social services and education, philanthropists are already experimenting with this new big idea: wealth building for the poor.[5]

The truth is that we tend not to trust the poor with money. We treat them like the panhandler to whom we give a sandwich instead of a dollar because we fear he'll squander the dollar on alcohol and drugs. Our services model provides education and advice and not funds to low-income people. Even micro-lending programs under way in the United States often follow this approach, whereas in many developing countries, actual funding arrives earlier into the hands of the needy. Advice and counsel accompany but do not often replace the real transfer of capital in developing countries. This is not to say that education in financial literacy does not improve chances of success with new assets, but advice needs to accompany the transfer of assets, not replace it. Just as acquiring assets changed the lives of the middle-income groups, it could transform some of the lives of those with the lowest incomes.

How would this work? Methods could be developed that both encourage and match savings toward mortgages for the poor. Philanthropists at all levels could contribute funds to build pension accounts for the working poor, particularly those who work for very small businesses or the nonprofit sector and currently get no pensions. As a donor, my gift to these efforts would not be spent right away, but, like an endowment, it would grow at the rate of growth of the economy. Over time my gift would reach a higher value to the individual recipient and to society. Again, over time, it could become routine practice for companies to grant stock not just to their highly paid executives, but to all employees. Perhaps under certain conditions, like five or more years of satisfactory work, some companies would match stock purchased by low-income employees so as to encourage their savings toward home ownership and eventually portfolio diversification.[6] Why would shareholders approve such decisions? For the sake of the greater good. Because we are all better off if taxes remain moderate *and* the quality of life of our bottom quintile improves significantly in self-sustaining ways. Like the rest of us, over time, with some ups and downs, the poor would grow their own capital, have something to fall back on, lend to their children when they needed to buy a house, have something more to retire on.

As we have seen, some programs that accomplish parts of this goal are already in place and working, but we need a new awareness of what this new big idea would mean if it became a major part of our national action, private and public, to reduce poverty and dependence. Generous people all over the country should have the chance to consider how to fund wealth-building opportunities for the poor in their communities. People of diverse ethnicities should consider how to add the features of the community economic development structures from their native countries to those developing in their U.S. communities. Undertaking this new model will require adapting Grameen banking and other credit-lending methods that have been used successfully over several decades.[7] We must believe that we are capable of designing instruments and the support structures that would make wealth-building work for low-income people.[8] Over time, our economy will grow better if a larger percentage of those in precarious lives can acquire and build, in partnership with generous citizens, the wherewithal beyond their incomes to become self-sufficient.

As asset building for the poor begins to make sense and work, a new consensus can emerge around poverty programs that offer a more effective use of tax funds than welfare programs of the more recent past that so many citizens have seen as dependency building. A new confidence might reengage Americans who currently hold back on support to the poor because they have lost confidence in the settlement house model. This new big idea could also inspire larger donations, especially if the donor's larger gift became part of a longer-term opportunity to make lasting change in the life of the receiver. Perhaps inspiration would be greater if the recipient matched a portion of the donor's gift.

Michael Sherraden, the director and founder of the Center for Social Development (CSD) at Washington University initiated thinking on this idea. In 1991, Sherraden authored *Assets and the Poor: A New American Welfare Policy.* Since the publication of this book, which proposed matched savings for the poor in individual development accounts (IDAs), pilot programs have begun to develop. The Corporation for Enterprise Development (CFED) launched an eight-year pilot project to test individual development accounts. IDAs are special savings accounts designed to help people build assets to reach life goals and to achieve long-term security. Account holders receive matching funds as they save for purposes such as buying a first home, attending job training, going to college, planning for retirement, or financing a small business.[9] This American dream project has been a partnership with the government, individual donors, and a set of major foundations.[10]

As Ray Boshara, director of the Asset Building Program at the New America Foundation, said in testimony before the Ways and

Means Committee: "We're not asking Congress to do something for the working poor that's not already being done for the middle class. Keep in mind that not one federal dollar is spent until low-income people work and save, and some private sector dollars are leveraged. IDAs are *not* a government hand-out, nor are they a new poverty program, but rather a true public-private-citizen partnership, one that expands our successful asset-building system to people willing to work and save."[11]

This, in my opinion, is the new big idea that can jumpstart philanthropy and our economy for the twenty-first century. We should keep it foremost in our thoughts as we approach every social problem and funding opportunity. This big idea, ironically enough, reflects the advice of Maimonides that he offered over a thousand years ago: make partnerships with those who need help. Engage with them as dignified equals. Give them the kind of help you would want if you were in similar circumstances. If it were me, rather than being limited to a handout that kept me going from one office to another to talk to counselors about the programs I could apply for—usually getting to the office by taxi because I have no car—I would prefer one site where I could see how to begin an individual development account. The IDA would nudge me to save, even the littlest amount, and get a match to accumulate the funds for my ticket out of poverty and dependence. The poor, we have agreed by our recent votes to terminate welfare services, are capable of taking responsibility for their own lives. Asset building is the "how."

Economist Paul Romer has wisely drawn attention to the power of ideas to create the most significant force for economic growth. In *The Greater Good,* I have taken a look at American history and the role played by the people and ideas funded by the generosity of individuals. We have seen the role played by the profound idea of guaranteeing each person life, liberty, and the pursuit of happiness. America's exceptional history distinguishes itself by the entrepreneurial spirit of each age that saw what needed to be done and did it with optimism and high expectations. We may need a second revolution for life, liberty, and the pursuit of happiness for those who have not achieved these yet in our democracy. A second revolution where we would redouble our already admirable efforts but go further to carry out the age-old Hebrew expression *tikun olam*, "to repair the world," and save rather than lose lives, build rather than waste capital—human, physical, and intellectual. We are facing a moment like that now, as I trust the previous pages have suggested. We need a generosity revolution.

In the remainder of this final chapter, I will offer some thoughts on the best targets, leadership strategies, and policy tools for wealth-building investment. My goal is to provoke you to develop your own agenda with your fellow citizens, to launch a debate that is informed by our American history of philanthropy and economic growth and one that emphasizes the risk-taking, highly rewarding role of gifts in our economy. Revolutions start with vigorous debate.

TARGETS

Number One: More Home Ownership for Low- and Lower-Middle-Income Citizens

Increasing home ownership for low-income families is essential to generate equity development and wealth accumulation for current and future generations. In 1880, 36 percent of the U.S. population owned their homes. The national average in the 1940s was just below 50 percent. By 1990, 63 percent owned their own homes. By the third quarter of 2000, home ownership stood at 67.7 percent, the highest level in U.S. history. This percent represents 71.6 million home owners in the United States. For African Americans, however, the rate is 48 percent; for Hispanics, 46.7 percent; for whites, 74 percent.[12] The average white family has a net worth of $84,000, while the average black family's net worth is $7,500. Why do these statistics matter? Because home equity is the major vehicle for wealth accumulation in the United States. If people cannot buy homes, they have impossible difficulties accumulating financial resources and becoming more productive for themselves, their communities, and the country. In 2001, home owners all over the nation withdrew almost $80 billion in home equity and reused it to buy new things, take trips, and pay off credit cards, so that ultimately $50 billion was plowed back into the economy. This activity created a bigger economic stimulus than the tax rebate. Home ownership mobilizes capital to the benefit of all.

Home owning also impacts quality-of-life issues such as children's achievement.[13] Studies show that children in home-owners' families are less likely to get involved in the criminal justice system, drop out of school, or have babies out of wedlock. Infusions of philanthropic gifts to home ownership reserve funds would significantly improve the lives of low-income families and advance the common good.[14] "Home ownership" as Franklin Raines, CEO of Fannie Mae, said recently, "creates more stable households in safer neighborhoods. Better schools. More cohesive communities. Citizens who are more active and involved."[15] Communities with higher levels of home ownership have lower crime levels, lower expenditures for support to their criminal justice systems, and more secure tax bases.

What's more, 83 percent of American families say that it's their goal to own a home. They believe it will make their lives better and their families safer. More than 60 percent of Americans say that, in order to buy a home, they would be willing to take a second job. Eighty-one percent say that they would make a longer commute, and 91 percent say that they would drive a less-expensive car. Sixty-seven percent say that they would put off retirement for up to ten years in order to own their own home. Americans want home ownership.[16]

The capacity of middle- and lower-income Americans to achieve ownership is vitally linked to their capacity to gather a down payment and keep up a mortgage so their wealth can grow each year. The obstacle for the working poor is gathering the down payment. It is a problem that continues through generations. Even well-educated black and Hispanic young people cannot go to their families for financial help with their first down payments like many of their white classmates can, so they buy their first homes later in life and have less time to build their investment.

My research suggests that current programs focus on government tax credits for new home owners or for corporations that give them loans. These are fine ideas—but as we've seen time and again, they are slow and low-risk ways to tackle an urgent issue. We need more direct approaches.

- We need to set a national goal for home ownership by households in the bottom two quintiles of the income distribution.
- We need widespread adoption of one or more of the financial structures now available to prepare potential home owners and to give incentives to potential lenders, both institutions and generous individuals.
- We need a major nationwide organization to spearhead the dissemination of these pro–home ownership ideas into every neighborhood in the country.
- We need to establish community home-ownership trust funds. These funds would be used to offer no-interest loans to new home owners who need help with the down payment or the first few years of the monthly mortgage payments and house repairs. Citizens who are finishing their mortgages might keep giving the same sum for a period of time and offer it as a gift-yielding tax credit to the local home-ownership trust fund.
- We need religious institutions in communities to commit their energies to this mission as a way to help the poor and build up our social strengths as a nation and our economy.
- We need a program, especially in the urban slums, to put vacant buildings back into use as owner-occupied homes and condominiums. This could have a striking effect.

Flexible, low-cost housing capital is an investment in the common future, the larger economy. Working-poor families will finally be able to leverage the dollars they have been spending on housing and build equity wealth, assets to help launch their adult children's home ownership and to secure loans for other large investments that build the economy.

Number Two: Community Centers

This second investment is a form of *community* wealth building. It supplements home ownership by improving the functioning of the community and therefore the value of each home in it. The average white home owner in this country has $120,000 of equity, while the average black homeowner has $58,000 of home equity. This is largely because, for too long, African Americans have been unable to own homes in communities where property values go up. We need to address the *value* of the home that a person is able to buy, as well as their ability to buy it. One way is by creating a public space for community activity.

Too many communities today lack safe, up-to-date facilities for people to gather for cultural events, neighborhood activities, and sports play. We don't need more gates; we need more common space. We don't need more sports arenas and convention centers that stand empty for days at a time and mainly generate jobs filling soft drink cups. We need sports facilities where more people can play rather than spectate. We need facilities that welcome families and singles, young people and the elderly, where activities continue throughout the day and evening. People who are building IDAs, or becoming first-time home owners need familiar, accessible places to develop financial literacy. Others need access to computers and technology training; still others need to study English so they can sustain their own culture and language and still function effectively in the United States. Still other neighbors can teach and learn new skills, from parenting classes to hobbies and arts, including the settlement-house offerings of music lessons.

Local community centers could teach citizens how to monitor their local governments for how well local ordinances are enforced. Typically, as I learned in working on community development in my own city, local ordinances on property maintenance are well enforced in middle- and upper-income neighborhoods. In poor neighborhoods, slumlords are left unbothered by the city manager as they leave their properties to decay and depress the quality of the blocks where they are located. Financially secure citizens do not tolerate this situation. The more transient, more precarious renters living in poor neighborhoods are less equipped to fight for their rights in their local neighborhoods. Community centers could assure them the power of the group to defend and build their property values.

Given what we have learned over the past century, these new community centers could be places where neighbors house their own community neighborhood foundations—grassroots institutions that give the low-income neighbors the responsibility to fund and distribute financial support where they believe it deserves to go in their communities. These funds should be matched by citizen donors who have already achieved security and comfort in American society. These new ventures will probably reflect some of the ways the cultures of new immigrant groups have built economic assets in their native settings. The strength of their neighborhoods would be greatly advanced in their stabilizing and pride-building settings.

Such venues develop in wealthy communities, but few low- and middle-income neighborhoods can point to similar resources. People who lead lives that are connected to the lives of others tend to be happier, less isolated, and less involved in antisocial behaviors that may put them in trouble with the law. They are more likely to be productive at work and positive forces at home. They are less likely to cost fellow taxpayers through their needs for social services or criminal justice system expenses.

With the goal of building community strength and lowering the costs that slums create for the tax base provided by working citizens, a number of cities are beginning to sponsor the development of community centers. These centers typically include the contributions of generous citizens and some foundation and corporate giving. Albuquerque and Indianapolis are two good examples. Centers will take time to affect the health and economic strength of poor neighborhoods. The key difference between these centers and settlement houses resides in the role of the needy population. In the new model, the local neighbors play central roles in developing and managing change. The young citizens, instead of just receiving benefits, volunteer, save, and support the work of the center. They become part of the solution and are not just left to be part of the future problems of a poor community.

- Major hotel chains could play a role in helping to build this idea in communities and engage food-service companies and the hospitality and sports industries, in general, in helping.

- Banks and credit unions need to play a much more prominent role under their Community Revitalization Act responsibilities by working with local non-profits to mobilize capital, both that saved by neighbors and that donated by citizens and institutions, to the benefit of asset building in depressed neighborhoods.
- Various other industries with related expertise should expand support for this work with generous citizens willing to make gifts of their own funds to create community centers.

Number Three: Children

Children, as they say, may constitute only 20 percent of the population, but they make up 100 percent of our future. No moral justification exists to permit one in five American children to be living in poverty. No economic justification, either. As economist Gary Becker says, our wealth is in our educated populace, our human capital. Educated people produce ideas, the fundamental economic asset in Paul Romer's new model, and we need ever more new good ones to deal with the challenges that await us. The nation is currently losing vast quantities of precious human capital through inadequate investment in the earliest years of life of its people.

Hernando De Soto's groundbreaking book *The Mystery of Capitalism* shows that capitalism fails in third-world settings because, in part, people cannot capitalize on what they possess. De Soto notes: "The poor inhabitants of these nations do have things, but they lack the process to represent their property and create capital. They have houses but not titles, crops but not deeds, businesses but not statutes of incorporation. It is the unavailability of these essential representations that explains why people . . . have not been able to produce sufficient capital to make their domestic capitalism work."[17]

In the United States and elsewhere, what most of the poor have is potential *human* capital that current systems do not develop. Our economy can use every bit of human capital we can produce, but we waste that capital early because poor children start school as developmentally delayed youngsters, seriously behind their peers. We continue to waste human capital by offering insufficiently strong support to children during their K–12 years to assure that they will graduate from high school with skills and knowledge that are adequate to enable them to advance in demanding jobs and succeed in life. Low-income people suffer, and American society pays for this waste. An example is our current severe shortage of nurses. According to the U.S. Department of Labor, an additional 450,000 registered nurses will be needed through the year 2008. At the moment, employment companies are recruiting nurses in South Africa and India, taking from those countries in crisis their own desperately needed human capital. Could a group of generous citizens undertake to raise funds for scholarships and other needed support to increase the number of nurses and doctors' assistants, drawing, as did the leaders of Provident Hospital, on the resources in poor communities to fill these important jobs?

Asset building, human and financial, makes economic independence and self-sustaining social justice available to those to whom we now offer mainly services. As good as they may be, they cannot match the dignity of independence.

- Ray Boshara suggests that for $8 billion a year, every child born in America could receive a $2,000 interest-bearing lifetime savings account that gets increased at graduation from grade school and from high school. Children can be asset builders if we decide we want them to escape poverty.
- We need to make available to children of low-income families cradle-to-classroom education of the same quality as children of middle- and upper-income people receive. Corporations with their own child-care centers need to share the expertise, teacher education, and perhaps even some facilities with the child-care and early-childhood-education centers serving low- and moderate-income families. Why? To keep taxes low, to help assure that a productive workforce develops naturally in our society. To provide well-to-do families with normalized daily contact with less-advantaged families. To advance the greater good, social justice, in this democracy—and these reasons are not necessarily listed in their order of importance.
- Health insurance, immunizations, and preventive medicine should be normal parts of children's lives at all income levels.

Local citizens need to know the availability of these resources and assure that what is available to the poor is what these citizens would accept for their own children or grandchildren.

- Schools need the support to become family centers offering parenting education that includes ways to stimulate cognitive development and language skill in young children as well as ways to encourage stable emotional growth.
- We need an organization with the power and force of the AARP, or perhaps the AARP itself, to take up the cause of advocacy for children's needs as they have done so successfully for older Americans. The intergenerational engagement would be very important to the future of America because the good example set by older Americans in connecting their agendas to the agendas of children would teach generations in between how responsible Americans carry out their roles in this democracy.

You will have noticed that my top three choices happen to reflect some rather traditional targets of generosity, following the topics I developed in the first half of this book—investments in people and investments in physical assets. Now I'll turn to the final category, intellectual assets. Good ideas.

Number Four: Good Ideas

Inspired thinkers and risk-taking, open-minded donors need to build new ideas and inventions, our intellectual capital. Remember Mary Lasker, Julius Rosenwald, Eugene Lang, and all of the others mentioned here. Each of these and thousands of other donors have identified a pressing need and contributed to answering it, either directly or through a contribution to someone else's good idea. The next March of Dimes, or MADD, or EDF is waiting to be launched. In addition to the ideas in earlier chapters, some recent "new" ideas follow.

- The Aspen Institute's Microenterprise Fund for Innovation, Effectiveness, Learning and Dissemination (FIELD) collects information on the best practices for building wealth among low-income Americans and then shares it with organizations and individuals who can fund or develop programs in local communities. Funding and developing resources such as FIELD gives every community the opportunity to find solutions efficiently in a marketplace of diverse ideas. We need to think creatively and entrepreneurially about how progress can and should be made toward this big idea, a big idea that I think is central to the American economy in the coming decades.

- Despite amazing gains against heart disease, diabetes, cancer, and HIV-AIDS, there are still significant limits in our medical research and critical delivery systems for drug treatments around the world. The Gates Foundation has focused on these gaps, funding research on diseases where the marketplace for drugs has not yet tempted the private sector. For instance, the foundation is working on developing delivery projects to get HIV-AIDS and tuberculosis drugs to patients—and to ensure that patients take the drugs correctly. We need to continue to invest our philanthropy in cutting-edge medical research, especially the research that cannot find funding in the private sector.
- Over the past two centuries, the American economy has in large part relied on fossil fuels to power the actual machines of business. The consequences have been considerable, but as long as fossil fuels are cheaper to use than other forms of energy, it is unlikely that large-scale innovations will be adopted by the government or for-profit sector. The Global Philanthropy Partnership and the Synergos Institute, among others, marshal the support of individual philanthropists to invest in the development of renewable energy sources. We need to continue to find new innovators who may literally invent the technology and industries that power and drive our future.
- In 2000, CNN founder Ted Turner and former Senator Sam Nunn launched the Nuclear Threat Initiative, a philanthropic foundation dedicated to disarmament and nonproliferation of nuclear, chemical, and biological weapons. The foundation thinks globally rather than nationally to identify insecure weapons stockpiles around the world; build coalitions between

governments that can allow for transparent information about threats and know-how; and develop pilot projects that all governments and businesses can use to help reduce the threat of accidental or terrorist use of weapons. In the next two decades, global security will have a dramatic impact not just on the political and military decisions of our government but on the day-to-day economic life of American citizens. We need to develop more organizations that can serve as watchdogs and catalysts for government action, especially when many nations must be involved.

POLICY TOOLS

We will need considerable expertise to achieve this revolution. Personal accountability will be critical, but so will the tools of policy and management.

First, we must establish an annual report on the social health of the nation to supplement our reports on traditional economic indicators, including the annual GDP, the Dow, the NASDAQ, the Consumer Price Index, the Index of Leading Economic Indicators, and others. With this data, we will be able to measure our progress—and set benchmarks for infusing the economy with philanthropic capital. We can do better and we would if we could see the relationship between social costs and losses of the benefits of human capital, between social health, economic health and the strength of our democracy.[18]

Marc Miringoff and his team at the Fordham University Institute for Innovation in Social Policy have been collecting data for twenty years on the social health of each state and compiled that data for the nation. This data show where the problems are. The Corporation for Economic Development founded in 1979 by Robert Friedman has been developing solutions, as have a number of other organizations. For those who are motivated to fix what is broken in the general area of social health, all of this work offers excellent starting points for setting goals, whether for increasing home ownership among the bottom quintile or reducing teen pregnancy.

Second, we need to set measurable goals in specific time frames. This approach models the entrepreneurial strategy used by President Kennedy when he announced: "Man on the moon by the end of this decade." He gave the nation a hard goal—hard because it was difficult, but hard and fast in that it was so specific. The who (man), the where (on the moon), the when (in less than ten years) left no room for slippage or misunderstanding. Hard goals sharpen dedication and effort. While hard goals offer special complexity in social and economic progress, it might be easier to enlist the full cooperation of business and industry, the nonprofit sector, and the community members being served by the change if goals and time frames were as clear as were Kennedy's for the space program.

So, should our national goal be that only 6 percent of American children, instead of 20 percent, be living below the poverty line in 2010? That would still leave six European countries providing better lives for their children on the international scale, but it might be realistic. What about home ownership for the bottom quintile in income distribution? What are the right targets? We need a debate.

Third, we need to establish a Council of Social Health Advisers to report annually to the nation and to keep the president and Cabinet advised of our progress in building social health just as the Council of Economic Advisers does in the area of the economy. Change occurs where clear data presents measures of progress. All these issues are complex and need interdisciplinary insight from the most advanced thinkers in various relevant fields. Citizen donors deserve to know that the country has a serious commitment to tracking and improving these urgent problems that cost our economic strength.

Fourth, we need to support changes in tax policy that will increase our generosity as citizens. Respectful of the great demands on the national budget, I would advocate that these changes in tax laws be made for a ten-year experimental period, with intermittent studies designed to discover how much social progress is actually being achieved in this approach to partnership with the private sector.

- We need to create a social investment tax credit, fairly narrowly circumscribed like the mortgage deduction is. This tax credit should be limited to ventures that build human capital, physical/facilities capital, and intellectual capital or new ideas. In each category, the credits would go to projects that build current social health. Tax credits currently go to investments in low-income, first-time home-owner trusts and renovations of depressed neighborhoods. They could be extended to other areas that would address weaknesses in the social health of the nation. They might also go to scholarship funds for students whose family incomes are at the poverty level and to building community centers in low-income neighborhoods. Avoiding handouts, these social investment credits would literally build partnerships to enable all concerned to connect their own inputs of effort and self-discipline, along with matching funding, to advance in society.

- The statistics should be carefully monitored by more than one organization, perhaps one governmental and one private, in order to ascertain that the credits end up reducing the expenditures that weak social health indicators cost. The tax credits should bring relief to the tax rolls as the investments in people, property, and ideas yield tax dollars and reduce social costs.
- Charitable deductions should be extended to nonitemizers. This change in tax law is controversial and has had extensive consideration. Abuses are always possible, but benefits for our society outweigh the dangers. Increases in giving by those in the lower-income bands respects their dignity as givers and shares with them the joy and the task of giving. Much of their giving goes to religious institutions. If concerns about this issue threaten to derail the change in tax laws to permit charitable deductions to nonitemizers, arrangements could be designed to minimize contributions to strictly religious organizations. In this democracy, significant giving by people at all economic levels is important, and such a change in tax law would increase giving by low-income givers who, because they do not itemize, get no tax deductions and no governmental encouragement to give as citizens at other economic levels now do.
- An increase in the amount of charitable giving that taxpayers may deduct would help to encourage more giving. Limitations

now cause an understatement of the amount that is given away each year as an unknown number of wealthy people give more than is statistically accounted for.

- I would also advocate social investment tax incentives for corporations involved in partnerships with individuals, non-profits, or governments working on some element of the revolution in generosity, especially the parts focused on the reduction of poverty and the improvement in the social health index. On average, corporations give about 4 percent of the donations received in the United States each year and receive a tax benefit for this wonderful generosity. New incentives should apply to giving beyond that 4 percent. The real goal is not only a larger amount of funds available to support the new big idea, but also to enlarge the amount of money corporations learn to give and shareholders learn to accept as a wise investment in the economy and our society—an investment they see as self-interest rightly understood.
- We should attach new incentives to generous corporate matches of any giving by a company's employees.

Changes in law on controversial issues such as capital gains taxes, estate taxes, and double deductions need to be considered in light of whether Americans can believe that the recipients of tax relief, if granted, will voluntarily distribute a larger portion of it to those whose social health is in jeopardy. To what extent are a higher percentage of us willing to make this poverty situation our own problem, to see it as a problem for our highly productive economy and powerful democracy? If our life of plenty has definitively separated us from fellow citizens in distress, the government has no choice but to slow the progress of what will eventually distort and put in jeopardy our way of life.

Tax policy is merely a tool in the revolution—a powerful one, but still merely a tool. The revolution in generosity can occur only if a fundamental personal change happens in the minds and consciences of a large number of Americans. After all, only individual citizens making good (and generous) decisions can maintain the fragile balance between capitalism and generosity. We are the only ones who ever have. Philanthropy can accomplish dramatic enhancement of social health. Perhaps, in fact, it can generate more positive change than only an adoption of higher tax rates. We need democracy as well as capitalism to continue in a healthy balance based on our entrepreneurial spirit and our investment in upward mobility. We need to reenergize our commitment to social progress and economic prosperity, especially for America's children.

LEADERSHIP STRATEGIES

The leadership for this revolution should come from individual donors. As a group, we give 75 percent of the gifts in the United States each year. Historically, our insights on big and small projects have propelled America forward. Our generosity is a significant engine of social and economic advancement in America. We have, of course, had moments in our history when elected leaders have provided important direction, usually in times of crisis and war. President Lincoln had the vision and the courage to lead in this way at a critical time. So did FDR at another and quite different critical time. But often, the critical leadership must come from citizens.

During the Progressive Era, citizens made the dramatic changes that led to the rise of national institutions with hundreds of local chapters. These new structures mobilized local citizens to lead progress on broad problems the country faced. Using national models, goals, and other resources, and local energy and funds, not only did these citizens improve conditions but they gave the country a more unified sense of what "we" stood for. The repercussions of this citizen leadership still resonate across the land. United Way, the Red Cross, the first Community Foundation, Boys Clubs and Girl Clubs, among many others, started during this period.

A revolution in generosity will require commitment and planning. It will not happen overnight. We need to identify and prioritize the key targets of opportunity. Lead organizations will need to gather and plan a dual approach: increasing the numbers of givers and increasing the size of gifts. Since 89 percent of Americans already make contributions to tax-exempt organizations and causes, there is little gain to be made in increasing the number of us who give. The real gains need to be made in expanding the size of our gifts. What approaches will cause Americans willingly to make greater sacrifices of their own needs and comforts to provide for the needs of others? We require leadership and personal commitment. It will not be easy to mobilize higher levels of personal giving among Americans, and especially the wealthy, but the Capping the Wealth strategy that Ken and Judy Dayton prepared offers an excellent place to start. Ideas like the 1 Percent Clubs also have the power to increase giving in predictable and impressive ways. Organizations like Rotary and chambers of commerce and others could take up the cause of starting and managing 1 Percent Clubs in their communities.

Creative personal generosity is essential now as it always has been in America. A new generation of major philanthropists such as Bill Gates and Jim Barksdale are stepping up to follow the philanthropic innovations of Ken Dayton, Ted Turner, David Packard, David Rockefeller, and George Soros. But this is not enough. We need a greater surge of generosity into our economy to ensure continuing prosperity. We have to become at least twice as generous as we ever have been as a nation if we hope to conquer the problems that we face today. More than ever, in a time of some economic downturn, we need to believe with considerably more conviction that personal generosity is *the* tool for ensuring a viable and just capitalist democracy going forward. *Tikun olam:* We have the ability to repair our world.

The civil society, or citizen sector, has and will have stunning amounts of wealth, income, and education to make the leadership their own, both the financial and the programmatic leadership. The top 20 percent of Americans in the income/wealth distribution will have especially significant financial capacity and management acumen to lead a new partnership effort to "fix what is broken" in the United States. This group will have the ability and connections to develop partnerships with corporations, major non-profits, and the government. It is essential that they do so.

Fundamentally, generosity is a way of being in the world that puts others on a par with oneself, loving one's neighbor as oneself. It means refusing to be more patient with someone else's pain and poverty than we would be with our own or our child's. It means living in a state of friendship and respect for others regardless of their circumstances. This takes moral fortitude, courage, and patience. It involves helping others develop what they need to ease their suffering and/or to advance their potential, as Robert Payton, founding director of the Center on Philanthropy at Indiana University, has said. But since the only ones people can ever really change are themselves, each of us needs to start on a personal level.

The commitment to acts of generosity affirms the choice individuals can make to mitigate the negative forces of capitalism. It also promotes the happiness of self and others, including our children. If we all make time for sports and entertainment and travel, we can probably find time for new levels of generosity as well. The vast majority of Americans are not being asked to sacrifice to defend our country by serving in the military. We can serve our nation through increasing our generosity. The impact on the nation's economic growth and social well-being would be significant.

The busiest person can become a catalyst for strengthening generosity. Ask yourself: What are my skills and what do I know that I could invest in for the advancement of others? What am I currently investing in others with greater needs than I have? Am I investing in what I value most? What do I most want to change about modern life? What moments in a week or a month bring me a sense of meaningfulness and happiness in my life? Then compare your giving to your values and your moments of meaning and evaluate the amount of your donations in relation to your net worth, other obligations, and future capacity.

Each of us is a part of a "family" and some belong to families with their own foundations. We should share wisdom about generosity in these groups. This idea involves having each member of the family (or, with adaptations, the company or organization) write a short reflection on the meaning of generosity in his or her life once a year. The holiday or the New Year season often works well for this project. Each person's annual reflection is sealed and put away for some period of time that the person designates, perhaps ten years, or even until after the person's death. Like building value in an endowment, these thoughts become more precious each year as family members grow up, move through life, and pass on. Over time, as the reflections from one year are put away and those from the next are opened and shared, the family members can see how the generous sharing of the aspirations and struggles, the achievements, and even the failures of the past, inform the present and help prepare for the future. The wisdom endowment future generations inherit may eventually be valued as highly as the financial portfolio from which they will benefit. This wisdom endowment shapes the values and therefore the democracy and the economy in which younger family members will live and work.

We are members of all kinds of organizations—including businesses, faith-based settings, Rotaries, and chambers of commerce, as well as community and family foundations. As leaders in these organizations, we can elevate and broaden discussions of generosity. Then we can move these groups from talking to reading, writing, and ultimately to improving the actions and the outcomes of the philanthropic efforts we undertake. All of us have a crucial role to play as future leaders for the greater good.

CONCLUSION

The ultimate goal of *The Greater Good* is to inform readers that we are rich because we are generous and then to inspire a dramatic increase in personal generosity over the next thirty years. The majority has achieved levels of comfort that additional wealth alone will not spin into higher levels of happiness. Generosity is the key to assuring that America, and Americans, can keep thriving, improving, and setting a better example in the global society of the twenty-first century. A hundred years from now, will Americans of the first decades of the twenty-first century be hailed as the generation that rebalanced capitalism and philanthropy?

We are at a crossroads. Will our economic success make us more generous or more self-absorbed? More idealistic about the aspirations of the founding fathers and the work of our own forefathers in making American life what we so comfortably inherit? Or will the diminished need to struggle as hard as other generations lessen our imagination about how to address the needs of others and fix what is still broken in our society? Either scenario is possible. One will build our society; the other will erode and slowly degenerate it over the first decades of the twenty-first century.

A careful examination of the projects currently under way in the nation to voluntarily and creatively redistribute opportunity, income, and wealth indicates that hope is not lost. We need resolve and leadership to make philanthropy bold again, as it was in the early decades of the twentieth century. Will you begin the task?

NOTES

INTRODUCTION: HOW PHILANTHROPY SAVES AMERICAN CAPITALISM

1. Winthrop, *A Modell of Christian Charity,* pp. 31–48.
2. Cotton Mather, *Essays to Do Good; Addressed to All Christians,* revised and improved by George Burder, 2nd ed. (London, 1808).
3. Benjamin Franklin, *The Political Thought of Benjamin Franklin,* ed. Ralph Ketcham (Indianapolis: Bobbs-Merrill, 1965), p. 341.

1: DEMOCRACY, CAPITALISM, AND GENEROSITY: THE FRAGILE BALANCE

1. Fleishman, "Philanthropic Leadership."
2. Fukuyama, *Trust,* p. 7.
3. David Hume, *Treatise of Human Nature,* vol. 3, pt. 2, sec. 5 (Baltimore: Penguin, 1969), p. 573.
4. Putnam, "The Prosperous Community."
5. Alexis de Tocqueville, *Democracy in America,* vol. 2, sec. 2, chap. 8 (Chicago: University of Chicago Press, 2000), p. 501.
6. Thomas Hobbes, *De Cive or, The Citizen,* 1651, sec. 7–8 (New York: Dutton, 1950), p. 105.
7. Mueller, "Democracy vs. Capitalism."
8. Two particularly important books are: Arnove, *Philanthropy and Cultural Imperialism*; and Odendahl, *Charity Begins at Home.*
9. Both scholars are part of the Boston College Social Welfare Institute.
10. Miringoff, Miringoff, and Opdycke, *The Social Health of the Nation.*
11. Cox and Alm, "By Our Own Bootstraps," pp. 6–7.

2: MAKING THE MOST OF PEOPLE THROUGH EDUCATION: HUMAN CAPITAL, PART ONE

1. Organization for Economic Cooperation and Development, "The Well-being of Nations," 2001, p. 18.
2. Gary S. Becker and Andrew M. Rosenfield, "An Investment in Education Pays the Best Return," (working paper, 1999), pp. 6–7.
3. Gary Becker, *The Economics of Life* (New York: McGraw Hill, 1997), p. 301.
4. "How Much We Earn—Factors That Make a Difference," Bureau of the Census, Statistical Brief. On line at http://landview.census.gov/apsd/www/statbrief/sb95_17.pdf. A different statistic comes from the Current Population Survey, "The Rewards of Staying in School": "$45,678 [is the] annual average earnings in 1999 of adults age 18 and over with a bachelor's degree. This compares with an annual average of $24,572 for those with only a high school diploma." "Current Population Survey," Census 2000 and the Statistical Abstract of the United States, U.S. Census Bureau Public Information Office. On line at http://www.census.gov/Press_Release/www/2001/cb01fff11.html.
5. Aristotle, *Politics.*
6. Curti and Nash, *Philanthropy in the Shaping of American Higher Education,* p. 7.
7. Ibid., p. 8.
8. Wilkinson, "Plural Ends, Contested Means," pp. 316–17.
9. "The Case for Yale College," *Treasurer's Papers* (New Haven: Yale University, December 1, 1831).
10. Leitch, *A Princeton Companion.*
11. Campbell, "Benjamin Rush and Women's Education," p. 13.
12. Wilkinson, p. 318.
13. Ibid., pp. 307–8.
14. Sander, "Sharing a Love of History."
15. Curti and Nash, p. 81.
16. I am grateful to Ronald Wells for access to details of the Phelps-Stokes Fund work.
17. The Phelps-Stokes Fund Report, p. 5.
18. UNCF Annual Fund, pp. 36–37.
19. Wiley Hall, "Reinventing Black Colleges."
20. An interesting list of a few would include: Ralph Waldo Emerson, Debbie Allen, Alice Walker,. Oprah Winfrey, Bella Abzug, George McGovern, Richard Nixon, Ruth Bader Ginsburg, Jacob Lawrence, Saul Bellow, Shirley Chisholm, W. E. B. Du Bois, Bill Clinton, John Updike, Patricia Harris, Angela Bassett, Mary McLeod Bethune, Morton Gould, Mark Rothko, Leontyne Price, Ruth Westheimer, Gregory Peck, Dizzy Gillespie, Diahann Carroll, and Irene Dunn.
21. We probably know the American Legion best as the sponsor of baseball.

The organization has been the breeding ground over the decades for thousands of amateur and professional ball players. It began by sponsoring the American Legion Baseball League in 1925. Today, over 60 percent of professional baseball players are graduates of that program. Over 89,000 high-school age students play on Legion-sponsored teams annually.

22. Wilkinson, pp. 310–11.
23. National Center for Educational Statistics. On line at http://nces.ed.gov/pubs2002/2002167.pdf.
24. The College Board, "Financial Aid Facts." On line at http://www.collegeboard.com/article/0,3341,6-30-0-402,00.html?orig=rel.
25. National Center for Public Policy and Higher Education, "Losing Ground."
26. Myrna Oliver, "Crispus A. Wright; Son of Ex-Slave Became Lawyer and USC Benefactor," *Los Angeles Times,* December 11, 2001, p.10.
27. McCarty, *Simple Wisdom for Rich Living*, p. 18.
28. Oseola McCarty, quoted in University of Southern Mississippi press release, July 1995. On line at http://www.pr.usm.edu/oola1.htm.
29. Montgomery Brower, "Helping Hands: For a Host of Philanthropists Inspired by a Common Dream, Charity Begins at School," *People,* October 7, 1987, p. 76.
30. All of these statistics on the "I Have a Dream" program are from research conducted by the Arete Corporation, "Report Card, Report on 10 City Studies and Evaluations," Fall 2001. On line at http://www.ihad.org/reports.php.
31. Sack, "Ex-Netscape Official Starts $100 Million Literacy Drive."
32. The Heritage Foundation, "Research: Education School Choice, 2001 Mississippi." On line at www.heritage.org/Research/Education/ Schools/mississippi.
33. Pruitt, "Literacy Is the Key."
34. A Better Chance, "Human Diversity and Academic Excellence: Learning from Experience," Annual Report 2000. On line at http://www.abetterchance.org/PDFs/00_Ann_Rpt.pdf.
35. U.S. Department of Justice, Office of Juvenile Justice and Delinquenct Prevention, Annual Report 2000.
36. Anderegg, "Juvenile Crime."

3: MAKING THE MOST OF PEOPLE BEYOND EDUCATION: HUMAN CAPITAL, PART TWO

1. Sander, *The Business of Clarity,* p. 63.
2. U.S. Bureau of the Census 1975, p. 128.
3. Sander, p. 71.
4. "Labour Economics," *Encyclopaedia Britannica* 2003. On line at http://search.eb.com.
5. Spain, *How Women Saved the Cities,* p. 15.
6. Addams, *Newer Ideals of Peace,* p. 206.

7. Trattner, *From Poor Law to Welfare State.*
8. Spain, p. 43.
9. Irwin S. Kirsch, et al., *Executive Summary of Adult Literacy in America* (Washington D.C.: National Center for Educational Statistics). On line at http://nces.ed.gov//naal/resources/execsumm.asp.
10. U.S. Department of Justice, Justice Management Division.
11. Community Resources for Justice, "Adult Correctional Services."
12. The Enterprise Foundation, Annual Report 2001.
13. Rentschler, "Lock 'Em Up and Throw Away the Key," p. 24.
14. Twist, "The Economics of Truth in Sentencing."
15. "Returning Inmates: Closing the Public Safety Gap," policy brief, January 2001. On line at Community Resources for Justice, http://www.crjustice.org/rettex.htm.
16. The Enterprise Foundation, Annual Report 2001.

4: EXPANDING THE BUILT ENVIRONMENT: PHYSICAL CAPITAL

1. Foster, *Robert Wood Johnson.*
2. Jeremiah 29:5–7.
3. Johns Hopkins University, "About Johns Hopkins." On line at http://webapps.jhu.edu/jhuniverse/information_about_hopkins/about_jhu/a_brief_history_of_jhu/index.cfm.
4. Johns Hopkins University Communications and Public Affairs, "Bay Area Economics Study." On line at http://www.jhu.edu/news_info/reports/impact. Most of the statistics in this summary are quoted from an independent analysis commissioned by the Johns Hopkins Institutions and performed by Bay Area Economics. The report, using data from fiscal year 1999, focuses primarily on the two most readily quantifiable measures of economic impact: jobs and income. Indirect impact was calculated using economic multiplier models developed by the U.S. Bureau of Economic Analysis. The study assessed the impact on Maryland of the Johns Hopkins University, including its nine academic and research divisions, and the Johns Hopkins Health System, including its three acute-care hospitals and other subsidiaries. It also included the impact of affiliated research institutions drawn to Baltimore by Hopkins (the Space Telescope Science Institute, the Kennedy-Krieger Institute, the Howard Hughes Medical Institute Laboratory, the Department of Embryology of the Carnegie Institution of Washington, the Gerontology Research Center of the National Institute on Aging, and the Addiction Research Center of the National Institute on Drug Abuse).
5. Florida, *The Rise of the Creative Class.*
6. Harvard University, "A Considerable Impact on the Economy." On line at www.harvard.edu.
7. Curti and Nash, *Philanthropy in the Shaping of American Higher Education*, p. 52.

8. Cohen, *The Shaping of American Higher Education*, pp. 87–88.
9. Lorenzen, "Andrew Carnegie and His Charity Towards Libraries."
10. Wooster, "Julius Rosenwald."
11. Ibid.
12. Ibid.
13. Ibid.
14. Museum of Science and Industry, Chicago, "VisitMSI."
15. Metro Chicago Information Center.
16. Ibid.
17. Ibid.
18. Kinzer, "Arts in America," pp. 1–2.
19. Guggenheim Museum, press release.
20. Ibid.
21. Decker, *The Whaling City*, p. 76.
22. Peirce, "Rouse: The Great Oak Falls."
23. *The Inner Harbor Book*.
24. Peirce, "Rouse: The Great Oak Falls."
25. "The History of Habitat: How It Works." On line at http://www.habitat.org/how/historytext.html.

5: ADVANCING NEW IDEAS: INTELLECTUAL CAPITAL

1. Stewart, *Intellectual Capital*.
2. In developed economies the rates of growth may slow because they start from a more advanced base each year. Growth does continue, however. Whereas in developing economies, the rates of growth may be very high and slow as they reach certain levels of advancement—but continue growing if they are healthy.
3. Paul Romer, "Economic Growth," in David R. Henderson, ed. *The Fortune Encyclopedia of Economics* (New York, Warner Books). Available on line at http://www.standford.edu/~promer/Econgro.htm.
4. Miller, *Dollars for Research*, pp. x–xxi.
5. Robert Goddard, autobiographical essay quoted on the American Institute of Aeronautics and Astronautics website. On line at http://www.aiaa.org/HistoricalSites/content/PDF/Goddard.pdf.
6. John H. Davis, *The Guggenheims: An American Epic* (New York: Morrow, 1978), p. 158.
7. Ibid., p. 160.
8. Ibid., p. 163.
9. Ibid., pp. 169–70.
10. Jennet Conant. On line at http://www.northcountynews.com/Archives2002/12_18_02/2002_1218lifestyles1.htm.
11. Conant, *Tuxedo Park*, pp. 273–74.
12. The Mary Woodward Lasker Charitable Trust, Annual Report 2001, p. 1.

13. Carter, *The Gentle Legions*, p. 96.
14. "R&D Funding Forecast for 2003 Predicts Major Shift Ahead; Federal Government Spending More; Industry Spending Less," PR Newswire Association, Columbus, Ohio, January 2, 2003.
15. Benjamin Franklin, *The Autobiography of Benjamin Franklin,* chapter 9, "Schemes for Public Improvements." Online at http://www.usgennet.org/usa/topic/preservation/bios/franklin/chpt9.htm.
16. "Lessons Learned Along the Way: Starting a Non-Profit"; MADD History; About Us, Mother's Against Drunk Driving. On line at http://www.madd.org/aboutus/0,1056,1122,00.html.
17. National Highway Traffic Safety Association, 1996.
18. Florio, *Prohibit the Sale of Alcoholic Beverages to Persons Under 21 Years of Age.*
19. Terry Carter, "Mad and Madder," ABA Journal eReport. Online at http://www.abanet.org/journal/ereport/d13drunk.html.
20. Amon, "Long Island: Our Story."
21. Berg and Ferrier, "Meeting the Challenge."
22. Environmental Defense, 2001 Annual Report.
23. According to MoveOn.org, the ozone hole is shrinking: "In September, the Australian Commonwealth Scientific and Industrial Research Organization announced that the hole in the ozone is closing. It should fully recover by 2050 if current trends continue. At its peak, the hole was three times the size of Australia. A global ban on CFCs under the Montreal Protocol of the 1990's has helped reduce CFC usage to the point where their levels in the atmosphere have begun to fall. Scientists say that the closing of the hole demonstrates how well global environmental protocols work, which could help gain more support for the Kyoto Protocol." On line at http://www.aig.asn.au/ozone_hole_closing.htm.
24. Reed, "Environmentalist Fred Krupp Helps Crush the Ubiquitous Fast-Food Clamshell."

6: GENEROSITY AND THE FUTURE OF DEMOCRATIC CAPITALISM

1. Participants are chosen so that together they represent the U.S. population for the characteristics significant for economic study results. These include race and ethnicity among others.
2. Cox and Alm, "By Our Own Bootstraps," p. 4.
3. Ibid.
4. Alesina, Di Tella, and MacCulloch, "Inequality and Happiness."
5. Ibid.
6. Ibid.
7. Karlyn H. Bowman and Everett Carl Ladd, *What's Wrong* (Washington, D.C.: AEI Press, 1998).
8. Wilson, *Considerations on the Nature and Extent of the Legislative Authority of the British Parliament,* p. 108.

9. McCullough, *John Adams,* p. 121.
10. Francis Hutcheson, *An Inquiry into the Origins of Our Ideas of Beauty and Virtue,* 2nd ed. (London, Printed for J. Darby, A. Bettesworth, F. Fayram [etc.], 1726), p. 177.
11. Lipset, "Some Social Requisites of Democracy," p. 75.
12. McCullough, *John Adams,* p. 102.
13. Rabin, "Psychology and Economics," p. 11.
14. Ibid., p. 33.
15. Simmons, "Presidential Address on Altruism and Sociology," p. 10.
16. Ibid., p. 3.
17. Names and circumstances have been changed to protect privacy.
18. Fordham Institute for Innovation in Social Policy, "The Social Report," p. 66.
19. Ibid., p. 9.
20. Ibid., p. 57.
21. Miringoff, Miringoff, and Opdycke, *The Social Health of the Nation,* p. 57.
22. U.S. Census Bureau, "Share of Aggregate Income Received by Each Fifth and Top 5 Percent of Households, 1967 to 2001."
23. Just to clarify, individuals and families moved quickly through this bottom 40 percent of the income distribution during this period, but the average income for those remaining and those newly entering stagnated. Their conditions as a group did not improve. Upward mobility in the study I quoted by the Dallas Federal Reserve Bank operated effectively because those in this quintile had and took advantage of opportunities, and their incomes propelled them up and out of the quintile. But that fact means the success stories were no longer in the bottom quintile and those who replaced them had even lower incomes than those departing had when they were still in the quintile. The average income of the bottom two groups did not improve.
24. Wolff, *Top Heavy,* pp. 2–3.
25. Lane, *The Loss of Happiness in Market Democracies,* p. 36.
26. Ibid., p. 10.

7: THE CHALLENGE OF AMERICA'S WEALTH AND THE COMING WEALTH TRANSFER

1. "The Giving Boom: How the New Philanthropy Will Change America," *Think Tank with Ben Wattenberg,* July 12, 2001. On line at http://www.pbs.org/thinktank/givingboom_transcript.html; accessed September 2002.
2. Schervish and Havens wrote a twelve-point reevaluation of their calculations after the drop in the market in 2002 and reassured themselves and their readers that their lowest estimate is still probably too conservative. Boston College Social Welfare Research Institute press release, January 6, 2003. John J. Havens and Paul G. Schervish, "Why the $41 Trillion Wealth

Transfer Is Still Valid," *Journal of Gift Planning,* winter 2003, vol. 7, no. 1, pp. 11–15, 47–50.

3. Eugene R. Tempel and Patrick M. Rooney, "Repeal of the Estate Tax," The Center on Philanthropy at Indiana University, November 1, 2000. On line at http://www.philanthropy.iupui.edu/EstateTax.htm.
4. Report by the Consumer Federation of America, July 16, 2001. On line at http://www.consumerfed.org/newsrelease.pdf.
5. Melvin Oliver and Thomas Shapiro, *Black Wealth/White Wealth* (New York: Routledge, 1995).
6. Lisa A. Keister, *Wealth in America: Trends in Wealth Inequality* (New York: Cambridge University Press, 2000), p. 68.
7. "Giving Boom."
8. Tamara Durant and David Callahan, "Crossing Divides: New Common Ground on Poverty and Economic Security Policy," *Demos,* New York, 2002, p. 2.
9. Blakely and Snyder, *Fortress America.*
10. Keith Bradsher, "Study Says Height Makes SUV's Dangerous in Collisions," *New York Times,* May 16, 2001.

8: THE CHALLENGE OF DIVERSITY

1. "The Peopling of America," The Immigrant Experience.
2. William J. McAuley, "Covenants of Care," *Journal of Aging Studies,* June 2001, vol. 15, no. 2, p. 63.
3. As an aside to the central argument, I want to eliminate a common misconception about our currently diverse population. It is a common belief of whites, for instance, that people of color are receivers, not givers, of generosity. Significant controversy surrounds the attempts to account statistically for the giving levels of people of color in America. Many of these citizens give through mechanisms not connected to formal structures like foundations. Many do not seek or get tax deductions. Many give generously to neighbors and extended family members who need tuition or other help. This sharing has never been counted and is very difficult to account for. In one survey, the Independent Sector, a premier research and advocacy organization for philanthropy in America, notes that blacks gave at a rate of 53 percent while whites in the survey gave at 73 percent. Factors having an impact on these statistics would include the lower income/wealth holdings of blacks in America, lower levels of married house holders, and their lower level of higher education—all factors related to higher giving levels.

   In a detailed article, philanthropy researcher Lisa Duran writes: "Other studies found that, despite differences in income, blacks, Hispanics, and whites were equally likely to make charitable contributions and that the sizes of their contributions were about the same. The [Emmet] Carson finding differed, but it is especially noteworthy because its differences account not only for income but for net worth, wealth, or total assets. For example, white families in the United States with annual income of less than $15,000 are nevertheless likely to have net worth of $100,000; black families with the same income, however, show a median net worth of zero or negative (debt). At the other end of the income scale, white families with incomes of $75,000 show a median net worth of $140,200, while a black family with the same income has a net worth of $54,000. Despite this widening wealth gap, African Americans at all income levels continue to make contributions." Duran, "Caring for Each Other."

4. Kenneth Prewitt, director of the U.S. Census Bureau (1998–2001), "Demography, Diversity, and Democracy, The 2000 Census Story," *Brookings Review,* vol. 20, no. 1, Winter 2002, pp. 6–9. On line at http://www.brook.edu/dybdocroot/press/REVIEW/winter2002/prewitt.htm.
5. Camarota, "Immigrants in the United States—2002."
6. Ibid.
7. Statistics were gleaned from the U.S Census Bureau, 2000–2001.
8. "Chapter 6—Religion," *The First Measured Century: An Illustrated Guide to Trends in America, 1900–2000.* AEI Press (November 20, 2000).
9. Seager, *Buddhism in America,* p. 11. Martin Bauman, in *The Dharma Has Come West,* writes that in the mid-1990s there were roughly 3 to 4 million Buddhists in the United States, which includes 800,000 Euro-American Buddhists. He estimates five hundred to six hundred centers, and using a total population figure of 261 million, Buddhists represent 1.6 percent, which is significantly higher than any of the other countries he lists. Charles Prebish, in *Luminous Passage: The Practice and Study of Buddhism in America* (Berkeley, Calif.: University of California Press, 1999), also reprints Bauman's figures. The Pluralism Project Directory lists 1662 Buddhist Centers in the United States. Don Morreale lists over a thousand centers in the United States and Canada in *The Complete Guide to Buddhist America* (Boston, Mass.: Shambhala Publications, 1998). *Britannica Book of the Year* estimate for 2000 is 2.45 million. Between 1 and 2 million Americans formally practiced Buddhism in 2000, according to *Yearbook of American and Canadian Churches.*

   There are about 6 million Muslims in the United States, according to estimates adopted by the U.S. State Department. M. M. Ali, "Muslims in America," *The Washington Report on Middle East Affairs,* May–June 1996, vol. 15, no. 1, p. 13. The Pluralism Project Directory lists 1,729 Muslim mosques and centers in the United States.
10. Three faiths—Buddhism, Hinduism, and Islam—account for about half of those following other religions. According to the GSS, they totaled 0.4 percent in 1973–80, 0.7 percent in 1981–90, and 1.1 percent in 1991–2000. The ARIS found that the three religions were 0.7 percent in 1990 and 1.4 percent in 2001.

11. "The 1990 U.S. Census indicated that the number of Asian Indians in the United States (not all of them Hindus) increased 125 percent during the 1980s, rising to 815,000 (about 0.3 percent of the U.S. population). When non-Asian Hindus are incorporated into the equation, one arrives at a total of well over 1 million Hindus residing in the United States." Edwin Scott Gaustan and Philip L. Barlow, *New Historical Atlas of Religion in America* (New York: Oxford University Press, 2000), p. 272. The Pluralism Project Directory lists 646 Hindu temples and centers in the United States.
12. Blakeley and Snyder, *Fortress America.*
13. Havel, "The Future of Hope."
14. Timothy Besley, Stephen Coate, and Glenn Loury, "The Economics of Rotating Savings and Credit Associations," *American Economic Review,* September 1993, vol. 83, no. 4, pp. 792–810.
15. Chami and Fischer, "Community Banking, Monitoring, and the Clinton Plan."
16. Sika and Strasser, "Tontines in Cameroon," pp. 21–22.
17. Association for Creation of Employment, "Islamic Modes of Financing," Conference and Workshop Report, Peshawar, November 10 and 11, 2000. On line at http://www.ids.ac.uk/cgap/download/imof.doc.
18. Gibbons, *International Replication of Grameen Banking.*
19. Huntington, *The Clash of Civilizations and the Remaking of World Order.*

9: DANGEROUS DONATIONS

1. The term *dangerous donations* comes from Methodist Bishop Warren A. Chandler, an early and persistent critic of Northern philanthropy and its influence on the South and race relations. His tract, "Dangerous Donations or Degrading Doles, or A Vast Scheme for Capturing and Controlling the Colleges and Universities of the Country," was published in 1909. Quoted in Eric Anderson and Alfred Moss, Jr., *Dangerous Donations* (Columbia, Mo.: University of Missouri Press, 1999).
2. Addams, "A Modern Lear," p. 119.
3. Hiatt, "Around the Continent in 180 Days," pp. 18–24.
4. Darlene Clark Hine, *Black Professionals and Race Consciousness: Origins of the Civil Rights Movement from 1890–1955,* chapter 2 (Champaign: University of Illinois Press, forthcoming).
5. Details have been changed to protect the anonymity of these individuals.
6. Branch, "Philip Morris's Ad on Macaroni and Peace."
7. *Wealthfare* is a term invented by Minneapolis lawyer Paul Niemann.

10: WORKING SOLUTIONS

1. McGoldrick, "Service Learning and the Economics Course," p. 43.
2. Lawrence, *Family Foundations,* p. 37.
3. Major investment firms all give advice on how to establish a family founda-

tion. They also provide information on the financial regulations that govern these entities. A Merrill Lynch website called Family Foundations states: "No deduction restrictions apply to contributions made by will to a family foundation. An estate may claim an estate tax charitable deduction for the full amount of the foundation funding. For example, a family foundation can be listed as the designated beneficiary of an IRA, avoiding, at death, not only estate taxes that might have been owed if the IRA had been left to children but also the income taxes that were deferred during the person's lifetime. Because family foundations are tax-exempt organizations, assets transferred to the foundation can be sold free of capital gains taxes, as long as the assets are used for the charitable purposes for which the foundation was established. This feature can make more funds available for the foundation's work." On line at www.ml.com.

4. The Columbus Foundation, 1999 Community Foundation Survey.
5. A reminder if you are intrigued by the idea of giving through or to a community foundation: there is much potential for a "dangerous donation" here. Let me explain. While it is a fine idea to provide scholarship money for a local minority student to attend university, for instance, too much specificity can inhibit future stewards of the foundation from making use of the gift in the best way, or indeed using it at all. Don't specify the race of the recipient, or the school where the scholarship can be used, or the topic the student must study, or, God forbid, all of the above, or the gift may prove too inflexible for real use in the future.
6. Abdul Sm Rasheed, "What Would the Community Economic Development Expertise Act Do?," September 17, 2002, Testimony Before the Housing and Community Opportunity Subcommittee, p. 2.
7. Freedman, *Upon This Rock*.
8. Community development corporations can be helped with good strategies by organizations like the Industrial Areas Foundation, founded by Saul Alinsky, LISC (Local Initiative Support Corporation), initiated by the Ford Foundation.
9. American Assembly, "Cross-sectoral Partnerships," working draft (New York, June 2003), p. 26.
10. Rubin, Speech.
11. "Community Investing." On line at http://www.calvertgroup.com/sri_650.html.
12. Osborne, "A Poverty Program That Works."
13. Shapiro, "ShoreBank Corporation."
14. Osborne, *Laboratories of Democracy*.
15. AAFRC Trust for Philanthropy, *Giving USA 2002: The Annual Report on Philanthropy for the Year 2001* (Indianapolis: American Association of Fundraising Counsel, 2002), p. 59. On line at http://www.aafrc.org.
16. Ken Dayton, "Stages of Giving," *Independent Sector,* p. 5.

11: A PHILANTHROPIC REVOLUTION

1. Stephen Moore, "It's Getting Better All the Time," The Cato Institute. On line at http://www.bigeye.com/jj01221.htm.
2. John Knowles, "The Composition and Distribution of Wealth," lecture at Topics in Macro-Economics, University of Pennsylvania, 2002.
3. The National Council on Aging, "Facts About Older Americans." On line at http://www.ncoa.org/content.cfm?sectionID=106.
4. Testimony of Theodore R. Groom Before the Subcommittee on Employer/Employee Relations Education and Workforce Committee, September 14, 2000. On line at http://edworkforce.house.gov/hearings/106th/eer/pension91400/groom.htm.
5. In an article for *Esquire,* Ray Boshara, director, Asset Building Program, New America Foundation, called wealth building, "The Big Idea: Asset Building," December 1, 2002. He also published "The $6,000 Solution" in *Atlantic Monthly,* February 1, 2003.
6. After appropriate review and agreement, a specific income level and family size could be designated to create the right point for this support. Rather than one salary point for the whole nation, distinctions for different states and costs of living would make the definitions more workable across the country.
7. See chapter 8 of this book.
8. Several foundations have responded to the work of Professor Sherraden, and the donors interested in this approach pioneered the asset-building field, beginning in the mid-1990s. These include: The Ford Foundation, Charles Stewart Mott Foundation, Joyce Foundation, F. B. Heron Foundation, John D. and Catherine T. MacArthur Foundation, Citigroup Foundation, Fannie Mae Foundation, The Annie E. Casey Foundation, Levi Strauss Foundation, Ewing Marion Kauffman Foundation, Rockefeller Foundation, Charles and Helen Schwab Foundation, and the Moriah Fund.
9. What began in 1993 as a few, small, independent individual development account (IDA) programs has grown into a popular economic development strategy that is uniting community-based organizations, financial institutions, educators and trainers, national advocacy organizations, policy makers, and private foundations across forty-four states. At the center of the IDA field are 250-plus IDA programs that have sprung up in diverse communities across the nation. But what unifies these programs is a dynamic, multilayered network of initiatives that serve to build greater financial and political support for IDAs, increase the effectiveness of IDAs, connect IDAs with complementary economic development strategies, and remove obstacles to making IDAs available to all low-income individuals. Together these initiatives are transforming the economic development landscape.
10. Ford, Rockefeller, Mott, and Annie E. Casey, among others.

11. Ray Boshara before the Subcommittees on Select Revenue Measures and Human Resources, Committee on Ways and Means Hearing on H.R. 7. The Community Solutions Act, June 14, 2001.
12. U.S. Census Bureau. On line at http://www.census.gov/hhes/www/housing/hvs/qtr300/q300/q300ind.html.
13. The last 110 years have seen a very significant involvement of the federal government in housing policy and in provision and support of housing and home ownership. In the first years of the twenty-first century, Mrs. Russell Sage, a farsighted philanthropist, focused on improving the quality of life and made home ownership one of her goals. Although she had very modest success, she was on the right track, and her difficulties may have illustrated just how hard this goal would prove to be. Since 1995, the federal government has made home ownership a priority, and, more recently, Fannie Mae, a private corporation, and the federal government, have committed to contribute billions of dollars and new efforts in mortgage investments for minority families over the next ten years and to make significant investments in affordable loans for all lower-income Americans. The forms of investment in home ownership have continued. Many have been funded in partnership with national or state-based as well as faith-based arrangements, all focused on putting the assets of home ownership into the hands of low- and moderate-income citizens. Fannie Mae has recently pledged to make $400 billion available in housing loans to serve 3 million minority Americans over the next eight years. Flexible, low-cost housing capital is an investment in the common future, in the larger economy, as well as in the families who will finally be able to leverage the dollars they have been spending on housing and build equity—wealth that bring security and assets to help launch their adult children's home ownership and to secure loans for other large investments whose purchase builds the economy.

    For instance, the average sale price of a home in LeDroit Park in the Howard University section of Washington, D.C., in 1999 was $157,000. Three years later, the same houses were selling at $224,000. Owners had built their investment by $67,000 in just three years.
14. For a set of studies confirming these and other advantages to low-income families and to lowering demands on social support costs see Richard K. Green and Michelle J. White, "Measuring the Benefits of Homeowning: Effects on Children," mimeo (Chicago: Center for the Study of the Economy and the State, 1994); Peter H. Rossi and Eleanor Weber, "The Social Benefits of Homeownership: Empirical Evidence from National Surveys," *Housing Policy Debate* 7(1) 1996; and Denise DiPasquale and Edward L. Glaeser, "Incentives and Social Capital: Are Home Owners Better Citizens?" (Joint Center for Housing Studies Working Paper Series W97-3,1997).
15. Franklin Raines, "Remarks for the National Urban League," August 1, 2001, Washington, D.C.

16. Johnson, "The American Housing Finance System."
17. Hernando De Soto, *The Mystery of Capitalism: Why Capitalism Triumphs in the West and Fails Everywhere Else* (New York: Basic Books, 2000), p. 7.
18. This idea has been a consistent call of Marc Miringoff's. See his *Social Health of the Nation.* I agree with his notion that we will make progress on what we count and know about.

BIBLIOGRAPHY

BOOKS

Addams, Jane. *Newer Ideals of Peace*. London: MacMillan, 1907.

America, Richard F., ed. *Philanthropy and Economic Development*. Westport, Conn.: Greenwood Press, 1995.

Anderson, Eric, and Alfred Moss, Jr. *Dangerous Donations: Northern Philanthropy and Southern Black Education, 1912–1930*. Columbia, Mo.: University of Missouri Press, 1999.

Aristotle. *Politics*. Trans. Benjamin Jowett, bk. 6, pt. 5. On line at http://classics.mit.edu/Aristotle/politics.6.six.html.

Arnove, Robert, ed. *Philanthropy and Cultural Imperialism: The Foundations at Home and Abroad*. Boston: G. K. Hall, 1980.

Bauman, Martin. *The Dharma Has Come West: A Survey of Recent Studies and Sources*. On line at http://jbe.la.psu.edu/4/baum2.html.

Becker, Gary. *Human Capital: A Theoretical and Empirical Analysis,* 3rd ed. Chicago, Ill.: University of Chicago Press, 1993.

Becker, William E., and Darrell R. Lewis. *The Economics of American Higher Education*. Boston: Kluwer Academic Publishers, 1992.

Becker, William E., and Darrell R. Lewis, eds. *Higher Education and Economic Growth*. Boston: Kluwer Academic Publishers, 1993.

Behrman, Jere R., and Stacey Nevser, eds. *The Social Benefits of Education*. Ann Arbor: University of Michigan Press, 1997.

Bellah, Robert N., et al. *Habits of the Heart*. Berkeley: University of California Press, 1985.

Bercovici, Konrad, with an introduction by John Reed. *Crimes of Charity.* New York: Alfred A. Knopf, 1917.

Blakely, Edward, and Mary Ann Snyder. *Fortress America: Gated Communities in the United States.* Washington, D.C.: The Brookings Institution, 1997.

Booth, William James. *Households.* Ithaca, N.Y.: Cornell University Press, 1993.

Bowen, William G. and Derek Bok. *The Shape of the River.* Princeton: Princeton University Press, 1988.

Bremner, Robert H. *American Philanthropy.* Chicago: University of Chicago Press, 1988.

———. *Giving.* New Brunswick, N.J.: Transaction Publishers, 1996.

Brilliant, Eleanor L. *Private Charity and Public Inquiry.* Bloomington, Ind.: Indiana University Press, 2000.

Brown, Lester R., Christopher Flavin, and Hilary French. *State of the World 2000.* New York: W. W. Norton, 2000.

Burder, George. *Essay to Do Good.* London: J. Dannett, 1888.

Caplovitz, David. *The Poor Pay More.* New York: The Free Press, 1967.

Caplow, Theodore, Louis Hicks, and Ben J. Wattenberg. *The First Measured Century: An Illustrated Guide to Trends in America, 1900–2000.* Washington, D.C.: AEI Press, 2000.

Carter, Richard. *The Gentle Legions.* Garden City, N.Y.: Doubleday, 1961.

Caulkins, Frances Manwaring. *History of New London, Connecticut.* New London: H. D. Utley, 1895.

Chernow, Ron. *Titan.* New York: Random House, 1998.

Clotfelter, Charles T. *Who Benefits from the NonProfit Sector?* Chicago: University of Chicago Press, 1992.

Clotfelter, Charles T., and Thomas Ehrlich. *Philanthropy and the Nonprofit Sector in a Changing America.* Bloomington, Ind.: Indiana University Press, 2001.

Cohen, Arthur M. *The Shaping of American Higher Education: Emergence and Growth of the Contemporary System.* San Francisco: Jossey-Bass Publishers, 1998.

Conant, Jennet. *Tuxedo Park: A Wall Street Tycoon and the Secret Palace of Science That Changed the Course of World War II.* New York: Simon & Schuster, 2002.

Curti, Merle, and Roderick Nash. *Philanthropy in the Shaping of American Higher Education.* New Brunswick, N.J.: Rutgers University Press, 1965.

Dayton, Ken. *Stages of Giving.* Washington, D.C.: Independent Sector, 1999.

Decker, Robert Owen. *The Whaling City.* Chester, Conn.: The Pequot Press, 1976.

Doan, Mason C. *American Housing Production 1880–2000.* New York: University Press of America, 1997.

Draut, Tamara, and David Callahan. *Crossing Divides: New Common Ground on Poverty and Economic Security Policy.* New York: Demos, 2002.

Easterlin, Richard A. *Growth Triumphant: The Twenty-first Century in Historical Perspective.* Ann Arbor: University of Michigan Press, 1996.

Edward, Jonathan. *Charity and Its Fruits.* New York: Robert Carter & Brothers, 1852.

Florida, Richard. *The Rise of the Creative Class.* New York: Basic Books, 2002.

Florio, J. J. *Prohibit the Sale of Alcoholic Beverages to Persons Under 21 Years of Age.* H.R. 3870. Washington, D.C.: U.S. House of Representatives, Committee on Energy and Commerce, Subcommittee on Commerce, Transportation, and Tourism, 1983.

Foster, Lawrence G. *Robert Wood Johnson: The Gentleman Rebel.* State College, Pa.: Lillian Press, 1999.

Freedman, Samuel. *Upon This Rock: The Miracles of a Black Church.* New York: HarperCollins, 1992.

Friedman, Lawrence J., and Mark D. McGarvie. *Charity, Philanthropy, and Civility in American History.* Cambridge, U.K.: Cambridge University Press, 2003.

Fukuyama, Francis. *Trust: The Social Virtues and the Creation of Prosperity.* New York: Free Press, 1995.

Gaustan, Edwin Scott, and Philip L. Barlow. *New Historical Atlas of Religion in America.* New York: Oxford University Press, 2000.

Geiger, Roger L. *Private Sectors in Higher Education: Structure, Function, and Change in Eight Countries.* Ann Arbor: University of Michigan Press, 1986.

———. *Research and Relevant Knowledge: American Research Universities Since World War II.* New York: Oxford University Press, 1993.

———. *Single Donor Universities.* New Haven, Conn.: Institution for Social and Policy Studies, Yale University, 1995.

Gérard-Varet, L.-A., et al. *The Economics of Reciprocity, Giving and Altruism.* New York: St. Martin's Press, 2001.

Gladwell, Malcolm. *The Tipping Point.* New York: Little, Brown and Company, 2000.

Gordon, John Steele. *The Business of America.* New York: Walker and Company, 2001.

Gratz, Roberta Brandes, and Norman Mintz. *Cities Back from the Edge.* New York: John Wiley & Sons, 1998.

Greenough, William C. *It's My Retirement Money, Take Good Care of It.* Boston: Irwin, 1990.

Grogan, Paul S., and Tony Proscio. *Comeback Cities.* Oxford, U.K.: Westview Press, 2000.

Hall, Peter Dobkin. *The Organization of American Culture, 1700–1900: Private Institutions, Elites, and the Origins of American Nationality.* New York: New York University Press, 1982.

———. *Inventing the Nonprofit Sector and Other Essays on Philanthropy, Voluntarism, and Nonprofit Organizations.* Baltimore: Johns Hopkins University Press, 1992.

Hammond, Allen. *Which World? Scenarios for the 21st Century.* Washington, D.C.: Island Press, 1998.

Healy, Tom, and Sylvain Cote, with significant input from John F. Helliwell, Simon Field, and many other colleagues within the OECD Secretariat. *The Well-Being of Nations: The Role of Human and Social Capital.* Paris: Organisation for Economic Co-operation and Development, 2001.

Hine, Darlene Clark, and Kathleen Thompson. *A Shining Thread of Hope.* New York: Broadway Books, 1999.

Hosbawm, Eric, and Terence Ranger. *The Invention of Tradition.* Cambridge, U.K.: Cambridge University Press, 1999.

Hodgkinson, Virginia A., and Murray Weitzman. *Giving and Volunteering in the United States.* New York: The Foundation Center, 1998.

Huntington, Samuel P. *The Clash of Civilizations and the Remaking of World Order.* New York: Simon & Schuster, 1996.

Inner Harbor Book, The. Baltimore: City of Baltimore Department of Planning, 1984.

Jacobs, Jane. *The Death and Life of Great American Cities.* New York: Random House, 1961.

Joseph, James A. *Remaking America.* San Francisco: Jossey-Bass Publishers, 1995.

Johnson, James A. *Showing America a New Home.* San Francisco: Jossey-Bass Publishers, 1996.

Katz, Michael B. *In the Shadow of the Poorhouse.* New York: Basic Books, 1986.

Ketcham, Ralph L., ed. *The Political Thought of Benjamin Franklin.* Indianapolis: Bobbs-Merrill, 1965.

Kevles, Daniel J. *The Physicists.* Cambridge, Mass.: Harvard University Press, 1995.

Keynes, John Maynard. *Essays in Persuasion.* London: St. Martin's Press, 1972.

King, Cornelia S., compiler. *American Philanthropy, 1731–1860: Printed Works in the Collections of the American Philosophical Society, the Historical Society Of Pennsylvania, and the Library Company of Philadelphia.* New York: Garland, 1984.

Kohler, Robert E. *Partners in Science.* Chicago: University of Chicago Press, 1991.

Lane, Robert. *The Loss of Happiness in Market Democracies.* New Haven: Yale University Press, 2000.

Lawrence, Steven. *Family Foundations: A Profile of Funders and Trends.* Washington, D.C.: The Foundation Center, 2000.

Lesser, Eric, Michael A. Fontaine, and Jason A. Slusher. *Knowledge and Communities.* Boston: Butterworth-Heinemann, 2000.

Lim, David. *Explaining Economic Growth: A New Analytical Framework.* Brookfield, Vt.: Edward Elgar Publishing, 1996.

Locke, John. *A Letter Concerning Toleration.* Indianapolis: Haskett Publishing Company, 1983.

———. *Locke On Money.* Oxford, U.K.: Clarendon Press, 1991.

Machlup, Fritz. *Education and Economic Growth.* Lincoln: University of Nebraska Press, 1970.

McCarty, Oseola. *Simple Wisdom for Rich Living.* Atlanta: Longstreet Press, 1996.

McCullough, David. *John Adams.* New York: Simon & Schuster, 2001.

McMillan, John. *Reinventing the Bazaar.* New York: W. W. Norton and Company, 2002.

Miller, Howard. *Dollars for Research: Science and Its Patrons in Nineteenth-Century America.* Seattle: University of Washington Press, 1970.

Miringoff, Marc, Marque-Luisa Miringoff, and Sandra Opdycke. *The Social Health of the Nation: How America Is Really Doing.* New York: Oxford University Press, 1999.

Nie, Norman H., Jane Junn, and Kenneth Stehlik-Barry. *Education and Democratic Citizenship in America.* Chicago: University of Chicago Press, 1996.

Nielsen, Waldemar. *The Golden Donors.* New York: Truman Talley Books, 1985.

———. *Inside American Philanthropy: The Dramas of Donorship.* Norman, Okla.: University of Oklahoma Press, 1996.

Nisbet, Robert. *History of the Idea of Progress.* New York: Basic Books, 1980.

North, Douglass Cecil. *Institutions, Institutional Change, and Economic Performance.* New York: Cambridge University Press, 1990.

Noyes, Gertrude E. *A History of Connecticut College.* New London: Connecticut College, 1982.

O'Connell, Brian. *Powered by Coalition.* San Francisco: Jossey-Bass Publishers, 1997.

———. *Civil Society.* Hanover, N.H.: Tufts University Press, 1999.

Odendahl, Teresa. *Charity Begins at Home: Generosity and Self-Interest Among the Philanthropic Elite.* New York: Basic Books, 1990.

Osborne, David. *Laboratories of Democracy.* Cambridge, Mass.: Harvard Business School Press, 1988.

Ostrower, Francie. *Why the Wealthy Give: The Culture of Elite Philanthropy.* Princeton, N.J.: Princeton University Press, 1995.

Payton, Robert, et al. *Philanthropy: Four Views.* New Brunswick, N.J.: Transaction Publishers, 1998.

Phillips, Kevin. *Wealth and Democracy.* New York: Broadway Books, 2002.

Powell, Walter W. *The Nonprofit Sector.* New Haven: Yale University Press, 1987.

Pursell, Carroll W., Jr. *Technology in America.* Cambridge, Mass.: MIT Press, 1991.

Putnam, Robert. *Bowling Alone.* New York: Simon & Schuster, 2000.

Rawls, John. *A Theory of Justice.* Cambridge, Mass.: Harvard University Press, 1999.

Richardson, Jean. *Partnerships in Communities: Reweaving the Fabric of Rural America.* Washington D.C.: Island Press, 2000.

Robinson, Richard H., and Willard L. Johnson. *The Buddhist Religion.* New York: Wadsworth Publishing Company, 1997.

Romer, Paul Michael. *Human Capital and Growth: Theory and Evidence.* Cambridge, Mass.: National Bureau of Economic Research, 1989.

Rose, Mary B., ed. *Family Business.* Brookfield, Vt.: Edward Elgar Publishing, 1995.

Rose-Ackerman, Susan. *The Economics of Nonprofit Institutions.* New York: Oxford University Press, 1986.

Rothschild, Emma. *Economics Sentiments.* Cambridge, Mass.: Harvard University Press, 2002.

Salamon, Lester, and Helmut Anheier. *Defining the Nonprofit Sector.* Manchester, U.K.: Manchester University Press, 1997.

Sander, Kathleen Waters. *The Business of Clarity.* Urbana, Ill.: University of Illinois Press, 1998.

Schervish, Paul, et al. *Care and Community in Modern Society.* San Francisco: Jossey-Bass Publishers, 1995.

Seager, Richard. *Buddhism in America.* New York: Columbia University Press, 1999.

Sealander, Judith. *Private Wealth and Public Life: Foundation Philanthropy and the Reshaping of American Social Policy from the Progressive Era to the New Deal.* Baltimore: Johns Hopkins University Press, 1997.

Sears, Jesse Brundage. *Philanthropy in the History of American Higher Education.* Reprint edition, with a new introduction by Roger L. Geiger. New Brunswick, N.J.: Transaction, 1990.

Sizemore, Russell F., and Donald K. Sweaner. *Ethics, Wealth, and Salvation.* Columbia, S.C.: University of South Carolina Press, 1990.

Skocpol, Theda, and Morris P. Fiorina, eds. *Civic Engagement in American Society.* Washington, D.C.: Brookings Institution Press, 1999.

Spain, Daphne. *How Women Saved the Cities.* Minneapolis: University of Minnesota Press, 2001.

Steinberg, Richard. *Economics and Philanthropy: A Marriage of Necessity for Nonprofit Organizations.* Indianapolis: Center of Philanthropy, 1993.

———. *The Clash of Values in Civil Society.* Indianapolis: Center of Philanthropy, 1995.

Stewart, Thomas. *Intellectual Capital.* New York: Doubleday, 2000.

Stone, Gregory N. *The Day Paper.* New London, Conn.: Day Publishing Company, 2000.

Sullivan, William M. *Work and Integrity.* New York: HarperCollins Publishers, 1995.

Szirmai, Adam, Bart Van Ark, and Dirk Pilat. *Explaining Economic Growth: Essays in Honour of Angus Maddison.* New York: North-Holland, 1993.

Til, Jon Van. *Critical Issues in American Philanthropy.* San Francisco: Jossey-Bass Publishers, 1990.

———. *Growing Civil Society.* Bloomington, Ind.: Indiana University Press, 2000.

Timmons, Bascom N. *Jesse H. Jones.* New York: Henry Holt and Company, 1956.

Tittle, Diana. *Rebuilding Cleveland.* Columbus, Ohio: Ohio State University Press, 1992.

Trattner, W. *From Poor Law to Welfare State.* New York: Free Press, 1989.

Warner, Amos G. *American Charities: A Study in Philanthropy and Economics.* Reprint edition, with a new introduction by Mary Jo Deegan. New Brunswick, N.J.: Transaction, 1989.

Wilson, James. *Considerations on the Nature and Extent of the Legislative Authority of the British Parliament,* 1774, in Carl L. Becker, *The Declaration of Independence: A Study in the History of Political Ideas,* 1922, 3rd ed. New York: Alfred A. Knopf, 1969.

Winthrop, John. *A Modell of Christian Charity, 1630.* Collections of the Massachusetts Historical Society, Boston, 1838, 3rd series. Hanover Historical Texts Project. On line at http://history.hanover.edu/texts/winthmod.html; accessed September 2002.

Wolff, Edward N. *Top Heavy.* New York: The New Press, 2002.

Wolpert, Julian. *Patterns of Generosity in America: Who's Holding the Safety Net?* New York: Twentieth Century Fund Press, 1993.

Wuthnow, Robert. *Learning to Care.* New York: Oxford University Press, 1995.

Articles and Reports

Addams, Jane. "A Modern Lear" Survey. November 2, 1912, reprinted in Christopher Lasch, ed., *The Social Thought of Jane Addams.* Indianapolis: Bobbs-Merrill Co., 1965.

Alesina, Alberto, Rafael Di Tella, and Robert MacCulloch. "Inequality and Happiness: Are Europeans and Americans Different?" *Journal of Public Economics,* June 2002.

Amon, Rhoda. "Long Island: Our Story / The Anti-DDT Vanguard / Suffolk Activists Lead the Fight to Save Wildlife in the 1960s." *Newsday,* January 12, 1998. On line at http://www.elibrary.com.

Anderegg, Michael J. Congressional testimony. "Juvenile Crime." Washington D.C.: Federal Document Clearing House, Inc., 3-08-01. Electric Library; accessed February 2, 2002.

Arete Corporation. "Report Card—I Have a Dream®: The Impacts." On line at http://www.ihad.org/reports.php; accessed fall 2001.

Association for Creation of Employment. "Islamic Modes of Financing: Conference and Workshop Report, Peshawar, 10th–11th November 2000." The Microfinance Gateway. On line at http://www.ids.ac.uk/cgap/download/imof.doc; accessed September 2002.

Berg, David R., and Grant Ferrier. "Meeting the Challenge: U.S. Industry Faces the 21st Century." The U.S. Environmental Industry, Executive Summary. U.S. Department of Commerce, Office of Technology Policy, September 1998.

Berkner, Lutz, et al. "Student Financing of Undergraduate Education: 1999–2000." National Center for Educational Statistics. On line at http://nces.ed.gov/pubs2002/2002167.pdf.

Branch, Shelly. "Philip Morris's Ad on Macaroni and Peace—Kosovo Tale Narrows Gap Between Philanthropy, Publicity." *Wall Street Journal,* July 24, 2001.

Camarota, Steven A. "Immigrants in the United States—2002." Center for Immigration Studies. On line at http://www.cis.org/articles/2002/back1302.html; consulted March 3, 2003.

Campbell, Jodi. "Benjamin Rush and Women's Education: A Revolutionary's Disappointment, A Nation's Achievement." *John and Mary's Journal,* vol. 13. Carlisle, Pa.: Dickinson College, 2000. On line at http://chronicles.dickinson.edu/johnandmary/JMJVolume13/campbell.htm; accessed September 2002.

Chami, Ralph, and Jeffrey H. Fischer. "Community Banking, Monitoring, and the Clinton Plan." *The Cato Journal,* vol. 14, no. 3. On line at http://www.cato.org/pubs/journal/cj14n3-7.html.

Columbus Foundation, The. 1999 Community Foundation Survey. On line at http://www.columbusfoundation.org/comm_found_set.html; accessed September 2002.

Community Resources for Justice. "Adult Correctional Services." On line at http://www.crjustice.org/AdultOff.html.

———. "Returning Inmates: Closing the Public Safety Gap." January 2001. On line at http://www. crjustice.org/rettex.htm.

Cox, W. Michael, and Richard Alm. "By Our Own Bootstraps: Economic Opportunity and the Dynamics of Income Distribution." 1995 Annual Report. Dallas Federal Reserve Bank.

Current Population Survey. "The Rewards of Staying in School" Census 2000 and the Statistical Abstract of the United States. U.S. Census Bureau Public Information Office. On line at http://www.census.gov/Press_Release/www/2001/cb01fff11.html; accessed September 2002.

Davis, Andrew M. "The First Scholarship at Harvard College." *Proceedings of the American Antiquarian Society,* V.N.S., 1887.

De Long, J. Bradford. "Review of: *Growth Triumphant: The Twenty-first Century in Historical Perspective.*" *Journal of Economic Literature,* vol. 36, no. 1, March 1998, pp. 278–80.

Duran, Lisa. "Caring for Each Other: Philanthropy in Communities of Color." *Grassroots Fundraising Journal,* vol. 20, no. 5, 2001.

Enterprise Foundation, The. Annual Report 2001. On line at http://www.enterprisefoundation.org/about/annual/baltimore.asp.

Environmental Defense. 2001 Annual Report. On line at http://www.environmentaldefense.org/documents/360_AR2001.pdf; accessed September 2002.

Finn, Chester E., Jr., and Bruno V. Manno. "American Higher Education:

Behind the Emerald City's Curtain." Hudson Institute Briefing Paper Number 188, April 1996.

Fleishman, Joel L. "Philanthropic Leadership: A Personal Perspective." Presentation to HSBC Bank USA. On line at http://us.hsbc.com/privatebanking/wealth/pb_fleishman.asp.

Fordham Institute for Innovation in Social Policy. "The Social Report, A Deeper View of Prosperity." Tarrytown, 2001.

Frey, Bruno S., and Alois Stutzer. "Happiness, Economy and Institutions." *Economic Journal,* vol. 110, no. 466, October 2000, pp. 918–38.

Funding Exchange. "Our Vision for Social Change Philanthropy." On line at http://www.fex.org/1.0_ourvisionindex.html.

Geoscience News. Australian Institute of Geoscientists. On line at http://www.aig.asn.au/ozone_hole_closing.htm.

Gibbons, David S. "International Replication of Grameen Banking: What Can the Poultry Network Learn from It?" On line at http://www.husdyr.kvl.dk/htm/php/tune99/6-Gibbons.htm; accessed September 2002.

Guggenheim Museum. Press release. On line at http://www.guggenheim.org/press_releases/waterfront_site.html; accessed September 2002.

Hall, Peter Dobkin. "The Model of Boston Charity: A Theory of Charitable Benevolence and Class Development." *Science and Society,* vol. 38, no. 4, Winter 1974–1975, pp. 164–77.

———. "What the Merchants Did with Their Money: The Origins of Charitable and Testamentary Trusts in Massachusetts, 1800–1880." In Conrad E. Wright, ed. *Entrepreneurs: The Boston Business Community, 1750–1850.* Boston: Boston Massachusetts Historical Society, 1997.

Hall, Wiley, III. "Reinventing Black Colleges." *Focus,* October 1999. On line at http://www.jointcenter.org/focus/pdffiles/oct99.pdf.

Hanushek, Eric A., and Dennis D. Kimko. "Schooling, Labor-Force Quality, and the Growth of Nations." *American Economic Review,* vol. 90, no. 5, December 2000, pp. 1184–1208.

Havel, Václav. "The Future of Hope," address given in Hiroshima, Japan, on December 5, 1995. On line at http://www.hrad.cz/president/Havel/speeches/1995/0512_uk.html.

Hiatt, Mark D. "Around the Continent in 180 Days: The Controversial Journey of Abraham Flexner." *The Pharos,* Winter 1999.

Ho, David. "U. S. Prison Population Rising." ABCNews.com. On line at http://abcnews.go.com/sections/us/DailyNews/prisons000420.html.

Huddleston, Barbara. "Community-Based Development: A Cutting Edge for Innovation in the Nineties: A Colloquium Summary." In Neil G. Kotler, ed. *Sharing Innovation: Global Perspectives on Food, Agriculture, and Rural Development: Papers and Proceedings of a Colloquium Organized by the Smithsonian Institution.* Washington, D.C.: Smithsonian Institution Press, 1990.

Inglehart, Ronald. "The Diminishing Utility of Economic Growth: From Maximizing Security Toward Maximizing Subjective Well-Being." *Critical Review,* vol. 10, no. 4, Fall 1996, pp. 509–31.

Johnson, James A. "The American Housing Finance System: A Public/Private Success Story." John C. Whitehead Forum. The Council for Excellence in Government, January 6, 1998. On line at http://excelgov.org/usermedia/images/uploads/PDFs/Johnson_Transcript.pdf.

Kenny, Charles. "Does Growth Cause Happiness, or Does Happiness Cause Growth?" *Kyklos,* vol. 52, no. 1, 1999, pp. 3–25.

Kinzer, Stephen. "Arts in America: It's Museum Time Down South; from Virginia to Louisiana, a Building Boom for Culture." *New York Times,* December 18, 2001.

Kirsch, Irwin S., et al. *Executive Summary of Adult Literacy in America: A First Look at the Results of the National Adult Literacy Survey.* Washington, D.C.: National Center for Educational Statistics. On line at http://nces.ed.gov//naal/resources/execsumm.asp.

Kyriacou, George A. "Level and Growth Effects of Human Capital: A Cross-Country Study of The Convergence Hypothesis." New York: New York University, Faculty of Arts and Science, Department of Economics, 1991.

Leitch, Alexander. *A Princeton Companion.* Princeton: Princeton University Press, 1978. On line at http://mondrian.princeton.edu/CampusWWW/Companion/rush_benjamin.html; accessed September 2002.

Lipset, Seymour Martin. "Some Social Requisites of Democracy: Economic Development and Political Legitimacy." *American Political Science Review,* vol. 53, March 1959, pp. 69–105.

Lorenzen, Michael. "Andrew Carnegie and His Charity Towards Libraries." Other Library Science Papers, Library Instruction Staff, Michigan State University Libraries. On line at http://www.lib.msu.edu/lorenze1/carnegie.htm; accessed September 2002.

Lydenberg, Steven D. "Corporate Philanthropy and Affordable Housing." In Richard F. America, ed., *Philanthropy and Economic Development.* Westport, Conn.: Greenwood Press, 1995.

Mankiw, N. Gregory. "The Growth of Nations." *The Insitute,* no. 1, 1995, pp. 275–326.

Mary Woodward Lasker Charitable Trust, The. Annual Report 2001.

McGoldrick, KimMarie. "Service-Learning in Economics: A Detailed Application." *Journal of Economic Education,* September 22, 1998.

Metro Chicago Information Center. On line at http://www.mcic.org/htmls/new/clientinfo/mip_report.htm; accessed September 2002.

Moffit, Robert E., Jennifer J. Garrett, and Janice A. Smith. "Education School Choice, 2001 Mississippi." The Heritage Research Foundation. On line at http://www.heritage.org/Research/Education/Schools/mississippi.cfm.

Mueller, John. "Democracy vs. Capitalism." *The American Enterprise,* March 1, 2002.

Museum of Science and Industry, Chicago. "Visit MSI." Museum Fact Sheet. On line at http://www.msichicago.org/info/vtm/factsheet.html; accessed September 2002.

National Center for Public Policy and Higher Education. "Losing Ground: A National Status Report on the Affordability of American Higher Education." San Jose: The National Center for Public Policy and Higher Education, 2002.

Organization for Economic Cooperation and Development, Center for Educational Research and Innovation, International Indicators Project, 1995. Available on line at http://nces.ed.gov/pubs/eiip/eiipid31.html.

———. "The Well-being of Nations." Special Report, 2001. p. 18.

Osborne, David. "A Poverty Program That Works." *The New Republic,* May 1989.

Oswald, Andrew J. "Happiness and Economic Performance." *Economic Journal,* vol. 107, no. 445, 1997.

Oswald, Andrew J., and David Blanchflower. "Well-being Over Time in Britain and the USA." NBER Working Paper Number 7487. Cambridge, Mass.: National Bureau for Economic Research, 2000.

Peirce, James Neal. "Rouse: The Great Oak Falls." *County News.* April 29, 1996. On line at http://www.naco.org/pubs/cnews/96-04-29/37nealpe.htm#11.

"The Peopling of America." The Immigrant Experience: Ellis Island. On line at http://www.ellisisland.org/Immexp/indexframe.asp?ellisisland.org; consulted March 15, 2003.

The Phelps-Stokes Fund Report, 1987–1989.

Prewitt, Kenneth. "Demography, Diversity, and Democracy, The 2000 Census Story." *Brookings Review,* vol. 20, no. 1, Winter 2002. On line at http://www.brook.edu/dybdocroot/press/REVIEW/winter2002/prewitt.htm; accessed September 2002.

Primavera, Bill. "The Secret Experiment That Won the War." *North County News,* December 18, 2002. On line at http://www.northcountynews.com/Archives2002/12_18_02/2002_1218lifestyles1.htm.

Pruitt, Allison. "Literacy Is the Key: Barksdale Donation Receives National Attention." *The Daily Mississippian,* January 21, 2000.

Psacharopoulos, George. "Returns to Investment in Education: A Global Update." *World Development,* vol. 22, no. 9, 1993, pp. 1325–43.

Putnam, Robert. "The Prosperous Community: Social Capital and Public Life." *The American Prospect,* 1993. On line at http://www.prospect.org/print/V4/13/putnam-r.html; accessed September 2002.

Rabin, Matthew. "Psychology and Economics." *Journal of Economic Literature,* vol. 36, March 1998.

Reed, Susan. "Environmentalist Fred Krupp Helps Crush the Ubiquitous Fast-Food Clamshell." *People Weekly,* April 15, 1991.

Rentschler, William H. "Lock 'Em Up and Throw Away the Key: A Policy That Won't Work." *USA Today Magazine,* November 1, 1997.

Rubin, Robert E. "Speech to Local Initiative Support Corporation (LISC) Leadership Conference." Philadelphia, Pa., April 24, 2001.

Sack, Kevin. "Ex-Netscape Official Starts $100 Million Literacy Drive." *The New York Times,* January 20, 2000.

Sander, Kathleen Waters. "Sharing a Love of History." *FYI Online.* University of Maryland University College, Faculty Forum, September 2001. On line at http://www.umuc.edu/fyionline/september_01/fyionline2.html; accessed September 2002.

Schervish, Paul G., and John J. Havens. "Money and Magnanimity: New Findings on the Distribution of Income, Wealth, and Philanthropy." *Nonprofit Management and Leadership,* vol. 8, no. 4, Summer 1998, pp. 421–34.

Schwartz, Robert A. "Personal Philanthropic Contributions." *Journal of Political Economy,* November/December 1970, pp. 1264–91.

Shapiro, Joan. "ShoreBank Corporation: A Private Sector Banking Initiative to Renew Distressed Communities." Conference on Unemployment and Consumer Debts in Europe. Hamburg, Germany, September 22 and 23, 1989. On line at http://www.hanenkamp.de/pool/gab/eusoc61e.htm#V%20NEIGHBORHOOD%20REINVESTMENT:%20FROM%20THEORY%20TO%20PRACTICE; accessed September 2002

Sika, Jean-Marc, and Balz Strasser. "Tontines in Cameroon: Linking Traditional and Semi-formal Financing Systems." D+C Development and Cooperation, no. 1, January/February 2001.

Simmons, Roberta. "Presidential Address on Altruism and Sociology." *The Sociological Quarterly,* vol. 23, no. 1, 1991.

Smith, David. "Economics and the Pursuit of Happiness." David Smith's EconomicsUK.Com. On line at http://www.economicsuk.com/research/happiness.html.

Stapleton, Darwin H. "Archival Sources and the Study of American Philanthropy." *Nonprofit Management and Leadership,* vol. 5, no. 2, Winter 1994, pp. 221–24.

Sylwester, Kevin. "Income Inequality, Education Expenditures, and Growth." *Journal of Development Economics,* vol. 63, no. 2, December 2000, pp. 379–98.

Temple, Jonathan. "A Positive Effect of Human Capital on Growth." *Economics Letters,* vol. 65, no. 1, 1999, pp. 131–34.

Twist, Steven J. "The Economics of Truth in Sentencing." *The World & I.* News World Communications, Inc., February 1, 1995.

U.S. Census Bureau. "Share of Aggregate Income Received by Each Fifth and Top 5 Percent of Households; 1967 to 2001."

U.S. Department of Commerce, Bureau of the Census, Current Population Survey.

U.S. Department of Education, National Center for Education Statistics, 1995–96 National Postsecondary Student Aid Study (NPSAS: 1996), Undergraduate Data Analysis System. On line at http://nces.ed.gov/quicktables/Detail.asp?SrchKeyWord=income&Key=360&optSearch=exact&quarter=&topic=All&survey=All&sortby=.

U.S. Department of Justice, Bureau of Justice Statistics. On line at http://www.ojp.usdoj.gov/bjs/correct.htm.

U.S. Department of Justice, Justice Management Division. On line at http://www.usdoj.gov/jmd/budgetsummary/btd/1975_2002/2002/html/page117-119.htm.

U.S. Department of Justice, Office of Juvenile Justice and Delinquency Prevention. *Annual Report 2000.* On line at http://www.ncjrs.org/pdffiles1/ojjdp/188419.pdf.

Vickrey, William S. "One Economist's View of Philanthropy." In Frank G. Dickinson, ed., *Philanthropy and Public Policy.* New York: National Bureau for Economic Research, 1962.

Voluntary Support of Education, Council for Aid to Education, 2000. Available online at http://www.cae.org/vse/vse2000/t04.htm and http://www.cae.org/vse/vse2000/t11.htm.

Wells, Ronald Austin. "Donor Legacy: What Is It That History Teaches?" In Charles H. Hamilton, ed., *Living the Legacy.* Washington, D.C.: National Center for Family Philanthropy, 2001.

Wilkinson, Rupert. "Plural Ends, Contested Means: Student Financial Aid in American History." In Michael C. Johanek, ed., *A Faithful Mirror: Reflections on the College Board and Education in America.* New York: College Entrance Exam Board, 2001.

Wooster, Martin Morse. "Julius Rosenwald: The Case Against Foundation Perpetuity." *Alternatives in Philanthropy,* August 1997.

Yang, Hsiu-ling. "Education, Married Women's Participation Rate, Fertility and Economic Growth." *Journal of Economic Development,* vol. 25, no. 2, December 2000, pp. 101–18.

ACKNOWLEDGMENTS

The Greater Good is the result of the wisdom and insight added by many colleagues. I must begin by thanking my students over the years at Connecticut College who threw themselves into my course, "Literature, Service and Social Reflection," from which this book was born. Preparing and teaching the course first made me think about the role of civic and spiritual texts from many different cultures in the unique American tradition of generosity, and then generosity's contribution to economic well-being in the United States. My students, however, pushed me to be more demanding of myself and to implement—not just discuss—social justice in our New London community. They let me see how their citizen generosity continued the philanthropic engine. I am particularly grateful to Robert Coles and Thomas Ehrlich who both advised me on the development of the course and its reading list. They have been generous mentors.

I was privileged to work with a strong staff team at Connecticut College who supported the earliest stages of this book. Donald Filer, Lucas Held, Patricia Carey, Diane Bullock, Wendy Mahan, Robin Tucker, and Claudia Shapiro are all now dear friends. Thanks also to Blanche McCrary Boyd, Linda Herr, and Kristin Pffefferkon, Connecticut College faculty; and the college's Board of Trustees, especially Jerry Carrington.

Very significant gratitude belongs to Yale Law School Dean Anthony Kronman who responded generously to the concept of this book and provided me an appointment as Senior Research Scholar at the law school while it evolved. The excellent library, office space, and other support enabled my work to move forward efficiently. I am grateful as well for Dean Kronman's advice and encouragement. I benefited significantly from the counsel and cautions of various members of the Yale faculty, especially John Simon, whose early and persistent attention was critical to this work. Thanks also to Herb Scarf, Gus Ranis, Susan Rose-Ackerman, John Geanokoplos, Dan Kevles, Ian Ayres, Sandra Barnes, Drew Days, William Nordhaus, John Roemer, Robert Lane, and Hayden Smith and, at Yale Law School Library, the invaluable Gene Coakley.

Colleagues in philanthropy listened, argued, read, and advised as well as guided me to additional sources. My thanks to William Graustein, Ronald Wells, Paul Schervish, Richard Magat, Virginia Hodgkinson, Darwin Stapleton, Diane Neimann, Penny and Bill George, Marilyn Mason, Bill Massey, Ambassador James Joseph, Vartan Gregorian, Charles Halperin, Charles Terry, Brian O'Connell, John DiBiaggio, Margot Rawlins, Lew Feldstein, Eugene Steurele, Eugene Tempel, Patrick Rooney, and Robert Payton.

Thanks also to Sam Chauncey, Roger Horchow, Robert Putnam, Ben Barber, Peter Kelly, Cheever Tyler, Matt Simmons, George Milne, and Charlie Edmonds.

I am grateful to colleagues in economics Glenn Loury, Fred Carstensen, and Steve Ross.

For UNCF data, thanks to colleague and friend William F. Gray III and his colleague Kim Edlin. And for insights on economic development, Bart Harvey.

For personal support and consistent friendship for years and particularly as this book evolved, I thank New London–area colleagues Father Lawrence LaPointe, Jack Evans, Dick Schneller, Wendy and Stephen Lash, Walter Baker, Sigmund Strochlitz, Steve and Marilyn Percy, Michael Joplin, Deena Varena, Louise Endel, Sisters Peggy and Mary Jo, Damon Hemmerdinger, Dave Goebel, and Millie Devine. Thanks to Sandy Oney for research data on New London and to New London Librarian Alma Petersen for crucial books on the Whaling City.

Special thanks to dear friends Nellie Murstein and James Schulz.

I am deeply indebted to Kathleen Thompson and Hilary Mac Austin, as well as, more briefly, Cheryl Collins for invaluable professional support as research assistants. Kathleen and Mac cared about the subject as passionately as I did through every month of work and added immeasurably to the color and the precision the text achieves. Yale research assistant Deepa Varadarajan provided excellent support collecting data in the early stages of developing the thesis.

Tina Bennett, my agent at Janklow & Nesbit, provided critical encouragement and clear advice at various important moments. Robin Dennis, my editor, provided focused critiques and sharpened the argument of the book.

My son, Graham Burnett, provided advice gracefully and stayed interested through the various stages of this book. My daughter, Maria Burnett, loyal and clear-thinking, was intensely present to me as few daughters manage to achieve for their working mothers. Thanks is a highly inadequate acknowledgment to either one. I am grateful for all they have brought to me so generously through the years.

To David Burnett, who outlined and read and advised tirelessly, the thanks that only a soul mate could offer. To SGM, deep thanks for saving (thorn-removing) grace. And to my parents and siblings, I owe enormous gratitude for sustaining care, inspiration, and affection through the years, especially the last ones.

The blindspots, errors, and inadequacies remaining in the text are my own, especially given the valiant efforts made by the abovementioned to eradicate them.

Index

ABOUT THE AUTHOR

A senior research scholar at Yale Law School, Claire Gaudiani served as president of Connecticut College from 1988 until 2001, during which time the college's endowment quintupled and it was rated in the top twenty-five liberal arts colleges by *U.S. News and World Report*. A fellow of the American Academy of Arts and Sciences, she holds a doctorate in French literature and is the author of six books.

While president of Connecticut College, Gaudiani helped to found the New London Development Corporation, which is dedicated to building the tax base, creating jobs, and improving the quality of life for all citizens of New London. She served four years as the NLDC's volunteer president and currently sits on its Board of Trustees. Since 1997, NLDC has worked with governments and businesses, including Pfizer, Inc., to build a new R&D facility, improve after-school education, offer job-readiness programs, and create new housing. She has served on the boards of numerous for-profit and not-for-profit enterprises, including the Henry Luce Foundation, MBIA, Inc., the Shubert Theatre, Legal Services of Connecticut, Southern New England Telephone Company, the Lyman-Allyn Art Museum, Public Radio International, and Citizens Bank. Gaudiani is a frequent speaker both nationally and internationally on topics related to philanthropy, education, ethics, and the role of colleges in a civil society.

She lives in Connecticut.